KEEPING 007 ALIVE

Conversations with James Bond Continuation Authors

by

Mark Edlitz

Copyright © 2024 by Mark Edlitz

All rights reserved. No part of this book may be reproduced in any form or by any electronic or mechanical means, including information storage and retrieval systems, without written permission from the publisher, except by a reviewer who may quote passages in a review.
Cover design by Sean Longmore. Illustrations by Pat Carbajal.

This book is not authorized or endorsed by Ian Fleming Publications, Eon Productions, or any copyright holder. This work is not intended to be a replacement or stand-in for any of the continuation Bonds. I implore you to put this book down and head to your neighborhood bookstore or library if, at any point, you feel the urge to read a Bond novel.

DEDICATION

This book is dedicated to:

Suzie, Ben, and Doug
Mom and Elliot

All the Bond continuation authors, past, present, and future,
who boldly follow in Ian Fleming's footsteps

And to the fans who devour their books

AUTHOR'S NOTE

Bond fans are familiar with minor inconsistencies in the rendering of various elements, such as departments or titles. As you know, Ian Fleming himself sometimes referred to Bond's elite section as "Double-O" (capitalized and hyphenated), "Double O (no hyphen), and even "double-o" (hyphenated but no caps). Similarly, *From Russia, with Love* sometimes has a comma, but not always. For consistency, this text uses Double-O, and *From Russia with Love*. Franchise names like Star Wars, Doctor Who, and James Bond are not italicized. Finally, interviews have been edited for length and clarity.

TABLE OF CONTENTS

Author's Note 1
Preface 4
Introduction 5
Foreword by Bruce Feirstein 13

The Interviews
Corinne Turner 21
Remembering John Gardner with Simon Gardner 35
Raymond Benson 53
Charlie Higson 69
Samantha Weinberg 91
Sebastian Faulks 105
Jeffery Deaver 117
William Boyd 131
Steve Cole 145
Anthony Horowitz: Part One 167
Anthony Horowitz: Part Two 179
Kim Sherwood 193

Appendix
James Bond Works by Author 213
Notes 216

Afterword by David Lowbridge-Ellis, MBE 217
Acknowledgements 220
About the Illustrator 224
About the Cover Designer 225
About the Author 226

LIST OF ILLUSTRATIONS

Ian Fleming	5
Geoffrey Jenkins	6
Kingsley Amis	7
Arthur Calder-Marshall	8
John Pearson	8
Christopher Wood	9
Corinne Turner	21
Lucy Fleming and Kate Grimond	31
John Gardner	35, 37, 39
John Gardner's letter to Bill Kanas	51–52
Raymond Benson	53, 56
Charlie Higson	69
Samantha Weinberg	91
Sebastian Faulks	105
Jeffery Deaver	117
Raymond Benson and Jeffery Deaver	129
William Boyd	131
William Boyd and Sebastian Faulks	134
Steve Cole	145
Charlie Higson and Steve Cole	146
Anthony Horowitz	167, 169
London Launch for *Trigger Mortis,*	170
Kim Sherwood	193
Double or Nothing Book Launch, 2022	194, 197
Ian Fleming	212

PREFACE

Keeping 007 Alive: Conversations with James Bond Continuation Authors is my second book on the post-Ian Fleming world of James Bond continuation novels. The first, *James Bond After Fleming*, is a comprehensive overview of the 50-plus works that have been written by various authors over the last fifty years. That reference book offers a potted history of the series and provides an analysis and guide to each novel, short story, spin-off work, and novelization. *Keeping 007 Alive* is different.

    This volume includes interviews with every Bond continuation author from 1997–2024. The nine James Bond continuation authors who were generous enough to speak with me about their memorable works include Raymond Benson, Sebastian Faulks, Jeffery Deaver, William Boyd, Charlie Higson, Steve Cole, Samantha Weinberg, Anthony Horowitz, and Kim Sherwood. I also interviewed John Gardner's son, Simon Gardner, about his dad's work and Corinne Turner, the Managing Director of Ian Fleming Publications.

    My goal was to let these imaginative, talented, and creative authors share their personal connections to James Bond as they very graciously pulled back the curtain to give us a behind-the-scenes look at how a Bond continuation novel is conceived, crafted, and published.

    I hope you enjoy reading what they had to say about their experiences as much as I adored talking with them.

INTRODUCTION

Ian Fleming changed popular culture with his twelve novels and two collections of short stories about his super spy, James Bond. Numerous novels carrying on Bond's literary adventures have been published since Fleming's death in 1964. Those varied works include traditional books about the spy's fraught missions, as well as works about Bond's teenage years, Miss Moneypenny, a pseudo-biography, movie novelizations, and short stories.[1]

Ian Fleming
Illustration by Pat Carbajal

The Ian Fleming Estate controls the literary rights to Ian Fleming's works and has authorized the publication of these continuation novels. The day-to-day work of managing the copyright and upholding Fleming's legacy is performed by Ian Fleming Publications (IFP), formerly known as Glidrose Productions, and Glidrose Publications, who work on behalf of the family.

After Fleming's death, his estate chose Kingsley Amis to pen the first traditional Bond continuation book. However, simultaneously, Geoffrey Jenkins, a South African journalist and colleague of Fleming, was also lobbying Glidrose for permission to write his own Bond novel. Jenkins claimed that Fleming had supported the project and insisted that he would publish it with or without Glidrose's approval. As a result,

Glidrose signed a deal with Jenkins. Nonetheless, after Jenkins completed the manuscript, titled *Per Fine Ounce*, Glidrose exercised its contractual right not to publish it.

Geoffrey Jenkins
Illustration by Pat Carbajal

And so, the first traditional continuation novel, became *Colonel Sun* (1968), written by Kingsley Amis. Amis' two earlier Bond-related works, *The James Bond Dossier* and *The Book of Bond or Every Man His Own 007*, amply demonstrated his familiarity with and affection for Fleming's writing. *The James Bond Dossier* is an analysis of Fleming's books, while *The Book of Bond*, published under the pseudonym William Tanner, a recurring character in Fleming's novels, offers a lighthearted guide to living the Bond lifestyle.

Amis wrote *Colonel Sun* under the pen name Robert Markham because Glidrose initially planned for future Bond novels to be written by different authors under a collective pseudonym. However, this concept was scrapped soon thereafter, and subsequent continuation novels have typically carried authors' names.

Colonel Sun is one of the better-known early Bond continuation novels, but it wasn't the first. That honor goes to *The Adventures of James Bond Junior 003½,* a spin-off book that was published in 1967, a year earlier than Amis' thriller. In the children's book, 007's nephew suspects that his neighbor is involved in a recent robbery of gold bullion.

Kingsley Amis
Illustration by Pat Carbajal

So, without any help from adults, 003½ sets out to prove his theory and bring his neighbor to justice. It's best not to give too much thought to how 007, who—as far as Fleming established—has a nephew but didn't have any siblings. Nor is it wise to question why civilians know the adult Bond's true identity and his code number. Instead, we're asked to take *The Adventures of James Bond Junior* at face value and enjoy this boy's adventure series for what it is. R.D. Mascott's name appears on the cover, but the book's true author is English novelist Arthur Calder-Marshall.

John Pearson followed with *James Bond: The Authorized Biography of 007* (1973), an account of the spy's life and times. The unusual premise of the book is that Bond is a real person, and Fleming fictionalized his exploits. In *James Bond: The Authorized Biography,* M instructs Bond to share his life story with Pearson, who is also a character in the book. As Fleming's biographer, Pearson was uniquely suited to tell Bond's story, and Bond, who is on the verge of marriage, reveals the never-before-told story of what happened in between Fleming's books. The book also sheds light on Bond's childhood and explains his facial scar.

Arthur Calder-Marshall
Illustration by Pat Carbajal

John Pearson
Illustration by Pat Carbajal

When Fleming sold the film rights to his novels, he stipulated that *The Spy Who Loved Me* could not be made into a movie. Years later, Fleming's heirs gave the film producers permission to use the novel's title but not its plot. As a result, there are few similarities between the film and Fleming's book. Christopher Wood, who co-wrote the screenplay for Roger Moore's third Bond movie, was chosen to adapt the screenplay into a tie-in. The novelization was renamed *James Bond, The Spy Who Loved Me* (1977), to differentiate Fleming's book from the film. Novelizations are not generally considered great works of literature. Yet, Wood effectively channeled his inner Fleming and wrote a nerve-wracking torture scene that took aim squarely at Bond's manhood. Wood then turned his *Moonraker* screenplay into the book *James Bond and Moonraker* (1979).

Christopher Wood
Illustrations by Pat Carbajal

From 1981 to 1996, John Gardner wrote fourteen original Bond novels—more than Fleming himself—as well as the novelizations for Timothy Dalton's last Bond movie *Licence to Kill,* and Pierce Brosnan's first outing in *GoldenEye.* During Gardner's tenure, Bond would trade in his Walther PPK for an ASP, swap his Aston Martin for a Saab, fall in love numerous times, and rise in rank from Commander to Captain.

After Gardner handed in his license to thrill, Raymond Benson became the first American writer to write a Bond novel. From 1997–2003, Benson wrote six original novels, three novelizations, and three short stories. When he took over, Benson aimed to retain Fleming's character, vices and all, and insert him into movie-style adventures. In the short story "Blast from the Past," Bond investigates the death of his son, James Suzuki. Benson's first novel *Zero Minus Ten*, is set against the handover of Hong Kong from the United Kingdom to China. Benson's run was noted for the return of popular Fleming characters, such as Marc-Ange Draco and Tiger Tanaka, who returned in *Never Dream of Dying* (2001) and *The Man with the Red Tattoo* (2002), respectively.

After Benson's tenure, Ian Fleming Publications changed course and published two Bond spin-off series—Young Bond and The Moneypenny Diaries. On the surface, a series about Bond in his teenage years sounds like an ill-advised idea and an attempt to cash in on the success of Harry Potter. How could a writer transform Fleming's adult-oriented novels into "kiddie fare"? Incredibly, Charlie Higson found a way to elevate this undertaking in a series of five novels and one short story in his tenure which ran from 2005–2009. Higson sensibly refrains from pairing young Bond with a juvenile Blofeld or tiny Jaws. Instead, Higson's books deftly map out young Bond's emotional growth, with the Young Bond series acting as prequels to the Fleming books set against the backdrop of the 1930s.

Despite the somewhat misleading title, Samantha Weinberg's *The Moneypenny Diaries* are not Bond romance novels. Instead, they are a trilogy of absorbing thriller mysteries that were published from 2005 to 2008. Ten years after Moneypenny's death, her niece reads her aunt's secret journals and learns that M's secretary has a richer and more dangerous life than any imagined. Weinberg's works are set primarily around the events of Fleming's *On Her Majesty's Secret Service*, *You Only Live Twice*, and *The Man with the Golden Gun*. Each of these books is highly recommended. Weinberg (writing as Kate Westbrook) also gives Moneypenny a first name—Jane.

Then, Sebastian Faulks, Jeffery Deaver, and William Boyd each wrote a single Bond novel, none of which require any knowledge of the previous 007 continuation books to enjoy. With *Devil May Care* (2008), Faulks was tasked with writing his book in the style of Fleming. Deaver rebooted the series and set it in modern times. With *Carte Blanche* (2011), Deaver wipes the slate clean, and Bond must entertain the notion that his father might have been a spy who betrayed his country and was killed to keep him from exposing the Russian operation. Meanwhile, 007 must take on Severan Hydt, a man who gets a sexual thrill out of death. Boyd's *Solo* (2013) finds Bond confronting his 45th birthday and nightmares about his time during the war.

From 20014–2017, Steve Cole returned to the Young Bond series following Higson's work. In his four-book run, Cole emphasizes action and spectacle and nudges James closer to becoming a secret agent. In Cole's *Strike Lightning*, young Bond swaps his tux for an exoskeleton suit in a steam-punk-infused escapade.

Then, with the decision to publish a new adult Bond novel, Ian Fleming Publications faced the task of selecting a suitable collaborator. Anthony Horowitz, a Fleming admirer, jokingly admitted to *The Bond Experience* that he was watching Faulks, Deaver, and Boyd with "sheer jealously" and wondered, "Why not me? When is the phone going to ring?" He needn't have worried; as fate would have it, the family would call on him three times. From 2015–2022, Horowitz wrote a trilogy of Bond novels. *Trigger Mortis* (2015), set immediately after *Goldfinger*, finds Bond shacking up with Pussy Galore and going up against Jason Sin, who uses specially designed cards to determine the manner of death of those who cross him. In his first two Bond novels, Horowitz incorporated material that Fleming had written for an unrealized Bond television series. *Forever and a Day* (2018) is an origin story set before Fleming's first novel, *Casino Royale*. In it, James Bond is tasked with finding who killed the previous 007. Horowitz's third book, *With a Mind to Kill* (2023), explores how 007 was brainwashed before the events of *The Man with the Golden Gun*. Taken together, the trilogy spans Bond's career as a Double-O agent.[2]

Kim Sherwood wrote *Double Or Nothing* (2022), the first book in a planned trilogy about the next generation of Double-O agents. Set in the present day, Bond is missing. MI6 sends their best spies to track him down. There's Johanna Harwood (003), named after the real-life co-screenwriter of the early Bond films, Joseph Dryden (004), and Sid Bashir (009). The book also features some old favorites, including Felix Leiter, who hasn't lost a step, or his Texan charm. With witty banter and deep-Fleming cuts, Sherwood expands the stage and invites a new generation of spies to bask in the spotlight. It's not entirely accurate to say that Bond doesn't appear in *Double Or Nothing*. While he is "missing" in the present, Bond appears in flashbacks and is very much a focus of the narrative. Sherwood's second installment, *A Spy Like Me*, which followed in 2024, added new characters and continued the search for 007.

Higson returned with 2023's *On His Majesty's Secret Service.* It is a timely tale in which 007 must ensure that King Charles' coronation goes off without a hitch or a hail of bullets. Ian Fleming Publications' Corinne Turner had the lightbulb moment that it was time to celebrate the 60th anniversary of the publication of Fleming's *On Her Majesty's Secret Service* and Fleming's family quickly agreed. Higson's remit was to write a short story, but he submitted a novella instead. Published two days before Charles' actual coronation, Higson's work quickly sold out and went into a second printing. *On His Majesty's Secret Service* also marked Ian Fleming Publications' first foray into acting as their own publisher. They followed with the rerelease of Fleming's books and selected continuation novels.

The Bond continuation novels demonstrate the enduring appeal of James Bond. By offering diverse narratives and exploring new angles on the character, they ensure that 007 remains a relevant and exciting figure in popular culture.

FOREWORD

"When you get the call to write for James Bond"

by Bruce Feirstein

When you get the call to write for James Bond, the first reaction is pure exhilaration. Amazing! How great! It's an honor, I'm flattered, I can't wait to start! Then, an unsettling reality begins to creep in, like storm clouds gathering on a distant horizon: Jesus! How am I going to do this? How am I ever going to come up with a plot and a villain that makes sense for a British agent? And finally, the final moment of fear and terror presents itself: How am I ever going to come up with anything as good as Fleming, or the seminal Bond screenwriter Richard Maibaum, or even many of the authors interviewed for this book?

Over seventy years after the publication of *Casino Royale*, Ian Fleming remains the long shadow cast over all of us who foolishly attempt to take up his pen. This isn't to say that some haven't come close. But as I sat in London, feverishly trying to write Bond films, I was struck by the fact there were two Bonds: Fleming's cold, hard (and brand-obsessed) Bond, and Maibaum's, which was the Bond with the wit. This may seem like heresy. And it is in no way meant to diminish Ian Fleming, but it always makes me laugh when I hear someone who's grown up on the movies say, "Bond needs to go back to the books." But a story told to me by Richard Maibaum's widow, Sylvia, about Fleming and Maibaum meeting for the first time on the set of *Goldfinger* confirms it for me. According to Mrs. Maibaum, her husband was filled with anxiety about meeting The Author, worried about how Fleming felt about the liberties he'd taken with the character. So they were introduced on a sound stage at Pinewood. They shook hands and sized each other up. For once, Maibaum didn't know what to say. No Bond witticism leapt to his tongue. Then, there was a moment of uncomfortable silence, finally broken by Fleming, who said, "I like your Bond better than mine."

So with this in mind, I sat in my office in London, always trying to come close to two impossible benchmarks that I had pinned to the wall. The first was the brilliant first two paragraphs of *Casino Royale*:

> *"The scent and smoke and sweat of a casino are nauseating at three in the morning. Then the soul-erosion produced by high gambling—a compost and greed and fear and nervous tension—becomes unbearable, and the senses awake and revolt from it. James Bond suddenly knew he was tired.*

The second benchmark on my wall was the scene in *Thunderball* where the villainess Fiona Volpe (played by Luciana Paluzzi) is in a bathtub, naked, when Bond enters the room, surprising her. "Aren't you in the wrong room?" she asks. "Not from where I'm standing," Bond answers. Bemused, she replies, "Since you're here, would you mind getting me something to put on." And with that, there's a simple cut to Bond coming further into the room, reaching down, and offering her a pair of sandals. It's a brilliant moment of screenwriting, which captures his cheekiness, his insouciance, and his sexuality without uttering a single word. It's a near-perfect example of action as character.

I'll leave it for someone else to pass judgment as to whether I ever came close to those Bond moments. Personally, I don't think so. But damned if I didn't try.

Entering the world of Bond as a writer is an incredibly odd, head-spinning experience, not just in the way that fans are invested in the character, but the way you quickly become hyper-aware of how much Bond is woven into the larger fabric of our culture.

A cursory reading of almost any major newspaper's cultural or political coverage over the course of a month will bring up dozens of references to Bond, from fashion to politics to architecture to business sex. And that's before you get to all the speculation about who's going to play 007 in the next movie—which is 99.99999% of the time wrong and 100% of the time planted by that actor's PR agent.

Casting questions aside, consider all those supertall billionaire buildings on 57th Street in Manhattan. They're almost always described as apartments for Bond villains.

Is there a man anywhere on the planet who hasn't put on a tuxedo and turned to look at his profile in a mirror, thinking, "Bond. James Bond."

Even working inside the franchise, Fleming's impact spills over into real life. I won't name the city or the film—and the story may be apocryphal—but we were shooting a street scene when the local mayor threatened to shut down the production unless he received "Two million USD in a silver Haliburton suitcase." The local production manager had anticipated the need to pay the bribe and was prepared to pay far, far, far less—something closer to 1.5% of the two million ask—which the mayor immediately agreed to. But he wouldn't budge on the suitcase. "The silver Haliburton is non-negotiable," Why? "Because that's the way they do it n Bond movies."

So how did we get here? How did Ian Fleming's genius come to own so much real estate in our cultural landscape?

In the beginning, it was Ian Fleming's words, stories, characters, novels. He is far from being the only author writing about post-World War II/Cold War spy stories and international intelligence intrigue—think John Le Carré, for one—but his creation, Bond, resonated with readers in a way that none of the others did. Bond was daring. Manly. Sexy. The books were huge hits. Even President John F. Kennedy claimed that *From Russia with Love* was one of his favorite books—although Cubby Broccoli told me that was a PR stunt cooked up by his press secretary, Pierre Salinger, to make the elite, Harvard-educated member of Boston's wealthy upper class seem more like a regular guy, with common tastes. (In a funny way, you can connect the dots here from Fleming, to Kennedy, to Barack Obama filling out his March Madness basketball brackets.)

After the books came the movies. The girls, the guns, the gadgets. The sexiest man alive—who moved like a panther—Sean Connery. By the time *Goldfinger* was released in 1964, Bond and the Beatles were dominating pop culture, and there was the kind of merchandising—toys, clothing, product tie-ins—that wouldn't be seen again until Star Wars. This is one of the things the Matt Damon movie *Ford Vs Ferrari* got stupidly wrong: In real life, Henry Ford II didn't loathe James Bond. He shipped one of the first Ford Mustangs to Europe to be introduced in *Goldfinger*, where it was driven by Tilly Masterson (the actress Tania Mallet). And, according to the Bond historian, John Cork, Ford himself appears as an extra in the "She's dead tired" restaurant scene in Jamaica.

(And if I can digress for one moment here about *Goldfinger*: I can't speak for every Bond writer, but for many of us, that iconic scene of Shirly Eaton wearing nothing but gold paint is the bane of our existence. Why? For an entire generation of 13-year-old boys who would grow up to become book or film reviewers, this was probably the first time they felt a warm stirring of manhood in their loins. So every Bond adventure since then has been a disappointment. Sorry, but there's nothing—nothing—most of us could do to duplicate that particular moment in our lives.)

In any event, none of this really explains how Fleming's Bond became such a phenomenon and has resonated for so long around the world and across the decades.

So forgive me for using a little *French deconstructionist film theory* here, but I would argue that there was something else going on in the books and movies that endeared Bond to the rest of the world and made Bond such a cultural icon on every continent.

And for me, that begins with the fact that Bond was not an American. There are no B-52s, no Pentagon, no meet-and-greets in the Oval Office with Harrison Ford standing in for the current president at the end of the mission.

Rather, underneath it all—underneath the cars and the casinos and the girls and the glamour—there is an archetypal character and an archetypal story that has appeared in every culture on every continent for over 2500 years.

And that is the King—the Emperor, the tribal chieftain—has to send out a lone warrior to save a threatened nation. The archetype appears throughout Asian, Indian, Middle Eastern, African, and Western cultures. And in my view, this was Fleming's true genius, which was to plant Bond with these universal roots. Our current critics in America—always searching to take offense at something—see British Imperialism and Bond as colonizers. But the rest of the world saw the hero and the warrior. I run into this whenever I've been invited to speak at a progressive American university. The academics can't see their own cultural imperialism—"big bad Hollywood culture dominates the world"—and are inevitably flummoxed when presented with an alternate worldview.

All of this brings us to the ticking time bomb in the room. What is the literary and cinematic future for Bond? Will the character continue to resonate? Will Fleming's alter-ego still speak to the next generation, no matter who writes him, in any form of narrative media, from books to video games? Here are just a few of the challenges the next generation of Bond writers will face.

First, the practical challenges: In this age of ubiquitous surveillance, artificial intelligence, virtually no privacy, and instant facial recognition, is it even possible to be a 'secret agent'? All you'd need do is hide a camera in a coffee shop across from MI-6, and you'd have everyone's faces in a week or two. Short of growing up—from birth—with no digital interactions or footprint, there's going to be a data trail. Forget MI-6! Google itself can't entirely erase you or substitute a totally new identity, given biometrics and DNA identifiers. In reality, Bond couldn't get through an airport, let alone a casino, without being unmasked.

Then there's social politics underneath all of it. Every Bond writer faces the conundrum of dealing with the zeitgeist. In *GoldenEye*, I wrote a scene in a sauna where Bond pulls a gun on Xenia Onatopp. (A name, like Pussy Galore, I would never use today.) "You don't need the gun," she tells him, to which he replies, "That depends on your definition of safe sex." The purpose of the exchange was to place Bond firmly in the reality of 1995 when AIDS and "safe sex" were prime topics. It was a way of saying, "We know who we are, and we are very much living in this moment," rather than some perfectly preserved version of 007 encased in amber.

As I said, everyone struggles with this. It's the way both the literary and film versions of Bond have very much been a reflection of their times, from the Cold War, to the fall of the Soviet Union, to the post 9-11 era.

And finally, what of Ian Fleming? What of his legacy? After over seventy years of continuous publication, it's clear that Fleming and his writing have earned a place in the pantheon of important and enduring writers. Few authors from the 1950s are still in the library, let alone in the news.

Fleming was a man of the time. Those books and films accurately represent the way people thought, and talked, and acted. I'll concede that if Ian Fleming were alive today and writing in the same voice, with the worldview that he had in the 1950s, he'd be an easy and worthy target for cancellation. But I'd rather take a wider view of this.

Before he wrote Bond, Fleming was a newspaperman. A journalist. An intrepid traveler and adventurer who was relentlessly curious and inquisitive about the world, along with the how and the why of the way society worked and people functioned.

All of which is why I believe that if Ian Fleming were alive today and writing contemporaneously, he'd be a man of our time and hold the views and values of someone born in our world. And it wouldn't surprise me at all if he were to meet some of the gifted writers who had carried on with the adventures of his singular and towering achievement and remark:

"I like your Bond better than mine."

In the end, having been involved with 007 for so long, there are only two things I know that are absolutely true.

First, Carly Simon was right: Nobody does it better.

And second, is the line that appears at the end of every one of the movies.

James Bond will return.

Bruce Feirstein
Los Angeles, July 2024

THE INTERVIEWS

CORINNE TURNER

Managing Director at Ian Fleming Publications Ltd.

Corinne Turner
Illustration by Pat Carbajal

What does Ian Fleming Publications do?
A former iteration of Ian Fleming Publications [called Glidrose Productions] was established by Ian himself. On the advice of his accountant, he assigned the literary copyright to the books to Glidrose [in 1952] for tax reasons. He was way ahead of the curve on many things. He ran it and he wrote his books through the company. The film rights are not in it, they're outside, separate.

These days, we've carried that on. We have tried to protect and uphold his legacy with the literary side of things and the family side of things, the Fleming Estate. That's our goal. We've done that for a long time by ensuring that his books are published properly. We continue publishing his books as widely around the world as we can. We also do that by having authors write new books that bring in the younger and the next generations of readers to Ian's books. That's fundamentally what we're about—looking after the legacy and keeping it alive.

Given that, one of the reasons to publish the continuation novels is to keep Fleming's legacy alive?

Yes, definitely.

When did you join Ian Fleming Publications?
I joined in 1988. I went to work for the authors' division of Booker [originally, a sugar firm that expanded its interests to include acquiring and managing literary copyrights]. At that point, they owned all sorts of authors. Ian was the first one that they had bought. It's in literary lore that Ian played golf with Jock Campbell, the chairman of Booker. At that time, it was called Booker McConnel. They came up with this wheeze [plan] that for tax reasons, Booker bought a 51% shareholding in Ian's literary company. The idea was that Ian would get a nice chunk of money and he would continue to write the books for the company. It would be a great relationship.

Sadly, within six months of the deal being done, Ian died. Booker, then owned it and ran it. They went from that and had [made deals to own and manage] other authors like Agatha Christie, Robert Bolt (*Lawrence of Arabia*), Dennis Wheatley (*V for Vengeance* and espionage books), Georgette Heyer (Regency Romances), and they created this division of author's estates. I joined in a PA role [supporting] and worked across all of them and went up through the business to eventually become the chief executive of the division. That was exciting and great.

Booker fell into hard times and was looking to divest the bits that weren't their core business. So the family bought back Fleming relatively early on, even before Booker was actually divesting it. Booker was still managing it. I sold the rest [other author's estates] to various places, but mostly to a company called Chorion, which got Christie. At that point, I had a choice of whether I went with the rest of it or if I went with Fleming. I stayed with Fleming because they're a lovely family to work with. I wanted that family attitude to running a business rather than the big corporate attitude. It's been a long time.

You joined IFP in 1988, around John Gardner's *Scorpius*, which is in the middle of his run. What do you remember about that period?
Oh, goodness. Peter Janson-Smith [Ian Fleming's agent] was running everything. Peter was my mentor. He was wonderful. Things were not as complicated as they are nowadays. Peter and John had such a great relationship. John Gardner was wonderful. I think he was living in America at the time. It was straightforward. John would come up with his ideas, he would write the book, and Peter would give an awful lot of feedback on it. Peter was a great editor, as well as being a wonderful literary guru and an agent. We were dealing with Hodder, who were

brilliant UK publishers. Then we had Putnam, our publisher in America. It was all good. It was going wonderfully well. It was his seventh book, and he was very much in the stride at that point. He had made Bond his own. It was good. It was exciting and fun.

What's noteworthy about Gardner's tenure is that there was essentially a book a year. He took two breaks, but basically, it was a book a year. It's not a scenario you would replicate today, but there must have been a great deal of comfort during that period. IFP [Ian Fleming Publications] knows the author, and the author knows what's expected.
Yes, it was working. John wanted to write as many books as Ian had written. So that was his goal. It was one a year. It was all working. They had a routine. John wrote in that way, and he was great at doing it. It got edited, it went out and it produced a good book. Then you were on to the next one. It was a commercially successful and productive relationship that worked for the time.

How would you characterize your relationship with Eon Productions, the company that makes the Bond movies?
I quite often compare what we do at IFP with the film company Eon. Of course, we have a relationship with them. We have all types of relationships, contractual and financial. At the core, it's two separate families [the Flemings and the Broccolis] who believe in and love the product. We run in parallel, and we do our own things creatively. Interestingly, we do similar things.

On the literary side, everything comes from Fleming. On the film side, they've got the original Bond, Sean Connery. That's their equivalent of Fleming. We've got our John Gardner years, which are probably like their Roger Moore years. In some ways, they're similar. John brought his books to tie into the period which had a slightly more Safari jackets feel rather than dinner jackets. I'm not sure who to compare Lazenby to other than to say *On Her Majesty's Secret Service* is one of my favorite films. Pierce Brosnan is probably our Raymond Benson years—slightly more glossy. Then we all took a little hiatus. They came back with Daniel [Craig], and we came back with Sebastian [Faulks]. We took a step. Prior to that, we had been doing these series [Young Bond and Moneypenny Diaries]. It was the same with Raymond, where it was pretty much one a year. They were good, and they were straightforward. They were successful mass-market books. Towards the end of Raymond, it was,

"Has it run its course? Can we do something different?" We felt we needed a break from that approach.

How did that change in strategy come about?
Peter never believed that a literary bestseller [author] would consider doing Bond. They would have to give up some of the money [to the rights holder]. Why would they do it? We thought we'd have a break and have a rethink. We took that opportunity to do something different. We brought in a wonderful lady called Kate Jones, who sadly is no longer with us. [Jones passed away in 2008.] Kate had been the publishing director at Penguin, and she'd looked after Fleming. I'd been working with her on that. She wanted to change and get out. Because we wanted to give this all a shake-up, I said, "Come work with us for a bit." Peter was stepping back and retiring at that point. So we brought Kate in. We asked, "Is there something else that we can do, something completely different? Let's go at it a completely different way and give [adult Bond novels] a break.

We talked about it and Kate came up with the idea of coming to it from various routes. We decided to do something for children. We formulated this idea of *Young Bond,* and Kate found Charlie because she had worked with him on his previous books. I would probably say that *Young Bond* is probably our most successful series. It still is, and it still keeps going. They all keep going. Charlie's writing is accessible and enjoyable, but he had that slightly more literary take on it. He was also completely immersed in Bond, as was Raymond.

Charlie's books weren't "Bond thrillers." They were great "thrillers" with Bond in them. That's a slight difference. The originals were "Bond continuations" and "Bond thrillers," and they were good. These new ones slightly changed the focus. Charlie gave us that break and established Bond in a different way and for a different market, a younger market.

We also looked at Moneypenny and Sam Weinberg, who also had a more literary take. They were wonderfully done and are great books. I love them, although I would say that we got the positioning on that one wrong. We tried to be too clever in that we tried to hoodwink the public and pretend that they were real. Instead, we should have brought the press in on our joke and played that one better. Those were more literary and contained; it was just three books. Charlie's books were relatively contained [to a series of five].

We were also heading towards the 100th anniversary of Ian's birth, and we said, "Let's give it a go. Go for a big name; it's a big year." I always wanted Sabastian Faulks. He's a wonderful writer. He is a beautiful writer and he's done great thrillers. He's also good at analyzing and breaking down the writing. He was on a radio program at the time on Radio Four [called *The Write Stuff*], where they wrote something in the style of another writer. One of them was Fleming, and [you think], "Oh, amazing." Of course, you want to avoid pastiche. We don't want pastiche. We've always tried to avoid pastiche.

As I said, I was keen on him, and so was my colleague Zoë Watkins, [Publishing Manager], now Zoë Aqualina. We both felt that he was a strong person, and the Family felt that it would be a great idea. We had been advised by Sebastian's agent, Gillon Aitken, who is sadly no longer with us, "He's just finishing this long book. It's taken about five years to write, quite grueling, and it's about mental health and mental illness. This could be a really good refresher for him. Just give him a complete break, something lovely and different to do that wouldn't take that long. I'll ask him." He said yes. It was amazing.

From Charlie onwards, it was a big change for us from doing those regular series—which were fabulous—to doing some things that involved event publishing. It was the biggest event in publishing. We hit number one on the bestsellers list. It was the fastest-selling fiction hardback that any publisher had. I think we sold about 50,000 copies in the first four days. It was amazing. It set us on a different trajectory.

Sebastian wasn't immersed in Fleming the way Charlie or Raymond had been. He took it as an academic exercise…sort of, 'How do I make this work?' I remember when the manuscript came in, I sent a copy to Barbara Broccoli. I got this text from her in return saying, "Amazing. If you hadn't told me otherwise, I would have thought you'd found an unpublished manuscript by Ian." I was like, "Yes!" I pinged back, "Can we use that in the publicity." [Laughs.] It's the best thing you can have.

We've gone on from there to do a series of one-offs, but we're gradually doing a little more with series; obviously, with Double-O, we're going back to a series. We've worked with such amazing authors. Even with wonderful Anthony, we started in theory, doing the one-off with him, but he got it and enjoyed it. We loved what he was doing. Then it was, "Could I do one more?" Then, "Three is a better number than two, isn't it? I've got one more in me, and it's a trilogy." Yes, of course. We'd love it.

IFP has gone through several name changes over the years, including one where the word Glidrose was in parenthesis, as in "Ian Fleming (Glidrose) Publications Limited."
That was to keep Peter happy. He didn't want to lose "Glidrose."

Let's go back to selecting Amis to write the first adult Bond continuation novel. He seemed like a natural pick as he had written *The James Bond Dossier*, an appreciation of Fleming's work.
Yes, he was a friend of Ian's. From the correspondences I've seen, I can tell you that Kingsley was asked to do an editorial review. So he reviewed the final book [*The Man With The Golden Gun*, published after Fleming's death] and gave comments on it. We don't know how much of his comments were used. He wasn't asked to rewrite anything. From the correspondence I've seen, there might have been an exploration with somebody else. But they felt that Kingsley was the right person and that he would be able to do it well.

Do you know anything else about that exploration before Amis was ultimately selected?
It's one of the things that I'm doing at the moment. When I get the time, which is rarely, I'm working through the old minute books [the records of the meetings]. Just to try to piece things together and to sort out when things happened. That's one of the reasons we miss Peter so much. He just knew it all.

The surrealistic cover for Amis' book was designed by Tom Adams.
I really like the Amis cover.

Me too. It's striking, but it's not in keeping with the Fleming covers.
No, not all at all, which is interesting. When they started Gardner, they went back to the Chopping style. [Artist Richard Chopping worked with Fleming to design the original book covers.]

It's well-established that Ann Fleming had issues with the Bond books and that she was initially against the continuation novels. She thought that the character was Ian's and no one should try to take over his work. Continuation novels were not a part of popular culture the same way that they are now. It's not an unreasonable stance.
Ultimately, she left it up to the business to make the decisions. [At the time, Glidrose was run by Ian's brother Peter Fleming, who convinced Ann that allowing continuation books not only made good business sense but helped to secure the copyright.] I've got this letter from her in my desk drawer. Actually, it's a copy of it. I keep it as a reminder to me. She said that she wasn't sure [about publishing post-Fleming Bond novels], but she was happy for the company to do it on the condition that all the

directors read the manuscript and approve it. And do it with all the continuation works. If all the directors were happy with it, then it could happen. I thought that was quite good because, obviously, there were family directors as well. It was family and business. It was everybody agreeing on it. We've kept that the whole way through. We still do that today. No book will get an okay without all of our board of directors reading it.

They rejected the *Per Fine Ounce* book by Geoffrey Jenkins. From the pages I've read, it seems like it would have been entertaining. I would love to read it.
I wish I could find a copy of that.

What do you look for in a continuation author?
They need to like Fleming. You get the best books with a Fleming fan. Somebody who loves the originals. We've been fortunate with that but that's why we take it carefully when we approach people. We do a lot of research beforehand. We always expect them to read Fleming again.

Comparing it to the film company, whenever they start working on a new film, the scriptwriters go back and reread Fleming. They're coming from his point of view every time. That's our core. We will say to our writers that Fleming is our core and our starting point. It's got to come from him, that world, and that aesthetic. But we're not prescriptive. We will ask them to do an outline and bring that to us. We give them feedback on that. We will pick up on the Fleming elements and say, "Sorry, Bond doesn't drink tea, or he wouldn't wear tan slacks," or whatever. Otherwise, we let them do their own thing. If it's a straightforward Bond continuation, we look for them to recreate Bond. We go to them because we love their writing, and we're looking for them to bring their voice. How that comes about varies a lot. It's really up to what they want to do as well.

We chose Jeffery Deaver because he had written a wonderful thriller book based on the beginning of the war in Berlin around the Olympic games. It had such a wonderful feeling of that period. You could feel that he could do really well with a period Bond. He set Bond in the modern era and wrote a contemporary story, but you knew that he could do it, and he was a huge fan.

Anthony is so embroiled in all of Fleming and so wonderful. Anthony, of course, wanted to write him in a period. That's what he wanted to do. So that's a conversation we will have. Generally, we will give an indication of what we're quite keen to do and whether it is taking it back into period or whether it's something contemporary, for example. But it's got to be driven by the authors themselves. If you tie their hands too much, you will not get a good book. We let them run with it, really.

We're there to support them too, especially when you are starting something new, like Kim's Double-O books or the same with Charlie's Young Bond. For Young Bond, we'll have a proposal or pitch document that we've put together of what we think it is going to be. We'll take it to that author and say, "This is what we're wanting to do. Have a think, come back to us." We did that with Charlie, and he did come back with what he wanted to do. With that, it was period. We did it with Kim and said we wanted that series to be modern-day. She wanted that, too. That worked really well. We gave her the skeleton of what we were trying to achieve. Then we let her take it, pick it up, and it becomes hers. What I hope we're doing is giving the inspiration from Fleming, and then we're letting them bring themselves to it.

The harder part is getting the character right. What do you need to see?

I guess what we need to see is the literary Bond. He's flawed. He's human. But you don't want to learn too much about him. Fleming made him this blank canvas. He had a job to do, and he went and did it. You would see elements of his personality, his drinking, or "champagne and Benzedrine, never again." There would be moments like that. You had some introspection, particularly in *Casino Royale*, where he's questioning things, and that's really wonderful. You don't get too much of his history. You don't know totally who he is or what makes him who he is. You don't know why or how he can do what he does.

I think that's quite important. That's something we've worked on and one of the things that we take care with. I think that's the thing, not too much. The only time we have allowed that to happen is probably in *Young Bond,* where you see the child and you see how the child becomes the man. You see a lot of things, but Charlie is so clever about it. He put in all these little bits and pieces of Bond as a child that, if you are a young reader who hasn't read the adult books, will pay off later. So, when these younger readers get to Fleming, the adult Bond reader will say, 'That's amazing.' and they'll make all these connections. Charlie was careful about how he wrote about Bond and how he developed. For the adult Bond, it's not giving him too much personality. That is a key thing. That keeps him relatively the same throughout all the books.

We call these continuation novels, but what are they continuing?

Exactly. They aren't. If anything, they are continuing the franchise. They continue the character and the brand. They're not continuing the storyline or anything like that.

I think that it is a great decision that there is not an overarching story because it allows for more variety in the books, and you give writers more opportunities to follow creative decisions. Some Fleming fans might not always love that they don't all connect. It's a different approach from, say, Marvel or Star Wars, where they primarily try to have one interconnecting story across all media.
I love that Marvel and Doctor Who are all interweaving. I think that you can do that if it's work for hire, and you've got this central organization that's controlling everything. In that case, you're bringing in people to work for hire and suit what you need. That can be great. With ours, we say that an author cannot use something from another continuation author's canon.

You want something that works for the times in which the new book is coming out. It needs to stand alone and draw its own audience. It complicates matters too much if you've got Flicka from Gardner coming into another author's book. It gets too complicated. That doesn't work for us. That might have worked if we had started with that approach at the beginning and been more controlling about it. I don't think the books would have been as good.

Benson would refer to Gardner's works but only in passing. If Benson's Bond thought of past loves, then one of Gardner's characters might appear. But Benson never incorporated any of Gardner's story elements or villains. However, he did bring back key Fleming characters.
Exactly.

This has been a particularly fertile period for IFP. There have been three major works in a short period—Horowitz's last Bond, Sherwood's first book, and Higson's novella.
Absolutely. Part of that was that we were hit by the pandemic. Kim and Anthony's books were supposed to come out at considerably different times. But with the pandemic, publishing went into a hiatus and wasn't doing anything. So those two came together. [Hororwitz's first book came out in May 2022, and Sherwood's first in September 2022 in the UK.] It would have been much better to hold one of them in whichever direction it was going to be. But it is what it is.

Charlie's book was entirely different. In February [2023], I was listening to the radio one weekend. They were talking about all the things that were going to happen over the coronation weekend [of May 6, 2023] and the events that were going on. Suddenly, I had this moment of, "Bother!" although that wasn't the word I used.[3] I thought, "We should be doing *On His Majesty's Secret Service*. The more I thought about it, the more I thought, "We should be doing *On His Majesty's Secret Service!*" Then I thought, "How do we do this?" I went into the team, and we have an amazing team. Simon Ward is our publishing director who came on [in 2021], and he is brilliant. I went in, and I said, "Um, hmmm. [Sheepishly.] What do you think about *On His Majesty's Secret Service*? We should be doing it. We should have talked about this about six months ago, at least. Simon said, "Oh. It's a really good idea. We should try and do it."

Then you think, "How do we make this work?" The first thing we had to do was take it to the board and say, "We want to do this. Board, please support us." They said, "Yes, absolutely." The Flemings didn't want to cash in [on the coronation], and I didn't want to cash in. Then it becomes, can you do it for charity? So we'll look for a literary-related charity. So that frees you up. Then I needed to think, "Who could do this? Who has always wanted to write an adult James Bond book, and who is a good friend? And who could possibly do it quickly?" So I pinged a text to Charlie, "Have a chat?" He wrote back, saying, "I'm here now." I called and said, "Short story. *On His Majesty's Secret Service*. 15,000 words-ish. I need you to write it in the next three or four weeks. And I'm not going to pay you anything." This cuts out the negotiation element with his agent, who's lovely, but she negotiates well. Charlie said, "Let me see if I can come up with a plot. If I can come up with a plot, I'll do it gladly."

He took a couple of weeks just thinking it all through and talking to Simon about what the plot could be. Then he came back with the outline, the overview of the book. We took it to the Board and then he got on writing it. It took him probably four or five weeks in total. Rather than 15,000 words, he gave us 42,000. All of them are brilliant.

Now, we are a publisher. [In 2023, Ian Fleming Publications started publishing Fleming's novels through their own imprint.] If we had taken this to a publisher, however, no matter how wonderful they are, we'd still be negotiating the contract. Whereas we were able to say, "Right, we're doing it." Simon was on it; they got the covers done and everything else. We had it out on the fourth of May [two days before the Coronation and a date on which some of the action takes place]. It would have been better if we had come up with the idea a month earlier, but we didn't.

It was one of those moments, that we had to do it. Yes, we had so much else going on at the time, but it was a tribute [to the sixtieth anniversary of the novel On Her Majesty's Secret Service]. It was raising money for a great charity, and it was fun and exciting. We got a great book out of it.

Lucy Fleming and Kate Grimond
Celebrating 70 years of 007 at the London Library, 2023
Courtesy of Mark O'Connell, Catching Bullets

It is the first Bond novella. There was no real precedent for it. It did extremely well for you. It seemed like there was no way to anticipate the interest in it.
[Corrine points to herself.]

[Laughing.] Oh, you knew?
Yeah.

It sold out immediately. You couldn't print them fast enough, and it went right into a second print run.
We probably didn't realize quite how [in demand it would be]. I think we were cautious with the print run. Too cautious. We should have done more. That was because we are relatively new to publishing, and we were overly careful about the numbers. We talked to our distributors first, and they have a very good idea of what the figures should be. They will give us those figures. We pushed them up from that. We pushed it higher. From that point of view, I think you're right. We didn't have enough out there. But I did expect it to be pretty big because it's Charlie,

and it's a great book. It was fantastic. It was one of those sweet moments. Great title. It was worth it.

The novella is also an example of giving the fans something that they didn't know they wanted. If you were to have polled fans about what they wanted from a Charlie Higson Bond book, they would either say a period adult Bond or his War Years. A modern Bond novella would not be on the list.
No, and until he wrote it, he didn't know that's what he wanted to do. Charlie always wanted to explore the war years. He wanted to do period because Young Bond was period, and he wanted to do period. Now, he loves contemporary and wants to do more. He had good fun doing it. It's not what he expected to do, but it worked.

Can you talk to me about Ian Fleming Books, your in-house publishing arm?
When eBooks started around the centenary [of Fleming's birth], around 2007, our publisher was Penguin, and they only had print rights, which was a historic thing. We kept eBooks out [of the contract] because publishers didn't know what they were doing with them. Until they did, they weren't having those rights.

We published Fleming's backlist through Ian Fleming Publications Limited as eBooks. We created one of the earliest relationships with Amazon [in 2012] and with Apple [in 2015]. That was good and successful. The licenses are always on fixed terms [for a finite period]. When we did the new license with Random House [in 2012], obviously, all the publishers were truly on board with eBooks, and they made us an offer we couldn't refuse. It was also sensible to fold those in because they needed to put the money behind those books [in print form as well], and they needed those [digital] rights as well. So that was fine, and we folded those rights in for 10 years. We also did the backlist with Raymond's books and Gardner's in America. So we have already been established as Ian Fleming Publications. The publishing company is a subsidiary company called Ian Fleming Books, but the imprint is called Ian Fleming Publications. It's the same name, people know it, and it's not changing—it's IFP.

In 2023, you started to republish the back catalog of continuation novels. You began with Amis, Pearson, and Benson. The price for the third Moneypenny book on eBay is quite high. It suggests that there is a demand for these continuation novels, and they should

never be out of print.
That certainly seems to be the case. We have to look at it commercially with every single one. That's what we're doing starting with these three [Amis, Pearson, and Benson]. We'll have to see what the interest is. We're certainly not a charity and we have to make a business that works. The goal is to have everything in print and available that we can. The Gardners are already in print here [in the UK] through Orion. The film tie-ins were an arrangement with the film company, and the Christopher Wood's books were part of a license at the time. They've expired and won't come back into print. Of course, there are the Dynamite comics.

The Dynamite comics have been a productive relationship. There have been so many different titles and stories.
The comics are quite interesting because they allow you to do things that you wouldn't do in novel form. There's much more freedom with comics. It's a different market.

In comics, you have Bond's war years.
The family has never been keen to do the war years as a novel. That goes back to making sure that he's a cipher. It fleshes him out too much. It gives him too much of a backstory. If and when we do that as a novel, it will be a big step.

Talking about the periods of Ian Fleming Publications, we discussed the mass market period and the literary period. How would you characterize this new period with your in-house publishing and work like the non-Bond novel *Double Or Nothing*?
Exploratory. We've got goals. Bringing Simon [Ward] in was a distinct decision, and he is the Publishing Director. It's his vision moving forward. We are walking before we run. We still have relationships with external publishers. The circumstances of Charlie's book made sense for us to publish it ourselves. We're getting it right with the Flemings. That's straightforward. We already have a relationship with Harper [HarperCollins with Sherwood's series, among others]. We have something in the pipeline that's very exciting. We've got two projects in the pipeline. One's already commissioned with a publishing partner and the other one is in early development at the moment. We will take that out to publishers, but Ian Fleming Books will pitch for it as well. That's because we want to make sure we get the best offer for the author. With Fleming, we can do it on our own because it's all ours. However, when we have an external author, we've got to do the best we can for that

book. We can pitch for it, but we've got to show that we can do what a mainstream big publisher can do. We may not be ready for that yet.

I think we are in an exploratory period; it's expansion. Our next step is doing projects like the Double-O Series…it's diversifying. I love how Kim talks about creating this world of Bond, like a Marvel world, where we've got these spin-offs. It's taking characters and playing with them. There will be circumstances where we can be experimental in a way that a mainstream publisher won't. That's what the next 10 to 12 years are about.

Not all books have to appeal to all fans. You can target an audience like you did with Young Bond or Moneypenny Diaries. Hopefully, they have crossover appeal, but not every book needs to be for everyone. It's an opportunity to experiment.

The Double-O books are brilliant. We're trying to broaden the market, to bring in new readers to Fleming and new readers to the world of Bond. That's what we are trying to do with the Double-O books, and Kim's done a fantastic job. She's incredible. You've also got the traditional Bonds with Anthony that speak to the original readers and the core fans. He does that perfectly. Ideally, you're broadening it out and bringing it to a younger generation with a younger author as well. I don't expect everyone to like all of them. We're trying to offer different things for different people.

REMEMBERING JOHN GARDNER

Licence Renewed (1981)
For Special Services (1982)
Icebreaker (1983)
Role of Honour (1984)
Nobody Lives for Ever (1986)
No Deals, Mr. Bond (1987)
Scorpius (1988)
Win, Lose or Die (1989)
Brokenclaw (1990)
The Man from Barbarossa (1991)
Death Is Forever (1992)
Never Send Flowers (1993)
SeaFire (1994)
COLD (1996, US *Cold Fall*)

Novelizations
Licence to Kill (1989)
GoldenEye (1995)

John Gardner
Illustration by Pat Carbajal

This volume includes interviews with every Bond continuation author from 1997–2024. John Gardner, the author of 14 Bond books, passed away in

2007. Because he wrote more Bond novels than any other continuation author, I wanted to somehow acknowledge his contribution. So I reached out to his son, Simon Gardner, who agreed to discuss his father's work. Simon refers to his late father as "JG."

Simon Gardner

Your dad wrote more Bond novels than any other author, including Ian Fleming.
A few years back, someone sent me a message that said, "Your dad's in the Guinness Book of Records." I said, "What are you talking about?" They said, "Seriously, your dad is in the Guinness Book of Records." If you include the two film novelizations, he's written more Bonds than Fleming." It's sad because he passed by the time the record was announced, so he never got to know that he made it in.

Your dad, like Fleming, was a writer with a military background. Given that, it seemed like he was a natural choice to write a Bond novel.
He was a 42 Commando. He would tell these stories about being a Royal Marine Commando and a Weapons Officer. He was doing military service at the tail end of World War II and ended up in Hong Kong in the New Territories [the areas between China and Kowloon]. When he looked back, he still couldn't believe how he managed to do it. It almost didn't feel like something that he had actually done…he seemed slightly detached from it. But in his writing career, he could look back at it and draw from it. He also kept up his knowledge of weapons throughout his life. He did a lot of research on weapons. That was something that he did all the time.

From interviews and simply reading the novels, one can see that he wanted to incorporate firearms, tradecraft, and cutting-edge technology into his writing. You're suggesting that he had a personal interest in it, in addition to the fact that it was a professional requirement
Oh, yes. When he was doing the early Bonds, he was interested in C.C.S. (Communication Control Systems). They were the security guys who provided the hardware for the Silver Beast, the car that Bond drove. He would always talk to them.

I would imagine that when you're writing a Bond novel, doors open to people who are eager to help.

I think so, but then again, he was always wary of who he fed that line to. In retrospect, I think he had a harder time than current Bond authors. He couldn't reference the movies, and he could only use certain authorized characters. Not only did he have to make Glidrose (now called Ian Fleming Publications) happy, but he also had to please the American publishing distributors, the UK publishing distributors, and, in certain cases, some of the European ones as well. Everybody was critiquing the work. After talking this over with some of the other continuation authors, I feel like they have since started to lessen some of those restrictions.

John Gardner
Courtesy of Peter Vollebregt

I think back to some of the fights they had over *The Man from Barbarossa*. I'll be honest and say that I haven't read [the final versions of] all of my father's manuscripts. Some, I didn't like the sound of, but others I read in various stages in manuscript format. I'm told that what I sometimes read didn't turn out like that in its final form. But some, I've never picked up. But *The Man from Barbarossa*, that was my dad. I know some people hate that book, but that was my father writing there. You could see shades of his Herbie's books [Herbie Kruger, the five-book series about a British intelligence officer]. There was more of him there in *Barbarossa* and the Herbie books, as opposed to the detached John Gardner writing the Bond books. When writing Bond, he had to put on another hat because it wasn't his character. He had to think in a different way. In the early days, when he first discussed how he was going to write those books, I think he made a conscious decision about that.

What do you remember about him getting the writing assignment?
I think I was visiting him in Ireland when it happened, but I can't quite remember. I think he got this letter on *Basildon Bond* [high-end] notepaper from Glidrose asking, "Would you like to come and have a chat with us about it?" Then, he called his agent, Desmond Elliott, and said, "I can't do this; it's not for me." Desmond replied, "What are you saying? Don't be an effing idiot. Of course, you're going to do this. At least, you have to acknowledge it." My dad understood that, and he respected it.

He felt that it was a great honor to even be considered, let alone asked to do one. He maintained that feeling throughout, even if he found it extremely difficult at times. It was extremely hard work. It wasn't something you could do lightly. There were a few that he didn't feel were up to scratch, but he was determined. He would say, "I'm going to do Bond, and then I'm going to do one of my own." That's two books a year. He wouldn't shake away from that. He had to do it. He was driven.

His output was incredible. Even putting aside his non-Bond works, with two short breaks, he wrote a Bond book a year. I can only imagine the challenges of coming up with a new villain and a new threat and then having the concentration and effort to write it.
It was hard. I recollect that he was constantly making notes about possible scenarios and plot lines. If he had an idea, he would say, "I think this might work." He understood that locations are a big thing in Bond books. So he would rake his memory for places that he had visited that he hadn't used. He would say, "I've got that lot there, but how and when can we link it up?" Then my mother [Margaret Mercer] and father would go off on a vacation somewhere. Sometimes I would go along with them. But I could pretty much guarantee that any locations that we went to would be used at some point down the line. It might be three years hence, but he would use it. That would go on quite a lot.

When you're on vacation, he would say, "While we are here, we need to go to a certain castle to scout for locations."
Absolutely, but that wasn't a bother because my mother also loved history. She loved traveling. She was the first editor of all his books, including the Bonds. He would write a chapter, and the first person who would read it was my mother. Literally. He would ask, "Is there a problem with this plotline?" So the initial edits would be from my mother making notes and saying I'm not too sure about this," or "What happened to such and such a character because three chapters ago he was supposed to

do be doing something integral to the plot. But now, you seem to have forgotten about it."

John Gardner celebrating the release of *Licence Renewed*

He would give it to her as he went along as opposed to waiting until the first draft was completed.
Right, or if he got into the flow of things, he might save up three or four chapters for her to look at. If he was in a flow, he wouldn't stop to have it analyzed. But if he was having problems, he would almost do it chapter by chapter to have another set of eyes on it. He wanted to make sure it was making sense and to make sure that there wasn't anything that stood out as not being right.

She was great. But after her death [in 1997, following his final Bond book, *COLD*, he found it difficult to write. He didn't have that person there to look at it and give him feedback. He needed her. Sometimes I would think that the books should have said, "Co-authored by Margaret Mercer." She had a lot to say about what was good and what was bad and about what you could get away with and what you couldn't.

Did he have a notebook, or did he just write on any scrap of paper that happened to be there?
Occasionally, he would have a notebook. But in those days, he was quite a heavy smoker, so you would see cigarette packets with ideas written on them. Or napkins, that kind of thing. He would grab anything in sight.

Did he work on a typewriter or a computer?
He went through stages of having a manual typewriter to an electric typewriter. He wrote a book on a modified Atari computer, but I don't think it was a Bond. It had a word processor burned on an EPROM [a memory chip], and you would put it into the Atari. It had those large floppy drives, and he got less than a chapter per floppy. He was at the forefront of doing anything to make his writing life easier. He thought, *if I can edit on a screen, this is brilliant.* After the Atari, he had a word processor that never really worked properly. It might have been a Mac SE [a small personal computer] or something similar, like the Apple before the SE. But after that, it was Apple-Mac all the way.

Given the struggles, why did he keep writing the books? I imagine he got pleasure out of it.
Because they kept renewing the contract and offering him money, if I'm to be honest about it. There were times when I honestly thought he was going to walk away. Before he started writing one, he would complain. But once he broke ground on the book, you wouldn't see much of him. That would be it. We left him to it. If I was around, I'd be another set of eyes on a manuscript. I would maybe pick up stuff that my mother hadn't picked up. I didn't do it often, but it was always interesting to have a little view of the process.

So you were in your mid-twenties when he started writing them. What was it like to have a dad who wrote Bond novels?
I was proud of it. The people who I was working with knew and accepted it. But it's not something that I would voluntarily bring up. I was working as a graphic designer in publishing. Because I'll be honest, it could become a bit of a pain. It would be constant questions and you get to the point of not wanting to answer those questions. So I didn't volunteer the information in a lot of cases. Personally, it was very cool. I liked the idea that my dad was trying to turn him into a real character by bringing in tradecraft. That was eventually reflected in the movies. When I look at Daniel Craig's version of Bond, that to me is like JG's Bond. But maybe I am looking into it too much. I don't know, but I like the idea. I might be wrong. But as Fleming said, he's a blunt instrument.

My impression about your dad was that he considered himself a professional writer. That is to say, someone who enjoys writing, and when there is an opportunity to write something, he would. It sounds like some of the books were easier to write than others.

Some, a few, particularly the early ones, were difficult to write. The first one, *License Renewed*, is a lot of fun, and I love *Icebreaker*. Those two are a lot of people's favorites.

Why do you think they originally asked him to write the Bonds?
My dad was writing in the 1960s, and he had written this anti-Bond character, Boysie Oakes. So I think they thought that this Gardner character kind of knows that territory. I think that was one of the important factors.

Why do you think they kept on asking him?
I think it was easy for both parties.

Can you expand on that?
It was so easy to keep the ball rolling during those years. I think they thought, we'll go along. They would agree to a price for the next three books, and they would say, "Bang, done." They get 50% [of the sales], we get 50%, and Desmond takes his 15% [from Gardner's half]. In publishing, authors may also receive an advance payment on their expected royalties. Everybody's happy. But, as with any franchise, there's a moment when you go, "Hang on a second. Maybe we need some new blood in here." I think they were looking at the last few that he did and asking," What are the actual returns here? How many are selling well? How much money is being made?" At least two Bonds before the end, I remember my father telling me in Virginia [where he was living at the time], "I think I'm going to have to knock this on the head. It's going to be difficult. I'm not enjoying it." So when the contract came up again, he said, "Guys, it's been great. I'm really honored, and I have had a lot of fun doing it. But it's time to pass the baton on to somebody else. Somebody younger. Somebody with a different approach to it." I can see why Raymond [Benson], with his background, was the right choice to do it and become the next author.

By the time he got to *COLD*, he had mentally made up his mind that "I don't want to do this anymore. Now's the time for me to bow out gracefully." When he told my mother and me that he was going to jack it in [quit], we both said that we were surprised that he didn't do it two books ago.

You weren't surprised.
He wasn't enjoying it anymore. The thing that he could never forget was that it was not his character. It's Fleming's character. These are not people that he's created. One of the actors who played Bond said that

you're allowed a certain amount of time with this character, and you can inhabit that space for a certain amount of time. I think he realized that he had inhabited it long enough.

It had also gone full circle, it being difficult again for him. He still had other ideas. He still had Herbie. He still had other characters that he wanted to create. There were still health problems, although I can't remember when health problems started to hit him. But whether it was him or my mother, I think there were hints at that. I remember his saying, "But there are books that I want to write before I die and other characters I want to write about. I can't spend all my time on good old James Bond. It's time for me to get my characters up and alive again."

What was his sense of the reader's response and feedback to his work?
I'm so glad that his books were written all those years ago. I think that in this day and age, given social media and the amount of trolls, I can't imagine what it would be like for an author starting today. You're taking on a beast. That's got to be difficult. When my dad was doing it, he could choose to shield himself from some of the reviews. Some of the reviewers hated his stuff. As I found out over the years on Facebook and through social media, some people loathe his work. They think he's the worst thing that ever happened to Bond. On the flip side, some people love his stuff. I think people recognize that he laid the foundation for where the continuation authors are now. Of course, there was Kingsley [and *Colonel Sun*] but there was a long time where there was a void, and nothing happened. Then, Glidrose said, "JG, we want you to pick it up and reboot it for the 1980s. Go for it." Over those stretches of JG's books, he laid the foundation for every author who is now taking over. Without that foundation and his platform, you wouldn't have the other novels. I think that's the important thing. That's what comes to mind when I think of him and how proud I am of him for what he did with it. When he stopped, I think he thought, "I've got it this far. Come on, guys. It's up to you to take it wherever you want to go."

I personally know two people who wrote him a letter that he responded to.
He was pretty good about responding to fan letters until my mother died. Then after that, getting him to write anything was difficult indeed.

That's understandable.

Everything fell apart a little bit at that point. But I don't think he realized how big a fan base he had, not only for the Bonds but for the rest of his work. After his death, I met with our agent and said, "We have his website, and I'm going to keep an eye on things if everyone is happy with that." It was only after the John Gardner Facebook page that the world opened up to me that I only had a vague idea about it. So I thought that I'd do my best to keep the flame on, not just for the Bond stuff but for all of his work. I didn't realize the kind of love for JG that was out there. It was like, "Whoa."

There were loads of Bond fans, loads of Herbie fans, and loads of Boysie fans, bless him. I don't think my father had any idea of the fan base. Although, he knew that the fan base in the States was big. That's one of the reasons we spent time in Virginia. He loved being in America. Before that, he always said, "At some point in my life, I'm going to go and live in America." So we did, which was brilliant. But even then, I don't think he really got a take on how many fans were out there and how many enjoyed his work.

In interviews, I've heard him talk about the challenges of dealing with different editors that the publisher would supply. There was an editor for the UK edition and another editor for the American edition. If you look at the totality of his work, I will argue that, in some way, he had more freedom than any other writer that would follow. He wrote traditional Bonds like *License Renewed*, *For Special Services*, and *Icebreaker.*
Correct.

When you get to *Never Send Flowers*, it's a serial killer book. *The Man from Barbarossa* is about a Nazi trial where Bond takes a backseat. On some level, he was given a great deal of freedom.
That seemed to happen more with the later ones. There were all these restrictions right at the beginning. But slowly, novel by novel, he managed to push the barriers open a little bit. "Can we at least try doing this or doing that?" I think that, for him, was one of the big challenges. It got more and more to the point where he was saying, "I want to write these the way I want to write them. Not the way I'm being dictated to by Glidrose, by the UK publisher, by the US publisher, or other individuals who have a say in how these books turn out." For him, that was pushing against trying to make them different in some respects. He didn't follow the normal Bond formula. That is why there are a lot of people out there who hated the books because they thought, "This isn't Bond. Good God,

what's he doing? What is a serial killer doing with Bond?" There are people out there who think that if you're not following the formula, then you're rubbish at writing James Bond.

I think changing from the formula is a natural and expected result of writing a series of books. You can't only keep writing Bond versus a homicidal maniac over and over again. So after you write six or so traditional novels, you try something new.
You can't keep writing the formula over and over again. But some people love that. You have to do something different. The core elements have to be there. But you can change everything that goes around it. You have to mess with it; otherwise, people would lose interest. Nowadays, you also need to bring in new readers.

You said that *The Man from Barbarossa* had the most of your dad in it. Can you elaborate on that?
His style of writing on most of his Bond novels is so different to me from the Herbies or the *Secret Generations* trilogy. But the style of writing for *The Man from Barbarossa* feels closer to his style of writing on the non-Bond novels. When I read *Man from Barbarossa,* I see more of him in there. But that could just be me.

Your dad said it was his favorite Bond book. So what you're saying makes sense. Some silly questions. Did you go to Disneyland Paris? Is that how the park made an appearance in *Never Send Flowers*?
No, we didn't. But when he was writing it, I remember him getting plans. I don't remember him going there, but we had been to Disneyland and Disney World on several occasions. He was well immersed in the parks. I think he wrote that around when the park was officially opening.

Disneyland Paris opened in 1992, and Never Send Flower was published in 1993, which means it was probably at least partially written in 1992.
I could be wrong, but I don't remember him going. I think he had phone conferences and God knows what else.

I remember you saying that there is a photograph in some of the books that he didn't like. He is standing in front of the portrait of Fleming.

There are two different ones, but they look similar. In one, he looks pissed off. He hated that photograph with a passion. He looks pissed off. There is another one where he is standing next to the Fleming portrait and smiling. That's on the back of the UK Jonathan Cape editions of *License Renewed.* He doesn't look dour and pissed off. He liked that one. I generally post that on Facebook on the anniversary of his death.

There's another one that comes up a lot where he's wearing a hat. [Holds up book.]
That's a photograph I took. I might be credited.

[Reading the book.] "Photograph of the author, by Simon Gardner."
I'm not sure exactly where it was taken. It must have been shot in Charlottesville.

Was it a candid photo, or did you take it specifically for the book?
I probably had been asked to take it. I think I've done two or three different shoots for him. At a later date, I think my niece took over.

There's also one by photographer Richard Newton.
Richard is a photographer whom I knew. I shared a flat with him in London. He ended up making a name for himself in car magazines. He's a photographer specializing in automobile photography and he's still doing very well.

There's another one that indicates that the author photo is courtesy of Saab.
That's the one where he went up and took the Saab to the north or wherever. He went out and drove it around on the ice and stuff and had a thoroughly fun time, by all accounts.

You once said that he had an idea about a condom wrapper.
AIDS was a big issue at the time, and we were getting a lot of ads on TV saying that "sex kills." He thought, "Teen boys and young men read Bond books." He wrote in one that one of the love interests asked Bond if it was true that he has condom wrappers with gold rings on them as he did on his cigarettes. It was his way of saying that even Bond wears a condom. They went, "Oh, you can't do that." But my dad's argument was, "Hang on, every night we turn on the TV, and there are stories about people dying because of having sex. We've got to reflect this in the books and show that Bond is practicing safe sex." I can't remember, did he

sneak that into one of the later books? But at the time, they were like, "No, you can't do that." He was trying to reflect modern society.

Do you remember any other ideas that he pitched but didn't use?
I recall from my experience when I'd read one of the original manuscripts and compared it to the published book, the last two-thirds were changed. I don't remember which one but something had happened, and he said, "This is going to be a bit of a problem. We might have to rework all this."

He wrote a lot about anti-fascism, antisemitism, and the rise of neo-Nazi ideas. I gather that those matters were important to him.
I think that anyone alive at the tail end of World War II or at any point in time when someone like Hitler was doing what he was doing and attempting to do, I think that experience is going to be pretty much burned into your mind. If you're a good soul, you're going to rail against it. You don't want to be repeating what happened in the 1930s and the 1940s. He understood how evil that was, and I think that's why he referenced it quite a bit.

You don't have any of his manuscripts.
No, he sold all of that stuff. He wasn't good with money, and he ran into some financial difficulty. So he sold it.

That's too bad. The work should be made available so that others can study it, and better understand his methods and how ideas evolve. How do you think he would like his work to be remembered?
Once he went into writing the Bonds, I think he quickly understood and got a horrible feeling that "If I'm going to be remembered for anything, this is what I'm going to be remembered for. It's going to be one of two things. It'll be either 'John Gardner was shit, and he couldn't write to save his life,' or 'I really like what John Gardner did with the James Bond books.'" He resigned himself to that fact.

I hope I made it clear that he was honored to do it. I'm proud of what he did with it. It would be nice if he were also remembered for his other work. But I'm a realist, like my dad, but that's how it's going to be in the court of public opinion. Some people liked the first two and hated the rest. Some people hated the first three but liked two in the middle and hated the rest. There are people who pretty much like all of them, except for *The Man from Barbarossa*. But I think he would be quite happy that people remember him at all. I will be as well. Bless him.

That's beautiful. When I read interviews with him, I am aware of the challenges that he faced and some of the pushback that he got from readers. So I'd like to think that he would be gratified to see this new groundswell of appreciation for his work.
I've gotten used to the fact that if people are going to talk about him, then, obviously, Bond is the first thing that is going to be spoken about. But, more and more, people who like his Bond work also really like his Herbie books. They say, "I love these. They're great." Or they'll say, "I wanted to get a flavor of the 1960s, so I started reading the Boysie books." Sure, they're a little dated, but they're period pieces...flashbacks to the 1960s. They're little time capsules in that respect. So when people start with the Bonds, they might ask, "What other stuff did this guy write? Let's have a look at it. This could be interesting." That's good. That's all good.

I don't know if there's anything to say about this. But we are talking today on the anniversary of Fleming's death.
It's funny. I noticed that before we started. I thought, "Hang on a second." I was wondering whether you'd set that up.

[Both laugh.] Complete coincidence. There have been a lot of anniversaries of your dad's books. Ian Fleming Publications ensures that your dad's books stay in print. We continue to see new editions from other continuation authors as well.
It's a business. It's a franchise, and it employs a lot of people, even from the literary side. There are people whose jobs exist because of Ian Fleming's James Bond. You've got to keep that thing ticking over in one form or another. I hope that doesn't sound cynical.

I don't think that's cynical. You're sharing your perspective with insight into how it impacted your father. But it's up to Ian Fleming Publications and the Estate to manage these books, which they've been doing for more than half a century.
There aren't many icons bigger than James Bond.

It seems to me that you feel a sense of responsibility to spotlight and protect his legacy.
I do. My relationship with my dad was always pretty complicated, one way or another. I think that's the same with most relationships. After his death, I felt this groundswell of people saying that they loved his work. I thought we couldn't let this disappear. There is the John Gardner Estate

which needs to be managed. We have someone who does a brilliant job. I'm not a social media expert, but I realized that we have a website, even if it's more or less only a shopfront. But it's a presence that has to be there. You can link it to the Facebook page which is where I interact more with people. I keep thinking that I must do an Instagram at some point.

Luckily, there are anniversaries and announcements. There are so many people who mention that we're at the 35th anniversary of one or another. Thank you, I think. I must do something about that. I try to do that not only with the Bonds but with the other books as well. This way, there's a presence out there that says, "There is an author called John Gardner, and he did write some pretty cool stuff."

Some of them are extremely dated. But, as I say, they are time capsules. I'm waiting to see if they put sensitive readers on my dad's Bond [as they did with Fleming's] when they put out new editions. I know some people got into a state about it and said that they're being politically correct. Somebody said to me, "Why are you sitting on the fence about this?" I thought, "Well, it's not up to you guys. It's up to IFP [Ian Fleming Publications] and the Fleming Estate. It's not up to the fans.

They still need to get new, young readers. So if the way to do it is to rework them slightly, then they are doing that. It's also a way to get cash flow and maintain the franchise. That's business. I'm sure if sensitivity readers read some of my dad's Bond, they're going to find that they trigger people left, right, and center. But he would do stuff like that on purpose.

Beyond that, he's an author who has played a part in the history of an icon. James Bond is one of the biggest British icons ever. He's one of the biggest icons in the world. And for him to have played a tiny part in that, he's done pretty good. Boy did good.

John Gardner answered letters from his readers, as noted in the interview with his son, Simon. One of Gardner's fans, Bill Kanas, saved one such correspondence, and it is reproduced below as another way to include Gardner's voice in this book. For context, Gardner's letter was written on October 8, 1994, shortly after the release of his fourteenth original Bond novel, SeaFire, and before the publication of his GoldenEye novelization and final original 007 adventure, COLD.

His letter is short but illuminating. In it, Gardner discussed the challenge of writing the continuation novels, working with the publishers, his thoughts about introducing the subject of AIDs and safer sex into his novels, the ailing M's fate, the restructuring of the Double-O section, and concluding his tenure as Bond author. Gardner also disclosed if Bond would have wed Flicka von Grüsse, the Swiss intelligence agent who becomes the spy's professional and romantic partner.

Dear Mr. Kanas,

Thank you for your kind letter of September 25, which has only just been forwarded to me by Putnam.

I fear this will be a short letter, as my time is strictly limited. However, I can put your mind at rest over certain matters. First, I have absolutely no intention of killing off M. I agree, he is essential to all Bond books. Neither do I intend to marry Bond to Flicka, though the return of Flicka in SeaFire was an attempt on my part to draw attention to one regular partner in view of the AIDS menace. Unhappily, while my American publishers allowed specific mention of AIDS in *Never Send Flowers*, my British publishers - for some unknown reason - refused to allow me to make overt references.

The new Two Zeros and MicroGlobe One are conscious decisions. The point is that the British Secret Intelligence Service has undergone huge changes. Their downsizing has only amounted to 120 people - which I am sure has now been made up by the influx of new recruits and the new headquarters is much larger than the old Century House. You will be aware that all Western intelligence agencies now have more officers in the field, as they - have realized that satellite and electronic intelligence are not enough. The old order of human intelligence - real spies on the ground - has come to the fore again.

However, the largest change in the SIS is that while it retains a Chief of the Secret Intelligence Service (C in real life; M in Bond fiction) and five Deputy Chiefs, the entire Service is now answerable to a series of government committees. Those who own the literary copyright agreed with me that we should restructure the Bond fiction: hence Two Zeros and MicroGlobe One. These are a reflection of what is really happening. That I am personally appalled by this is neither here nor there.

To answer another query. Yes, I am to do the novelization of *Goldeneye*. My contract also calls for one more Bond novel - and here comes the bad news - after which there are no plans for future books. This could change if the movie *Goldeneye* takes off, but the main problem lies in the publishing market. We have watched the popularity of the Bond books wane over the past three years, and as publishers are driven by market forces, it may well be that we will close shop for a while.

This, of course, could easily change should the new movie be a spectacular success. I have mixed feelings about all this. I have enjoyed doing the Bond books, but I am not getting any younger, and I cannot deny that they get more difficult all the time. It is only natural that I have more love for my own work—Kruger, etc.—but I shall be sad to say goodbye to Bond, should that happen. We must wait and see once the next Bond is done.

I will try to find a photograph for you.

Again, with thanks.

Sincerely,

JG

John Gardner

Mr. William Kanas

October 8, 1994

Dear Mr. Kanas,

Thank you for your kind letter of September 25, which has only just been forwarded to me by Putnam.

I fear this will be a short letter, as my time is strictly limited. However, I can put your mind at rest over certain matters. First, I have absolutely no intention of killing off M. I agree, he is essential to all Bond books. Neither do I intend to marry Bond to Flicka, though the return of Flicka in **SeaFire** was an attempt on my part to draw attention to one regular partner, in view of the AIDS menace. Unhappily, while my American publishers allowed specific mention of AIDS in **Never Send Flowers**, my British publishers - for some unknown reason - refused to allow me to make overt references.

The new Two Zeros and MicroGlobe One are conscious decisions. The point is that the British Secret Intelligence Service has undergone huge changes. Their downsizing has only amounted to 120 people - which I am sure has now been made up by the influx of new recruits - and the new headquarters is much larger than the old Century House. You will be aware that all Western intelligence agencies now have more officers in the field, as they have realized that satellite and electronic intelligence are not enough. The old order of human intelligence - real spies on the ground - has come to the fore again.

However, the largest change in the SIS is that while it retains a Chief of the Secret Intelligence Service (C in real life; M in Bond fiction) and five Deputy Chiefs, the entire Service is now answerable to a series of government committees. Those who own the literary copyright agreed with me that we should restructure the Bond fiction: hence Two Zeros and MicroGlobe One. These are a reflection of what is really happening. That I am personally appalled by this is neither here nor there.

To answer another query. Yes, I am to do the novelization of **Goldeneye**. My contract also calls for one more Bond novel - and here comes the bad news - after which there are no plans for future books. This could change if the movie, **Goldeneye**, takes off, but the main problem lies in the publishing market. We have watched the popularity of the Bond books wane over the past three years and, as publishers are driven by market forces it may well be that we will close shop for a while.

This, of course, could easily change should the new movie be a spectacular success. I have mixed feelings about all this. I have enjoyed doing the Bond books, but I am not getting any younger and I cannot deny they get more difficult all the time. It is only natural that I have more love for my own work - Kruger etc. - but I shall be sad to say goodbye to Bond, should that happen. We must wait and see once the next Bond is done.

I will try to find a photograph for you.

Again with thanks.

Sincerely,

JG

Photo will be sent later.

John Gardner's letter to Bill Kanas
Courtesy of Bill Kanas

RAYMOND BENSON

Zero Minus Ten (1997)
The Facts of Death (1998)
High Time to Kill (1999)
DoubleShot (2000)
Never Dream of Dying (2001)
The Man with the Red Tattoo (2002)

Novelizations
Tomorrow Never Dies (1997)
The World Is Not Enough (1999)
Die Another Day (2002)

Short Stories
"Blast from the Past" (1997)
"Midsummer Night's Doom" (1999)
"Live at Five" (1999)

Raymond Benson
Illustration by Pat Carbajal

Before we talk about your Bond novels, let's talk about how you got to know Glidrose Chairman, Peter Janson-Smith.

I met Peter in August of 1982. I really didn't even know who he was at the time...he simply responded to a letter I had sent to Glidrose. I was doing research for *The James Bond Bedside Companion* [the 1984 overview of Ian Fleming's life, his novels, and the movies]. I had started the book on my own initiative, thinking, "There will be no problem with cooperation" [from Glidrose and Eon]. There had already been John Brosnan's book on the films [*James Bond in the Cinema,* 1972, and Steve Rubin's book [*The James Bond Films: A Behind the Scenes History,* 1981]. As I started the book, I reached out to Glidrose and Eon.

Eon's lawyer wrote me back and said, "You cannot do this book." I thought, "Okay, fine. I won't deal with them at all; I'll use photos from a photo agency," which is what Steve Rubin did.

Then I heard from Peter [on behalf of Glidrose]. Peter Janson-Smith. I had no idea who he was, but I made an appointment to talk to them. When I met Peter, he didn't say, "By the way, I was Ian Fleming's agent." What he did say was, "This is not something we would get behind." But then, I had a lot of Fleming connections in England. I arranged to speak to Ivar Bryce [author and Fleming friend], Peter Fleming [Ian's brother], Fionn Morgan [Fleming's stepdaughter], and Robert Harling [author and Fleming friend]. So I wrote Peter back and told him about the people I had lined up to interview, and he said, "Oh, well. Okay. Why don't you come by the office and let's talk."

I went to the office on the first day that I was there, and we had a nice chat. That's when I realized who he was. He asked me, "Do you have some of your manuscript with you?" I said, "Yes, I do." He said, "Well, why don't you leave it with me and go off and do your interviews this week? Then, let's meet again at the end of the week." I came back at the end of the week, and he had left a package for me. The note said, "I love what you're doing, keep going. You have our permission to use quotes, although there will be a fee. Keep in touch." So I did. And we did.

The James Bond Bedside Companion came out in 1984, and the Fleming family apparently liked it. We started staying in touch and communicating a lot. We became really good friends. I would do little odd jobs, no pun intended, for Glidrose. John Gardner was the author then. I wrote the *Casino Royale* stage play. I was commissioned by Glidrose to do it. Little things like that.[4]

You became a friend of the court, and Peter Janson-Smith would send you manuscripts of the Gardner novels for your reaction.

54

Yes. They were usually already bound proof copies. They must have been American-proof copies. He wanted my opinion. Every now and then, I would question something that didn't fit in with the Fleming mythos. I didn't ever say, "I don't like this book," or anything like that. That never happened. It's hard to remember, but I probably gave two or three suggestions on something. I don't know if they were ever really incorporated. But he appreciated my input.

Peter called me in November of 1995, right before *GoldenEye* came out. I was working for Viacom, and was in my office there. The phone rang, and it was Peter. He said, "Raymond, John wants to hang up his hat. He's tired of it. I was wondering if you'd like to give it a shot."

I never campaigned for it. I never asked for it. I never thought it was even in the realm of possibilities. I was shocked. But I could not say no. I said, "I would like to try that." He said, "We need you to do something. First, I need you to come up with a plot, an outline, for us to look at. It would be on spec. And I need to approve it. We also need to show it to the British publisher and the American publisher." I had to get approval from three different groups. Once the outline was approved, they wanted me to write the first four chapters on spec. It was an audition, although they didn't call it that.

When you came on as the writer, was it always assumed that you would continue where Gardner left off and that the novels would be contemporary?
Before I started the books and before I even started the first outline, Peter and I had a couple of discussions along the lines of, "What direction are we going to go? Do I continue as John Gardner did in the 1990s? Or maybe we should set them back in the 1950s or 1960s. We discussed it. Peter decided to make them contemporary. He said, "I think we should stay in synch with Eon because these new movies look like they're going to be big." He had visions that now that Gardner was not writing the books, maybe Eon would look at my books as possible adaptations for movies. We were both hoping for that. Maybe I was naïve. Peter wanted my books to be more like Eon's movies, with more action and more humor.

I insisted that I wanted my Bond to be like Fleming's Bond. I wanted all of his vices intact. I wanted him to smoke. I wanted him to drink. I wanted him to womanize. Peter said that it might be anachronistic in the 1990s if Bond is the misogynistic dinosaur, but if you can make it work, fine. Let's see what you do. Apparently, I did. I made it work.

Another directive was that Peter wanted M to be a woman so that we would be in sync with the movies. Those were my only two directives. Make the books more like the movies so that they might be attractive to Eon and make M a female.

Raymond Benson at Misterious Book Shop, 1986
Courtesy of Gary J. Firuta

How did you come up with the plot for *Zero Minus Ten?*
It was November 1995, and I knew that the Hong Kong handover from the UK to China would happen in 1997, which would probably be when the book would come out if it was published. I thought it was an interesting milieu. I had no idea that Eon had considered a Hong Kong plot [which was the original story for *Tomorrow Never Dies*]. I don't think Peter did either. I'm firmly convinced that Glidrose had no clue. I don't know if Eon changed their plans after they heard about the plot of my book. Nobody will ever say.

Anyway, I said to Peter, "What about something to do with the Hong Kong handover? He said, "That sounds great." I spent most of November 1995 writing an outline. Peter read it and loved it. I think he approved it sometime in December. Then, I started working on the first four chapters and they were done around February of 1996. Then, they gave me the contract, and it was announced to the public in March of 1996 that I was the next guy.

You interviewed Gardner for *007 Magazine* in an expansive conversation that covered most of his Bond novels. What was your impression of Gardner?
I first met John when *The Bedside Companion* came out. My first book signing was in the Mysterious Bookshop in New York. Otto Penzler, who ran the place, set it up. John was in town signing the fourth book, *Role of Honour*. My book came out nearly simultaneously around the same time. We did a signing together, and that was great. John was very nice. We had started corresponding during the writing of my *Bedside Companion*. He knew who I was, and I interviewed him by phone but that was the first time we met in person. We may have had a little bit of contact for the rest of the 1980s.

Then, in the early 1990s, he was living in Virginia. I think Graham Rye [editor and founder of *007 Magazine*] suggested, "Why don't you try to get John Gardner to do a big in-depth interview." By that time, *Bondage*, the American fan club [that Benson also wrote for] was defunct. I contacted John and he said, "Why don't you come to Virginia for the weekend, and we'll hash it out." And I did. We bonded over that weekend and developed a friendship. I wrote the interview, and I guess John was pleased with it. [The interview appeared on Gardner's website for many years.]

Gardner wrote so many of them. Nearly one a year. What was your sense of his relationship to writing these books? I get the sense that he treated it partially as a job and a good one. I hope that it gave him pleasure but it was quite a pace.
I'm speculating here, and this is only my opinion, but I think he was getting tired of it towards the end. The first several were best sellers, and I think maybe four got on the *New York Times Bestseller List*. So that's good. That's an incentive to keep going. I think they probably did well enough in the 1980s, and I think starting in the early 1990s, the sales started to sag.

That's basically what Gardner said in an interview that I happened to read today.
I don't want to speculate, but I don't think that Glidrose wanted to change yet. As long as John was willing to keep going, they seemed happy to have him do it. I think the publishing philosophy at that time and even during my period was that they knew how many of these books would sell. They had an agreement with the American publisher and the British publisher. They knew the number they sold to a niche market. The

market was mostly Bond fans, but the general public didn't buy these books. So they knew how many books to print and they knew how many books would sell. They were always in the black. They sold less in England than they did in America. They sold a lot more in America.

My research also supports the notion that the American market was much more important at that time. Now, it's the opposite.
The American market was the market they concentrated on in the 1980s and 1990s.

Getting back to *Zero Minus Ten*, you have an effective scene where Bond is tortured with a cane. Where did that come from?
In the 1990s, there was an incident with a teenage boy [Michael Fay] who was caned in Singapore. It was all in the news [in 1994]. I read that China still did that sometimes. I thought, "We gotta have a torture scene. It might as well be something like that."

After Zero Minus Ten, you wrote The Facts of Death.
And in between, I wrote the *Tomorrow Never* Dies novelization.

Let's come back to that. For *The Facts of Death*, which was published the next year, did you start with the setting in Greece or the idea of the cult?
I would take a large map of the world and figure out the hotspots that Britain was concerned about. Then, through talking with friends and networking, I thought, what type of story could I develop? I would always start with a location and then develop the story from there.

I had to answer the question, Why did Britain own Hong Kong in the first place? Why were they giving it back? So I had to do the research. I learned that Britain and China had a war over opium in the 1800s, and Britain won the war. In the treaty, they gained the landmass that became Kowloon in Hong Kong. When they were writing the treaty, some fool in England said, "We'll give it back to you in 100 years." Britain was getting ready to honor the treaty. I thought, here are six million people who have lived under British rule, a democracy, for 100 years. Suddenly, they are being handed over to a communist country. How are they going to feel? How are British businesses and businessmen going to feel? That's how my villain developed. He's a British businessman whose business would be seriously affected. That's how I developed that story. I used that approach with all the books.

With the second one [*The Facts of Death*], I already knew about Cyprus. Cyprus is a divided country. The southern half, Cyprus, is

58

governed by Greece, and the northern half, the Turkish Republic of Northern Cyprus, is governed by Turkey...but it's also kind of Greek. The Brits police it. They police along the borderline there. It's like a North and South Korea situation. It's been that way since 1974. There's always been tension. With the Brits acting as policemen, I wondered if something happened there, what would the Brits do?

When *Zero Minus Ten* was in the works, I was online with these primitive chat groups, and there was a Bond fan there, a Greek guy named Panos Sambrakos. He's a big Bond fan, and we got friendly over chat. I reached out to him, and I said, "I'm thinking about setting my next book in Greece and Cyprus. Do you have any ideas?" Mainly, I was looking for places to go. Just like a movie, I was looking for cool locations to set scenes and set pieces. He had a lot of suggestions.

As far as the plot, Panos was helpful with Greek history and mythologies, about Pythagoras and stuff like that. He was a source for my research. Then, he agreed to be my guide if I came to Greece. [Benson named Bond's guide after Sambrakos.] For my first book, I went to Hong Kong, China, and Macau. I didn't go to Australia, but I didn't think I needed to. For my second book, I went to Greece and Cyprus.

For the first book, Bond gets his assignment from M, and he goes off. For this second book, you altered the formula. Bond's access to it is through M, who has been shaken down.
I wanted to humanize M a bit and show her personal life.

Today, authors like Faulks, Boyd, Deaver, and Horowitz are directed to largely ignore Eon's movies and stay true to Fleming. In some ways, you were told the opposite.
Yes. For my second book, I tried to do an Eon story. There's some goofy stuff in it. It's my least favorite of the six books. I love them all; they're all like my children. There's some really good stuff in it, but it's more like an Eon movie than the other books.

What was the initial spark for *High Time to Kill*?
The third book came about with the idea of mountain climbing. I thought Bond supposedly loved mountain climbing, but you never see that in any of the books. I thought, "Gosh, let's do that." I developed the plot to go around the MacGuffin. The MacGuffin was the formula for the skin of the airplane. I knew a guy from Lockheed who was a main, top-brass guy. I contacted him and asked, "Is this even possible?" I worked with him to develop the MacGuffin. It was "future-now" stuff.

What's noteworthy about the book is that Bond doesn't get to the mountain or his mission for a while. Instead, you set up a game of golf with an old rival from school. Their relationship pays off later, but there is plenty of pre-mission Bond living his life.

As I developed the story, I knew that I was going to have this other British guy be the villain. I also wanted to try to write a golf game, like Fleming did. I wanted to write a modern golf game. I don't even play golf, but my friend, Doug Redenius, is a big golfer, and he has connections at Stoke Poges, where Sean Connery played golf in the movie. I thought, "Let's use that course in the book." I was in England doing my research, and Doug was there. We had a caddy with us who worked at the club. The three of us walked the course. Doug would make suggestions about the kind of shots and clubs you would use. That's how the golf game came about. The Belgium part was simply me wanting to go to Belgium. I set that first part in Brussels because why not? It's a neat place.

How did you decide what car to give Bond?

Peter and I discussed which car should be Bond's. We almost went with the then-new Aston Martin but the Jaguar was hot at the time with the new XK8. I contacted Jaguar in England, and they set me up with one of the designers. He came up with the gadgets like color-changing pigments and the scout that comes out. By the way, the scout is what we now call a drone. In 1997 and 1998, we called it a scout.

***High Time to Kill, DoubleShot*, and *Never Dream of Dying* are known as your Union Trilogy because the evil organization, the Union, is featured in all three. When you were writing *High Time to Kill*, did you set off to write a trilogy?**

I did not. While I was writing it, I knew that I didn't want to resolve the Union just yet. At that point, I knew that I was going to use the Union again. Fleming probably didn't know he was going to write a SPECTRE trilogy per se. He used them again. I left it open at the end of *High Time to Kill,* suggesting they would be back in the next book, and they were. The leader of the Union, Le Gérant, was in the background. By the time I was writing *DoubleShot*, I figured that the next book would be the third Union book, and maybe I'd wind it up and kill off Le Gérant. By the time I started writing *Never Dream of Dying,* I knew that it would be a trilogy. The realization happened during the writing of the second one.

Normally you said that you start with a country or region that's a hot spot. But with *DoubleShot*, did you start with the notion of Bond and

his double?
Right. I was having a conversation with a friend about how doubles had been used a lot in movies. There's been lots of spy stories and mystery stories about a guy and his double. *The Man from UNCLE* had a double thing. In *Thunderball*, there's a double.

I also wanted to do a "Let's Kill Bond" story. That's the plot, the villains want to kill Bond. Fleming did it with *From Russia with Love,* and Gardner had his *Nobody Lives for Ever.* I wanted to do mine. So I thought, let's have the Union try to kill Bond. That's how it started. Then, I came up with the double idea. I wanted to see if I could do something different with it, something new. That was a challenge that I set for myself.

Then, the locations came about. I had already established that the Union was in Morocco. That idea came out of my head, out of a hat. This time, I realized, "Well, I guess I gotta go to Morocco." Before that, I had no plans to ever go to Morocco. But then I realized that if this story was going to develop into something, then I needed to go to Morocco. I always wanted to go to Spain. I had friends in Northern Spain who could help out with the locations. I thought, let's do Spain. At the heart of the plot is Gibraltar, which is a British hotspot. Gibraltar is like a stone in the shoe of Spain. Spain doesn't like that the British owns Gibraltar. They would like to control it again. They're friendly about it now, but at the time, I thought, "What if some nationalist guy wants to get Gibraltar back?" That's how the villain came about.

You wrapped up the story with *Never Dream of Dying*.
I wanted to do a story where I brought back Marc Ange Draco, Bond's former father-in-law [*On Her Majesty's Secret Service*]. He was from the Corsican mafia. One of the ideas was how he would feel about losing his daughter. We never learned how he felt. Would he blame Bond for Tracy's death? I think he probably would.

I know a lot of the fans think about the movie version of Marc Ange Draco and think he's a nice, lovable guy. When the book came out, some fans didn't like what I did with him. I don't think they were thinking about the real Marc Ange Drago from Fleming's books. In Fleming's books, he is a killer. He's the head of the Corsican mafia. He's a drug smuggler. He's a criminal. He's a bad guy. The only reason he befriends Bond is because he wants to help his daughter, and he thinks Bond can do it. So they become allies. I thought it was perfectly reasonable that he would hate Bond now that they no longer had Tracy in common. He would want to bring about Bond's demise.

Peter loved that idea. He loved the idea that Marc Ange Draco would become a vengeful father-in-law. He said, "This is terrific. This is fantastic." I went, "I'm glad that you like it because that's what I want to do." That all ties in with going to Corsica, which was amazing. That was one of the best trips. I also wanted to include the Cannes Film Festival because I wanted to go there. I wanted a plot about movies, and including the Cannes Film Festival would be a good target.

You also have a scene where Bond is locked up in the villain's lair and he bites a rat so that he can make a weapon from its bones.
I thought that was hardcore. I thought, "What's he going to do? Here's this damn rat that's bothering him." Bond thinks, "There's a sharp bone in that rat's body. I'm going to bite the bullet," so to speak. I thought that that was hardcore—Bond biting the backbone off of a rat so that he could have something sharp to kill somebody.

The Union trilogy doesn't completely wrap up the storyline after three books.
There were some leftover plot threads from the fifth book that got into the sixth book. Goro Yoshida, the guy who hires the bad guy in the fifth book is still alive at the end of that story. He becomes the villain for the sixth book. It's almost not a trilogy.

The villains' plot in your sixth and final book, *The Man with the Red Tattoo*, involves weaponizing mosquitoes.
I thought using genetically altered mosquitoes would be an interesting delivery method. I was prescient in that the West Nile virus became a big thing either at the time I was writing it or when the book came out. That was luck.

I wanted to take Bond back to Japan. I wanted to deal with his past and what happened with him and Kissy Suzuki [*You Only Live Twice*]. My Bond was Fleming's Bond. I wondered what memories he would have of his time with her and living with her. We know from Fleming that she got pregnant. I dealt with that child in my short story "Blast From the Past." I thought that would haunt him in many ways. I wanted to explore that.

In the end, Bond's experience in Japan offers him some closure. A quantum of solace, if you will.
Yeah. Yeah.

You mentioned "Blast from the Past," which was originally published in *Playboy* in an abridged version and then later in the 2008 collection *The Union Trilogy*.

"Blast from the Past" started as a Playboy commission. *Playboy* had published Fleming in the 1960s, and they had a relationship with the Bond movies. They had been in bed with Bond for many years. I had gotten to know Heffner after I sent him a copy of *The Bedside Companion* because I knew that he was a Bond fan. I was of age in the 1970s and 1980s when I had a subscription to *Playboy*. After I sent him the book, he wrote back to me. He said, "I love this book. If you're ever in Los Angeles, let me know, and you can come to the mansion." So I did.

We became friends. Anytime my wife and I were in LA, I'd always go to the Playboy Mansion. Before my book came out, I suggested to Peter, "Why don't we hit up Hef? I'll ask if they want to do a short story." Peter said, "That sounds like a great idea." I wrote to Hef and suggested it. He said, "By all means. Absolutely. Let's do it."

I wrote the short story, and then Playboy said, "It's too long. We can't fit the story into one issue, and we don't want to spread it over two issues. We want to do it in one." It was published first in truncated form. They cut out a third of it. They did it judiciously. I thought they did a nice job. Alice Turner was the great fiction editor at *Playboy* and she was the one who did it. When I got the chance to do the anthology books, we published the full-length version.

What do you remember about the writing experience?

At the time, I was writing *Zero Minus Ten*. I had already written some of it. I was in the process of writing it. I had to put it aside and write the short story. That was done pretty quickly. I think I had to write it around April of 1996, and then Playboy saved it for the January 1997 issue. That was their big issue. January was always a big issue for them.

That must have been tough to stop the momentum of writing your first novel to write the short story.

I had that experience several times. I had to write the film novelizations in the middle of writing the original novels. I had already started *The Facts of Death* when I had to write *Tomorrow Never Dies*. I had already started *DoubleShot* when I had to write *The World Is Not Enough*.

I feel the premise of "Blast from the Past"—Bond is investigating the death of his son—is strong enough that it could have worked as a novella. In it, Bond's past is coming back to haunt him, as does Draco's past in *Never Dream of Dying*.

Yes, I liked exploring that stuff. John Gardner never did. Kingsley Amis didn't. I liked exploring Bond's past and those loose ends. I wanted to explore how Bond would feel about those events. They would have been traumatic. This was before Daniel Craig's Bond movies. They didn't go into his past, but they are introspective. When I was writing them, they didn't do that in the movies. I thought that was unique to my Bond books. At one point, I was considering doing something with his parents. I think Peter may have said, No, let's, let's leave that alone." But I can't recall the particulars.

That's interesting because Jeffery Deaver's *Carte Blanche* and Steve Cole's *Red Nemesis* explore the backstory of Bond's parents. As the mandates of Ian Fleming Publications change, so too can the content of the books.
I know John Gardner wanted to do something about Bond's son. At some point, John proposed it. But he wasn't allowed to do it because of the show *James Bond, Jr.,* and Eon owned any offspring of Bond. Peter and I talked about it. I said I wanted to do it. He asked, "How can we do this?" I said, "What if Bond's son is dead? What if he's a corpse? If he's a corpse, he's not a character." Peter said, "That's the way to do it." Maybe he consulted a lawyer or something. I don't know. He said, "Go ahead, make him a corpse." That's how we did it.

Your second short story was "Midsummer Night's Doom."
That one was commissioned by Playboy. They came to us. I think Hef and I were talking at a party when I was there. The 45th anniversary of *Playboy* was coming up, and they were going to do a big, special issue. Hef said, "You should write a story where James Bond comes to the Playboy Mansion and meets me." He was joking; he was being facetious. I said, "We could do that. Probably. Maybe…let me talk to the bosses." I approached it as a novelty story. It's only a joke. A lot of fans thought, "This is trash." But it was meant to be no more serious than *Bond Strikes Camp* or *Alligator* [the 1963 and 1962 parody works].

That's another example of context dictating form. Then your third published short story was "Live at Five."
It was commissioned. *TV Guide* approached Glidrose. *TV Guide* came to them and said, "We're doing this special issue in November with Pierce Brosnan. We've interviewed him, and he's on the cover. Would you like to contribute a short story?" We said, "Sure." They said, "We'd like it to have something to do with television." I thought about that and thought

that I could set it here, in Chicago, because that would be easy. Keep in mind that I was in the middle of finishing up edits for *High Time to Kill*, starting *DoubleShot*, and *The World is Not Enough.* 1999 was my busiest year. I had two short stories and two novels come out in 1999.

So I set "Live at Five" in Chicago. I knew Janet Davis, who was an anchor at one of the local stations, and I wanted to use her as a character. She was gorgeous, and she was perfect as a Bond girl. She agreed to lend her name to it. She had to ask permission from the TV station for the character to sleep with Bond.

The story itself was short. They said that it couldn't be more than so many words. *Playboy* never did that with "Blast from the Past." That's why that one was so long. *TV Guide* said that "Live at Five" has to fit in a certain amount of space.

Your fourth Bond short story, "The Heart of Erzulie," was originally unpublished. You updated it, removed Bond, and it appears in a revised form in your 2015 collection *12+1: Twelve Short Thrillers and a Play.*

That was a story that I came up with and wrote. By that time, Peter was kind of out of the situation, and Ian Fleming Publications was being run by Corinne Turner and Zoe Watkins [publishing manager]. They felt like it was more of a pastiche. They weren't interested in pursuing it. I thought it was a pretty good story. That was fine with me. I still had another novel to write, and I was working on *The Man with the Red Tattoo* at the time. I was about to go to Japan to do the research, so I let it go. Years and years later, I took out all the references to Bond, made it a different character, and published it in my anthology.

You changed Bond to a character named Brock, but it's easy to imagine Bond as the hero. When you do, I think it's a fun Bond short story.

I agree, and John Cox [Bond expert and creator of the fan site The Book Bond] really likes it, too. He has been a big supporter of mine. When the story wasn't published [in 2001], I used the villain's name in my book *Sweetie's Diamonds* (2006). I thought it was a cool name. I also used some of the voodoo stuff and Erzulie stuff in another book, *Torment: A Love Story* (2018).

The Bond books were your first published novels. What a way to start.

The Bedside Companion was my first book. In the 1980s, I had written a couple of short stories that weren't published. But then I got into the whole computer gaming world. I was a writer, creating story-based adventure games and role-playing games. Writing those games involves incorporating and creating universes, storylines, dialogue, characters, plots, obstacles, puzzles, and everything that goes into writing a thriller. That's really where I honed my fiction writing. Peter was well aware that I was doing this.

In the late 1980s, I did try writing a novel. My first novel was a mystery detective story. Peter read it. He had complimentary things to say about it. He said, "I think you've got a great plot here. Maybe the characters need developing." Or something along those lines. "As a first novel, it's not bad, but I don't think it's publishable." I had some people read it here in the States. Got the same feedback. I put it in the proverbial drawer. But Peter knew that I could start and finish a novel. That was all before he asked me to write Bond.

It's also notable that he didn't think your novel was ready, but he still saw something in you as a writer who could write a Bond continuation. He also saw someone who understood Fleming and someone he could work with, which is also a factor in selecting a continuation author.
We were good friends, and we had a great rapport. I knew the Bond universe, the movies, and the Fleming books really well. I think John Gardner might not have really known the Fleming works. He saw the movies and enjoyed them. But he wasn't into the Bond phenomenon like I had been since I was nine years old. I think that had a lot to do with it.

Did being the first American present any problems?
That was tough for the first couple of books. By the time I got to number three, I think I was doing pretty well. I would spend a lot of time in England. Peter probably thought, "We'll be editing him, and he'll have a British editor. If any Americanisms slip in, we can fix that." I think some Americanism slipped in anyway. I got better as the books went along.

Since Bond, you've had a long career as a novelist. You've evolved as a writer since your Bond books. With all those skills you picked up, I wonder what you would bring to Bond now.
I think about it too. I think I'm a much better writer. I've got a lot more experience under my belt. I've written a lot of novels. I'm sure that if I went back and read my Bond novels, I'd probably wince a few times. I

don't know. I have no idea. I think they're pretty darn good if I say so myself. I think by the time I was writing *The Black Stiletto* books [2011–2014], I'd honed what I had done. *Black Stiletto* is my magnum opus.

After six original novels, three novelizations, and three short stories, your tenure came to a close. It also signaled a change in how Ian Fleming Publications would treat the release schedule. After your tenure, there would be a break, and they wouldn't publish a new Bond each year.
The publishing philosophy at the time was to do a book a year and get it out there. Then Peter retired, and the company started changing some of their approach. 2003 was going to celebrate the 50th anniversary of *Casino Royale*. They decided to stop my books and celebrate that anniversary by reissuing all of Fleming's books. Basically, they thought my contract was over, I had my six, and they were going to start focusing on different directions and changing their philosophy. They got the Young Bond books going. They did the Moneypenny books. They didn't even think about doing another adult Bond book until about six years later with Sebastian Faulks' book [2008's *Devil May Care*]. I think they were thinking of going with a big-name writer like Faulks to do one book at a time. I'm speculating here. I don't want to speak for them.

Who do you think the continuation novels are for? The general public or hardcore Bond fans.
When Sebastian's book came out, it was promoted as this big new Bond book. It was almost like, "This is the first Bond book since Fleming." The general public was seeing it that way. It sold very well. I have no idea how subsequent books have done. I don't know if they were bestsellers or not. I do know that the Bond reader fans scarf them up. Bond reader fans collect them and get all the different editions. A lot of libraries carry them. Are the people who are buying Tom Clancy spin-offs and Lee Child books also picking up the new Bond? I have no idea.

Your Bond books came out immediately after Gardner and close enough to Fleming that Bond's age almost lined up. You had to adjust the age a bit and mention the gray in his hair. As with the first wave of Eon films that directly linked Connery to Moore to Brosnan, your books were linked from Fleming to Gardner to you.
Gardner didn't say how old Bond was, but he would have been too old. My Bond would definitely have been too old. We say that he's a little older and wiser, just like in the movies. The first five actors up through

Pierce Brosnan were supposed to be the same guy. They are. I think with Daniel Craig they started over and did a whole different bubble that's separate from the rest of the series.

I was thinking that the Bond novels were written at the start of your career. Your book *The Mad, Mad Murders of Marigold Way* (2022) is as good as anything you've ever written.
It's been tough. It's been tough because the people who read my Bond books don't read my other books. The people who read my other books don't read the Bond books. They are different audiences. There are some fans like you who have read both. Some people follow me and read all my stuff. However, the reading community, especially the mystery community and the thriller community, don't read both.

Why is that?
I don't know, but Bond fans only like the Bond stuff. Maybe if I was doing hard-boiled spy stuff, that might interest them. After I finished Bond, I decided I didn't want to write anything like that. I didn't want to create my own secret agent. There were a lot of people telling me I should do that. They said, "Now that you're no longer writing Bond books, why don't you create your own guy? Just write Bond books that aren't Bond books." I've done Bond, and anything else would be an imitation. I would be doing something like *Our Man Flint*, which is an imitation of James Bond. I don't want to do that. My interests went more towards Hitchcockian thrillers, more of an everyman-caught-in-extraordinary-circumstances kind of story. That was more of what I wanted to do, more personal stuff.

What has your time with Bond meant to you?
It's going to be my footnote in history. It's what I'm going to be remembered for. I would love for it to be *The Black Stiletto* or one of my other books. After I'm gone, it's going to be "Raymond Benson has died. He was the first American to write James Bond."

Not too shabby.
That's not too shabby. No, it's okay. I'm fine with that.

CHARLIE HIGSON

SilverFin (2005)
Blood Fever (2006)
Double or Die (2007)
Hurricane Gold (2007)
By Royal Command (2008)

Short story:
"A Hard Man to Kill" (2009)

Novella:
On His Majesty's Secret Service (2023)

Charlie Higson
Illustration by Pat Carbajal

The Young Bond books were quite a departure for the series. How did you get involved?
I wrote four adult crime thrillers in the early 1990s [*King of the Ants* (1992), *Happy Now* (1993), *Full Whack* (1995), and *Getting Rid of Mister Kitchen* (1996)]. I then moved into a career doing comedy for TV, which took up all my time. I had a fantastic editor called Kate Jones, who was brilliant. She left publishing for a while; when she decided to get back to

work, she ended up at Ian Fleming Publications [IFP], the Fleming Estate.

The Estate was looking at all the anniversaries that were coming up for Fleming and Bond. Because the film franchise was being relaunched with *Casino Royale* [in 2006], the Estate wanted to remind people that it all started with Fleming. They wanted to drive people back to the books. They also wanted to revamp the continuation novels. Some of the continuation novels had done quite well, particularly the early ones. They felt that it would be good to get proper literary authors to work on the adult Bond books. Eventually, the first one in the revamp was written by Sebastian Faulks. They also felt it would be a good thing to try and do a strand of Young Bond books.

At the beginning of the Millennium, there was a resurgence in books—particularly in books for boys—that were exciting thrillers and adventure stories. Before that, they had been slightly frowned upon. I think what happened was that children's fiction in the 1970s had been written in the voice of the 1950s and 1960s. It was those "Boy's Adventures" books—all colonialist, imperialist, dubious xenophobic adventure stories for boys. There wasn't much for girls. So publishers said, "If we start publishing the books that boys *and* girls might want to read, there might be a switch." And lo and behold, you start writing books for girls, and girls start reading them. But boys stopped, and it swung too far the other way. Then there were some forays into boys' books and, obviously, on the back of the huge success of Harry Potter, suddenly kid's books were a respectable area to be in. And the kids were reading a lot.

Suddenly there were two main writers, mainly in the thriller field, who were writing for boys. There was Anthony Horowitz with his Alex Rider books [about a teenage spy]. Obviously, Anthony went on to write three of the adult Bond continuations. He makes no bones that his Alex Rider books were about a teenage James Bond in the contemporary world. He called him Alex Rider, and the implication was that he was the son of Honeychile Rider and James Bond. Of course, he couldn't officially say that. There was also the CHERUB novel series about a teenage secret agent figure by Robert Muchamore, which was a huge hit in the United Kingdom.

The Fleming Estate thought, "We've got James Bond. We've got the character that they're all copying. We should be doing our own teenage spy series." So they started looking around for writers to do those books. I'm pretty sure they did speak to Anthony about doing

Young Bond, and I'm pretty sure he turned them down. He had Alex Rider, and it was doing well, so he didn't need it.

But Kate Jones, my old editor, is working for the Estate. She knew me, and she knew my writing. I've always loved American stripped-back, hard-boiled fiction that was direct, punchy, and to the point. Kate felt that style would work well for kids because there are not a lot of flowery descriptions or internal monologues. Instead, it's people doing things. Kate also knew that I had three boys who were the target age and that I was a big James Bond fan. She suggested me to the Estate, and they decided to talk to me. I was vetted in a secret MI6-style meeting with Kate, and she sounded me out. Eventually, she was able to tell me what the project was and would I be interested in it.

Where did the idea of *SilverFin*, the first book, come from?
The idea for *SilverFin* sprang fully formed into my mind. I had been looking for something to write for my boys. Something along the lines of an action-adventure story with a young boy. It was perfect for me. It also came at the right time, when I was slightly scaling back on the TV front. My kids were at the age where I wanted to spend more time with them. The idea of being able to write something that would have been cool when I was a kid and something that would be cool for my kids was appealing. I jumped at the chance.

I put forward a plan for the book and how it might work, even over the series. That plan was submitted to the Fleming Family and the Estate. Then I went to the Fleming headquarters. The big money in the Fleming family is from the banking side of the family. They had these huge, swanky headquarters, a kind of Bond villain thing. It was built on top of a glass-roofed dining area, and it was all ornate. There was a uniformed staff. It was like a meeting with a Bond villain, except that they were very nice. They didn't try to feed me to piranhas. I was vetted both on the writing front and the type of person that they would like to work with and would get on with. I hadn't written for children, but I had written for adults, and I had a profile for writing for TV. I was considered a serious author, and I was media-friendly…which was a big help.

What was the writing process like?
I had a lot of fun writing the book, actually sitting down and writing the words, "Bond, James Bond." It was really exciting. I got to write the actual James Bond. I'm not writing about his nephew or someone who is like Bond. I had the luxury of writing the first book, delivering it, editing it, and getting it ready for publication before it was even announced.

It was understood with IFP that, whilst I didn't need to submit every chapter for scrutiny, if they felt it wasn't working, then it wouldn't see the light of day as a Bond novel. If that happened, I could always change Bond's name and publish it [as an original novel, without any reference to 007]. Luckily, everybody liked it. Then, it was all systems go, with the publisher lined up, and then we were going to announce it. Suddenly I thought, "Oh, my God. This is badly wrong. This is James Bond, one of the best-known characters in the world…of all time." I had avoided looking at the fan sites but when things were announced, then I started to look. I then realized how big and fanatical this Bond community is and how they scrutinize everything closely. I thought, "Let's see how this goes."

What was your perception of the Bond community's reaction to the idea of the books?
Of course, when it was first announced that I was writing a Young Bond novel, the Bond community was up in arms. They had the idea of a Harry Potter-style James Bond book. They were taking the piss out of it. A lot of them said, "I have no intention of ever reading this book. But I will, of course, buy it so that my James Bond collection is complete." The world of the male James Bond collector must have every single edition of every book and as much as the obscure stuff as they can get a hold of. I thought, "I don't care if you read it or not, as long as you bought it."

Luckily, when the book came out, they universally changed their tune. They actually liked it. They realized that I had been faithful to Fleming and that I tried to channel his worldview. I didn't try to write in his style; that would have been impossible. Yet, I wanted to have the feel of Fleming, have nods to Fleming, and be respectful to him. I tried to write the story in a way that he may have written if he had been writing them. Of course, there is no implication in Fleming's books that James Bond started being "James Bond" in the 1930s.

Your book came out in 2005. When did you first meet with IFP? Would that be 2003?
It probably would have been about then.

To get approved in the first place, was it a two-part process? You had to get the approval of IFP and the Estate?
Yes, but the family has always been very involved in the Estate, particularly when it was set up [and renamed] as Ian Fleming Publications because the Estate had rested with someone else. [For

years, a company called Booker owned 51% of the rights.] The family had brought it all in-house. Fleming's nieces Lucy and Kate were still very involved, perhaps slightly less now, as they're older. There are now younger members of the family involved in that process. There is also a small team who do the day-to-day work, which is run by Corrine Turner. At the time, Kate Jones had been brought in to revamp the whole literary side. While working on *SilverFin*, I worked with Kate and a good editor at Puffin called Rebecca McNally. Having the two of them together was fantastic. The book would go through Corrine and through the Estate and I'd get feedback from them.

What was important to them?
The brief was to stick as closely as possible to any of the facts and any of the backstory that had been included in Fleming's books. That's slightly tricky because Fleming tried to keep Bond roughly 35 years old, over 10 years of writing books. So the backstory doesn't always line up from book to book. Fleming was writing them in the pre-internet days with no thought that people would actually sit down and study these books, make timelines, make it all work out, or write academic papers on them. He would have been absolutely delighted but amazed that the world of Bond studies exists now. When he was writing them, there were continuity errors between books. Things he said in one book would be completely contradicted in the next one. Nobody bothered about it as long as we're caught up in the story.

How did you determine the setting?
We settled that my books would be set in the early 1930s. We could have gone with the early 1920s. I thought that the 1930s was a more interesting period, historically, because you had everything that was going on in Europe. It was the rise of fascism, the rise of communism, depression, disruption, and how radical politics were becoming. I thought that was a more interesting background than the 1920s.

How did you begin?
I reread all the Fleming books in chronological order and just noted down any facts. There are few mentions of him as a child. There's a mention of him at a beach making sandcastles in one book and going to see the cinema as a kid. It's tiny, tiny things except for the famous obituary in *You Only Live Twice*, which is really the only time that Fleming gives us a backstory for Bond. The backstory was the perfect one for a kid's book because it makes him an orphan.

In kids' books of this style, the kids are always orphaned. Just like in a fantasy book like Harry Potter, the kids are always orphaned or separated from their parents and separated from that domestic world. This way, they can go on that great adventure. I think going to boarding school plays well with that. The kids are not at home with their mom and dad. They're not dealing with pesky brothers and sisters. They're in a community of children who run their own world. I think that's the appeal of boarding school stories like Harry Potter.

My Bond went to Eton; his mother was Swiss; his father was Scottish, and they died in a climbing accident. I knew that I had to somehow deal with the incident between him and that maid at the school. I worked out from the start about how I would handle that [in the final book in the series]. It was quite fun having something to aim towards.

So that was the stipulation—stick as closely as possible to the Fleming books, to not contradict anything in them, and, if possible, try not to bring in anything from the films that weren't in the books. It had to remain completely Fleming-based to be true to the spirit of Fleming. Kate had known him when they were younger, so it was great to have that actual connection to him. They would make some interesting comments on the books like "He wouldn't have liked that" or "He would have loved that." I initially wrote a dog into the book. I thought it'd be great. Kids' adventure stories often have dogs. But they said that Ian hated dogs. So I had the dog put down. Little things like that were great so that it had an authentic flavor.

You've spoken about what you retained from Fleming, but what did you change?
I did change quite a lot. The Young Bonds don't have that xenophobia that's in the Fleming books because Eton at that time was reasonably diverse. A lot of wealthy foreigners and foreign royal family members would send their kids to Eton. Kids came from different parts of the empire, and Bond would have mixed with a reasonably diverse bunch of extremely wealthy and posh people. So young Bond doesn't say nasty things about foreigners, and he doesn't yet have Fleming's extreme views on women.

What did you want to highlight about Bond's character?
What I wanted to do in the books was to show what damage this kid goes through that might make him grow up to be the adult Bond, one who is a damaged character. To show why he might mistrust people and why he might always, in the end, come to rely only on himself; to see himself as

being the only person he could trust.

Can you talk about the document that outlined your vision for book one?

As a written document, it was fairly short. It was written mainly so that I could go into the meeting and talk about it with the family and talk it through. I used it to explain that I wanted to tell a James Bond story on a level that kids could relate to. So all the familiar aspects of Bond's world would be there but in a form that kids could understand.

The structure goes back to what Umberto Eco said about a classic James Bond plot being a chess match [in his essay "Narrative Structures in Fleming," 1965]. That was my model for the actual story. The document I wrote said that he's going to Eton, but he's not going to officially be a teenage spy. It's clear from Fleming that he only joined the service in World War II. But for one reason or another, he would get involved in Bond-style adventures.

Initially, I was worried about him going to Eton and worried if kids would relate to this posh boy in a uniform, which was a black tailcoat and a bow tie. I decided that's James Bond's superhero outfit. That's the prototypical look for him. I thought, "Okay, that's great." Then I wondered, what is Bond famous for? Driving a fast car. So it seemed obvious that in the first book, he would need to learn to drive a car, even if he's underage. He does it on his uncle's land in Scotland; it's private land, and he can do what he wants. When things happen in the story, he has to actually drive a car on the roads in order to get away. As for firing guns and shooting people, I avoided that through all the books. The villains get killed, but I don't think that Bond ever actually kills any of them himself.

Right, they tend to get hoisted on their own petard.

Exactly, I couldn't have a 13-year-old shooting people. I think he does get a hold of a gun and a couple of weapons but only uses them to break and destroy things. The guns are there. The villains have guns. We didn't have him smoking, although kids at Eton in those days would have been smoking. For alcohol, he couldn't officially be drinking. But in one of the books, I had it so that the villain is torturing him by forcing him to drink spirits. That's a rite of passage that many teenagers go through the first time that they sneak a bottle and start drinking it with their mates. They wind up sick.

As for having sex with lots of women, the book can't explicitly depict sex. I did make sure that there's a strong and interesting female character who gets involved in his adventures. He has respect for her and enjoys being with her. So it was a matter of bringing everything down to that kid's level so that they could relate.

How many pages was that document?
A couple of pages because it was more of a verbal presentation about my approach to the whole series.

That's interesting because other authors had to submit much more detailed documents. Gardner submitted detailed outlines. Benson had to submit chapters as he went.
I think back in those days they were dealing with a different Estate and a different approach. From the start of this, there was the understanding that if they accepted my basic idea and took me on board, "We're not going to look over your shoulder. We trust you." There was mutual respect. There was also that "get out clause," which was that, in the end, if the book didn't work for them, I'd get it all back. He wouldn't be James Bond, but I could publish it elsewhere.

That's what happened with Geoffrey Jenkin's *Per Fine Ounce*; his manuscript was rejected. Although the circumstances of that book were quite different than yours. With *SilverFin*, you start with Bond at school in Eton, and you establish his world. Then, later, you get into the particulars of Bond's life. You don't start with the end and then put him in school. You do a lot of world-building, and then more than halfway through the book, you get into the plot and the villain's story.
My books are longer than Fleming's because he came up with a fantastic device. On the first page of his book, Bond can go into M's office, and M can say, "This is the villain. This is what he's doing. Can you stop him?" For a standard thriller, the first half is finding all this out. But M has done that for all of us. This way, we can get on to the fun bits where Bond goes in and sorts the villains out. It's a neat and economical way of writing a thriller. *From Russia with Love* is different.

I couldn't do that because he's a teenage boy and he's at school. I always had to arrange it so that somehow, through his life and what was happening at school or just outside of school, he gets involved in this big, outside plot. In *SilverFin*, the villain is introduced early on, and there is the standard competition between him and Bond [in the form of a school race], and Bond can turn the tables on Hellebore.

I had to create a world that's my fantasy version of the 1930s. It's a slower build up but in the end, it did help that he was at Eton. They have their own rules, their own way of doing lessons—well, their own way of doing everything. It's such a strange school…there is a bit of Hogwarts about it. At first, it was difficult to get inside that. Any books about Eton are written *by* old Etonians *for* old Etonians. So, they're not bothering to explain how the school works. Luckily, a friend of my father-in-law had been at Eton, and he had this book, which was a year in the life of an Etonian boy. It was a day-by-day recounting of what they go through and how it all works. That was very useful.

The other thing that was useful is that the head librarian at Eton at the time was a huge Bond fan. Eton is proud that Ian Fleming—and Bond—went there. It gives them a certain level of cool. They have this amazing collection of Fleming first editions as well as from other ex-pupils, like Shelley. The head librarian is also the keeper of the history of the school. I would go up and talk to him about stuff. He would say here's this, and maybe you might be able to use that in the book, or that would be a good plot. He would read the manuscripts of each book and would say, "You got that bit right. That's not quite right. This bit here is sort of right, but if you do this, it would be a lot of fun." He was able to help create that world. He was able to bring in some of Fleming's biography and the things he did at Eton. That's why Bond gets involved in the running race, which is the equivalent of the card game [in *Moonraker*] or the golf game [in *Goldfinger*]. It's an early competition in the book between Bond and the villain. One of the things that Fleming enjoyed doing at Eton was athletics, so I made Bond a runner. So through all of that, I thought I could build up to Bond getting involved in Hellebore's fiendish plot.

You were able to do so much world-building in book one that I think, in some ways the second book, *Blood Fever,* would be harder to write. The world-building gave you so much guidance and structure. Furthermore, you have to come up with another adventure that a young boy could plausibly be involved with.
There were things that I wanted to do. I wanted to send him abroad…somewhere exotic. I had to follow what goes on at the school. It had to go through the entire school year. He packs a lot into this first year. [Laughing.] He had to go somewhere abroad that he could travel to and back in the summer holiday. We're looking at the Mediterranean, and Fleming hadn't done Sardinia. I had been on holiday there, and I thought, "You could have a great adventure set here." Then it became setting up the story that would work with him going to Sardinia and getting involved in this Mussolini-style New Roman Emperor-type plot. In retrospect, the

second book is possibly a little dense. I probably tried to put a little too much into it. I could have streamlined the story a bit, but it was a chance to do Bond going somewhere exotic.

What was your inspiration for your third book, *Double or Die?*
I wanted to have Bond get involved in gambling because that's a big part of what Bond does. I'd always wanted to do an adventure story based on cryptic clues. That's what we ended up using in this one. It was not a great idea. Because all the clues are verbally based and based on the English language, that made it untranslatable.

We were getting good sales around Europe, particularly in Germany, which was the biggest market outside of the UK. Suddenly, we had to ask, how do we deal with these word-based clues, which are all based on English words? Some of them were easier to translate than others, but you couldn't do a direct translation. You had to find a different way of doing that. As far as the Japanese edition, God knows what happened.

I also like the idea of his teacher being kidnapped and his friend [Pritpal] having to work out where he's gone. The villain comes to the school and then we have the actual card game where Bond bests the villain. I liked the idea of doing something in the London Docklands [the former docks on the river], which was a pretty extraordinary place at the time. There were a lot of interesting parts of the Docklands, secret parts that I could use.

Each book is a self-contained adventure but each book also builds on Bond's lore. In *Double or Die*, Bond has an opportunity to shoot a villain in cold blood and he opts not to. You make the point that, at this time in Bond's life, he is not prepared to kill.
I couldn't have Bond shooting people, particularly not in cold blood. But this is the next stage in his process of being the cold-hearted killer that he is as an adult. That's really where I left him at the end of the fifth book, *By Royal Command*. Everything has gone wrong, and his idea of the world has changed.

There's a moment at the end of the fifth book where he beats up the bully of the school. Bond beats the bully quite savagely. We're meant to think that he's gone a bit too far there. That's the closest I can get to having him shoot the bully, as it were. There's a distinction in *Double or Die*. He's not a child, but he's still a young teenager. That's part of the process that I was going through in the books. It's having these events happen to him that determines where his life goes.

In terms of Bond's development, the books are carefully calibrated. You are incrementally making him more isolated and damaged. In the coda, there is a special guest appearance by the adult Bond.
I don't know if I should have done that or not. I was itching to write a bit about the adult James Bond. When the book came out, some people thought that was the end of the series because we'd jumped ahead to him being an adult. I also wanted to tell people who Alan Turing was and what an important role he played in winning the war.

When Kate Jones first came to pitch the idea of writing Young Bond to me, it was all secretive. She starts by saying, "I'm working for the James Bond Estate, and we're trying to revamp the literary side." I was thinking, "Oh, God, she's gonna ask me if I want to write an adult continuation novel." At that point, I thought, "I couldn't possibly do that. What can I do that hasn't been done in any of the previous books and all the films? What can I bring to it? That would be so difficult." When she said it was about Bond as a young teenager, that was a relief. I thought, "Okay, well, that would be interesting. Ian Fleming didn't write about that. So there was space for me to bring my stuff to that."

I had this fantastic framework, scaffolding that Fleming had created that I could then hang on bits of my own and come up with new bits of James Bond lore. By the time I'd got to write that third book, I was so immersed in the world of Bond. I'd been writing him as a young man and thinking about him growing up. It's in the water. It's before Fleming starts writing about the adult Bond. I wanted to have a go at writing a bit of the adult Bond.

Did you check with IFP?
I said if you don't think this is right, I can easily take it out. But they were happy with it.

What was the creative spark with your fourth book *Hurricane Gold*?
I knew that the fifth and last book, *By Royal Command*, was going to be about the incident with the maid. So I knew I needed to fit in another adventure between the third and fifth books. I thought it would be fun to not have to go through all the rigmarole of being at school and somehow coming across a world-shattering event at Eton. I thought, let's go more Fleming and throw him into the adventure at the start. Let's have it have nothing to do with school and take him out of that environment. Let's have him on more of an adult-style adventure, with him as an individual [and not with his friends, as with the previous books]. Although, he does

team up with Precious Stone in *Hurricane Gold*. I thought, let's rip and have this tremendous adventure in Mexico.

It was also inspired by another book. My favorite book is *Pop. 1280* by Jim Thompson. He wrote another book called *The Getaway*, and Sam Peckinpah made a pretty good go of it [in 1972 with Steve McQueen and Ali MacGraw], and there was another version of it [with Alec Baldwin and Kim Bassinger]. Neither of those films dealt with the end of the book, which is really what it's all about. In the book, Doc and the woman do get away, but they get away to a state run by criminals. It is an island where criminals go to get away. Once they're there, they can't escape; they're trapped. *The Getaway* is an amazing piece of writing. It's desolate, and it's a version of hell. You can't escape from your crimes. I love the idea of a criminal mini-state that is run by a criminal and has all the criminals in it.

Fleming wrote about American gangsters in three of his books [*Live and Let Die*, *Diamonds Are Forever*, and *The Man with the Golden Gun*], although not always effectively. I wanted to write about American gangsters who have a lot of machine guns.

Young Bond is up against the human threat of gangsters, but an even bigger threat is nature. Having the hurricane and floods was an effective way to change the nature of the threats.

Fleming loved nature; he was fascinated by it. He put a lot of that into his books. Not only the underwater stuff, but he also wrote about Jamaican wildlife. The "Rat Run" in *Hurricane Gold* is inspired by the novel *Dr. No* and the rat run Doctor No built inside his base. There are also elements of Indiana Jones. I wanted to let it rip and have a full-on adventure where these kids go through this maze of death. *Hurricane Gold*, or maybe *SilverFin*, is probably the most popular book amongst kids. They particularly like the idea of the rat run.

Your final Young Bond was *By Royal Command*. You were five books into the series, but I felt like, creatively, you still had a lot of energy in your tank.

There could have been more. It had always been discussed as a five-book series. When we were getting to the fifth book, there were a lot of discussions about doing more. IFP wanted more. Penguin Puffin [the publisher] wanted more. I was in the position of thinking, "I don't want to spend the rest of my life writing someone else's creation."

Also, because of the deal with IFP, I wasn't getting all the proceeds, as it were. One of the other continuation authors said that writing the books was a bit like polishing somebody else's gold. [Laughs.]

As much as I love doing it, I wanted to write a series of books that were my thing. After having written the fifth one, I said, "Look, I want to go off and try something else." Never say never again. It would be good to come back.

Had you given any thought to the sixth book in the Young Bond series?

I did have an idea. It's the story of him going to Fettes and what happens to him in Scotland. I planted some seeds in the other books. As it was, my *Enemy* series [of seven books] took off and I felt that I had to dedicate my energies to that. Fleming did it himself with his fifth book, *From Russia with Love*, which was his last throw of the dice. He put everything he had into it, all his energies. It's certainly the best-written of his books. It's got that fabulous opening section where Bond isn't even there other than as a target. It was about the inner workings of the Russian Secret Service. Fleming [apparently] kills Bond at the end of it.

Fleming's books were successful. They were doing well in the UK, but they hadn't taken off in America. He always knew that success in America was what he needed to cement the series to avoid being another parochial little English crime series. He wanted to try to get films made because that would give the character longevity. He worked hard on *From Russia with Love*, putting everything into it, and then he leaves Bond dead. He also knows that if things pick up, then he can come back to it. "Oh, there's an antidote. Let's move on."

I was slightly in the same position on this, having built towards this fifth book from the start. It might have been looking at only a four-book series. I don't remember. But that's partly why *Hurricane Gold* slipped in. It's not part of the inexorable progress of the school year. So I was able to throw that in.

With the fifth book, I was doing the same thing as Fleming. I was thinking that I would make this as good as I can and as deep and interesting about James Bond as I can. Then, I'll leave him at a critical point in his life.

I suppose there had been similarities with Fleming in that the books were really big sellers in the UK and, as I say, in Germany and a couple of other places. They sold okay in the States. It was interesting that James Bond was not viewed by the Americans the same way that the English viewed James Bond. Obviously, for a start, James Bond is British, so he's seen as one of our great cultural artifacts. Whenever a new Bond movie comes out, there is this huge media interest. The James

Bond films are huge in America. *Thunderball* was seen by a third of the population in the cinemas. Adjusted for today, it shits all over the James Cameron films. Bond became part of the fabric of our lives when ITV got the rights to the films and started showing them at Christmas. It became part of the ritual of the English year. The dads would introduce their kids to James Bond. So it became a family thing in the UK. I may be wrong, but in America, it wasn't quite like that, "James Bond is for adults." Kids get into it, but it's for adults. So Bond is not viewed the same way in the UK and America. The Young Bond books were a bit different. The books did okay in the States.

Interestingly, *The Enemy*, the series that I went on to write, did much better in America than the Young Bond books. That's one of the reasons I stuck with it. For me, it was like, "Okay, if the fifth book does properly take off in America and we get huge foreign sales, that would be more of an impetus to carry on." It did okay. We have sold millions of books. But I felt, "Okay, I've done that. It isn't my thing. I need to do my own thing." It was time to move on.

Along those lines, in *By Royal Command*, you include two major events in Bond's life—his times with Hannes Oberhauser and the incident with the maid. If you wanted to, each event could have appeared in a separate book.
I was thinking, "Let's put it all in there and wrap it up." I liked that there was a callback to the first book. There is quite a lot going on in the books—a lot more stories and a lot more plotting than in the Fleming books, which are straightforward. There is no twisty plot or double-crossing in the Fleming books. Let's be clear on that front. If I had that inclination to write more, I could have [split them up]. In retrospect, I think, "Did I do the right thing?" I think I did because I had a lot of success with the follow-up series. Now, I'm finally in a position to be writing an adult Bond which is being announced tomorrow.

[Shocked.] Wow. Mazel Tov, congratulations.
It's a novella. It's a special thing that IFP is doing for the coronation [King Charles III)]. It's called *On His Majesty's Secret Service*. [Chuckles.] It's very exciting. I've had to write it quickly. But it wrote itself. I've all this Bond inside me, building up. I had been thinking about writing another one and it was a joy to write it. It's for charity. So I'm making even less money out of it than I did with Young Bond. I didn't do that standard IFP deal with writers. It's the standard deal [for continuation authors]. They say this is what we pay. It's favored nations [where all authors agree to

the same general terms]. This one we didn't have to get into any discussion about because it's for charity.

IFP wanted to do something for the coronation, and it is the 60th anniversary of *On Her Majesty's Secret Service.* I had about a month to write it. I've got to deliver it today. It's going to be in the shops on May 4th, two days before the Coronation.

What was the creative spark for the story *On His Majesty's Secret Service*?
Corinne from IFP said to me, "I want to do this book." She said that we should probably avoid anything about a villain trying to stop the coronation. I thought, "No, surely that's got to be the plot. Someone is going to try to stop the coronation or assassinate him before he's crowned." The story came to me quite quickly. I thought as long as Charles wasn't actually killed, it would be okay. [Laughs.] It would be crazy not to do that story.

It relates to the whole idea of genealogy, which is also what *On His Majesty's Secret Service* does. So, there are callbacks to that. It's about a guy who thinks he has a greater claim to the English throne than Charles because he can trace his ancestry all the way back to Alfred the Great. It's the Anglo-Saxon line, as opposed to the Norman line, which I've been quite obsessed with.

This novella is modern Bond, and your Young Bonds were all period pieces. Did you have to reconceive it differently?
It's a tricky thing, particularly because in *On His Majesty's Secret* Service, Bond is roughly 35 years old, as he has to be. But he's actually only five years older than my oldest son. One's idea of Bond is not only influenced by the books but also by the films. He's also a certain type of man, that let's face it, he's slightly square. But oh God, [in the novella], he's a Millennial.

I also have to preserve that Fleming-esque quality. I'm trying to channel Fleming's Bond but also think that he has to have the sensibilities of what a 35-year-old man would have. So he's a bit more "woke" than Flemings, but that's not hard to be. But not to such an extent where the reader is like, "Oh God, not a woke Bond." You're trying to do a balancing act between the literary Bond and the cinematic Bond. You can't pretend that the cinematic Bond doesn't exist. I hope I got the balance right. I think it comes across quite well. He is Bond.

Bond is obviously at the center of the whole thing. I enjoyed writing him and putting him on these adventures. Fleming famously said that he thought the success of Bond was down to the fact that he had an adolescent mind and that he didn't have an adult sitting on his shoulder, saying, "That's a bit far-fetched. I don't think that would ever happen." Someone would say, "Aren't you merely indulging in a school-boy fantasy." He says, "Yes, what's wrong with that?" He can do these mad things. He can fight with a giant squid [in *Dr. No*] or be involved in a plot to rob Fort Knox [in *Goldfinger*]. The criticism is a terribly English thing. John le Carré is much more a typical English writer than Fleming. His books are kind of dowdy and dull. It's kitchen sink realism. It's like le Carré is carrying a cup of tea while writing, and Bond is cocktail-writing.

Fleming is so unlike other English writers and other English crime writers. He's much more of an American writer, writing about these mad international adventures. It's not what we do. John le Carré is a better writer, but Bond is insanely entertaining. As I say, it's very un-English. Few other English writers have written the way that he does—those mad, mad adventures. I think that's why he was so successful then and is still.

Obviously, through the films, he created this whole idea of a big international jet-setting thriller. As I said, the adolescent mind is really useful. It was a great way to write the kid's books because you think, "I've just got to entertain." The kids don't want to get bogged down with boring details, and they will accept anything. So it set me free to send Bond in these fantastical situations.

Having gone through writing the Young Bond books, I found it quite easy to write this new story. Every time you begin to think, "Well, I don't know. Is that a bit much? How do we explain it" I would also think, "I could just do it." The films give you a slight *carte blanche* because they exist in that thriller, cinematic world where characters can charge around the streets of London shooting each other with machine guns, and it's not even in the news. That's what happens in these thrillers. However, the bulk of the story is set in Hungary because I was in Hungary recently, and I'm quite fascinated by the country. They're all charging around and shooting each other and blowing things up. Which is great fun.

In general, who are these Young Bond books for? Are they for adult Bond fans or are they for kids?
The Young Bond series was written for kids, and they are the main readership. They are still popular with kids, certainly in the UK. I think that's partially because they are historic novels. They are treated almost like fantasy novels. Whereas, if I made them contemporary, they might have become dated. To a kid, two years is a long time. It's like doing things that their older brother did, and that's uncool. I think part of the

reason that they are still popular is because they can't be dated in that way.

They're written for kids, but I was trying to put in as much of Fleming and Fleming's world as I could. There's a lot of stuff in the books that was written for people who know Bond and have read the adult books. A lot of adults have read and enjoyed them. With all my children's books, or whatever you want to call them, I didn't set out to write a "children's book." I set out to write a book in which a child is an essential character. So, I'm not patronizing. I'm not writing down for kids. It's a proper adult adventure that Bond goes on every time. The most important thing for me was that kids would enjoy the books. The books became their own thing. They became "Young Bond" as opposed to "James Bond."

What were your ideas for the Fettes years?
My idea for the Fettes series was to take him to the next stage of his life, taking him up to his 30s and up to Scotland. That would run through almost where the war breaks out and where he joins up and becomes a Double-O agent. I always wanted to write my original idea because Fleming didn't write about his wartime years and becoming a Double-O. The British commandos were training up in Scotland. So the idea was to keep that connection through the commando training and perhaps get some proper training of his own up there.

In the fifth book, it was revealed that his teacher works for the service. There's now a system in place for him to go on these adventures.
Yes, we know that his school teacher is working for the secret service and it allowed me to start to put him in a world where he could officially be sent on adventures. We wouldn't have to keep wondering why all these international criminals keep turning up at school in Scotland.

Would you call Young Bond a continuation novel?
I don't know. It feels like it's a different thing. It's "Young Bond." It's really interesting looking at the history through the continuation novels. Obviously, *Colonel Sun* and John Gardner's books were proper continuation novels. Fleming was writing contemporary novels, and so they were writing contemporary novels. Those were written at the same time [as if Bond was simply older and time had passed]. So it made sense that they were just carrying on. People have enjoyed those books. But as the process went on, it became more complicated. When you get

to the new ones, starting with Sebastian Faulks, you wonder, how does it work and who are these books for? Sebastian Faulks dealt with it as an academic exercise. Not *exactly* a pastiche but it is sort of a pastiche. It was this idea of him writing as Ian Fleming. Faulks has written a lot of pastiche, and he was involved in a long-running radio show where there was a parlor game, "Tell an Agatha Christie story in the style of James Bond." That type of game. He was good at that, and he loved that.

He set his book in the time of Fleming. So it's a historical novel. It's trying to be as close to Fleming as possible. In some ways, it becomes a curiosity. It did enormously well in the UK. I think it didn't do particularly well in the States, which is why they chose Jeffery Deaver [an American author] to do the second one. That was the idea. "We'll get this big American popular crime writer to do it, and that will sell books in America." Unfortunately, they chose an American crime author whose most famous character is a paraplegic who solves crimes with the power of his great brain. Which is about as far opposite James Bond as you can think. The book has its moments, but it did not work for the Estate in the way they wanted it to on that front. So the other books are trying to find a way into it.

It does come down to the question of, "Who is the readership for a modern James Bond book?" If you make it too much of it ["writing as Fleming"], as Sebastian did, then it does become its own thing. That was what was so great for me with the Young Bond books was that they didn't have to be a continuation thing. You don't have to know much about James Bond in particular to enjoy them. The Young Bonds were their own thing. They were much more in the tradition of adventure stories for kids that had fallen out of fashion. So we didn't have to worry about the continuation thing. The kids who are coming to them don't have to worry about the question, "Am I reading this as a heritage thing? Am I reading this because I'm interested in James Bond?"

For their adult Bond books to work, they've got to be standalone, really good, exciting thrillers in their own right. That you could come to without knowing anything about James Bond. Whether that's possible, I don't know. I'm interested to see what happens with this novella. I'll be interested to see who reads it if anyone reads it. I hope that it gets read outside of the community of people who have no intention of reading it but will buy it so they can say, "I've got all the Bond books on my bookshelf." [*On His Majesty's Secret Service* was a *Sunday Times* bestseller and quickly went it a second printing.]

I think that the Bond novels have to be true to Fleming, but for them

to be really good, the authors have to bring an equal measure of themselves to it.
That's why I thought I could do Young Bond. I thought I could bring my own stuff to that. I brought my own childhood, what I observed with my boys, and the things I'm interested in. You've got that solid structure, and you can put whatever you like on that.

When you look at the Batman movie franchise, the general public mark the eras by the actors who played the Caped Crusader, but I wonder if they should mark them by their filmmakers, too.
It's interesting to look at the recent continuation books and say that it says as much about the authors as it does Bond. I don't know if it's possible for any of them to fully transcend the iron hand of Fleming. With the films, they've managed to have different characters in the films. There's been enough of the core iconography that each incarnation of Bond has reflected the times that they were made and has reflected the sensibilities of the people making them.

So you have Fleming's Bond, the 1950s Bond, which is slightly stuffy English. He was so desperate to get a film made, but it was lucky for him that he didn't manage to make it in the 1950s. A 1950s Bond would have been made in England and would have starred someone like Stewart Granger, and it would have been a dull, under-funded, black-and-white English film. But in the 1960s, suddenly, it was cool, sexy, and cynical. Despite the fact that Sean Connery is in his beautifully tailored suit and has short hair, there is something anti-establishment about him. He seems to embody the energy of the Sixties.

I wonder what will happen when the character enters the public domain. I like that the Estate currently ensures that the author works within the framework of the character and that people don't go too crazy with the character. Or would that be fun? I don't know.
That's kind of what happened with the first *Casino Royale* [with David Niven and Peter Sellers]. That was like, "What if we go nuts with James Bond?" It didn't work. But they've managed it with the [Eon produced] films. In the 1970s, it became camp. Nothing's taken too seriously. In the 1980s, it became politically correct and a bit dour. The 1990s were a lads-mag era. It's the design of the world and there's a lot of money swirling around. Daniel Craig embodies the uncertain, dark times we're living through now. In the next phase, they can't get more dour or glum. Because you lose the fact that James Bond is this escapist fantasy. Maybe they need to say, "What we need is to be cheered up." I think the

most Bond-like films being made these days are *Mission: Impossible* films. Tom Cruise doesn't have these characters sitting around moping or worrying about what happened to his girlfriend. He's like, "Wow, look at that tall building, let's climb up it." That's what Bond should be again, that sense of fun and fantasy, an adventure. It's finding the right way to do that. You could get it right in the books. You can make it work. But you've got to somehow get rid of all that burden and say, "This would be a really exciting and fun story." People would read it in their own right.

In terms of continuation vs. spin-off, you could make the argument that Young Bond is not a spin-off. It's still on the same Fleming timeline, it's simply earlier. As Anthony Horowitz's *Forever and a Day* comes before *Casino Royale*, your books are on the same timeline, earlier, and at a different stage of life. It's the same character; it's not Moneypenny.
Yes, very much. The Fleming Estate has tried these other spin-off works, The Moneypenny Diaries and Kim Sherwood's books about the other Double-O agents. They're fun and entertaining, but you do keep wondering, where is James Bond? I want him to turn up and start shooting people. There's so much you can do in the world but if you don't have James Bond, what have you got?

You also had a *SilverFin* graphic novel.
That was great, and Kev [Walker] was great to work with.

You also did a learn-to-read version. [Holds up a copy of the book.]
I remember having discussions about that. But I've not seen it. I seem to remember giving permission for it. I think that any version it gets out there might encourage people to get reading which is a good thing.

Did you have to read any of the continuation novels?
The one thing that the Fleming Estate said to me was that I didn't have to read any of the other continuation novels. I didn't have to read John Pearson or any of those. Just Fleming. Nothing outside of that. Just the core, which was great.

When I first wrote you a note requesting an interview, I had a line saying that I hoped that one day you would write an adult Bond novel. However, I decided to delete that line because I didn't want to inadvertently suggest that the Young Bonds were in some way less than.

I'm pleased that they became a thing in their own right. I remember that we had an early meeting with Puffin, and everybody from Puffin was there. They were saying, "It's so exciting to be doing these books. We'll put James Bond in big letters on the front." A chill went through IFP members there. Puffin asked, "Is there a problem?" They said, "We can't put James Bond in big letters on the front." That was because EON has so many rights. So they had to brand it as Young Bond and put Young Bond on the front. In the long run, that helped. It made the series "Young Bond" and not a junior version of 007. It worked well for us.

I don't know how much you know about the relationship between IFP and EON. Essentially, IFP has the rights to the books and any of the books about James Bond [the literary character]. That's about it. They might have logo rights, but they don't have any merchandising rights, and they obviously don't have screen rights. At least, that's my understanding.

What's your overall impression of your tenure?
They were good Bond books. I think they were good books in their own right, whether they were James Bond books or not. I had my own space to put my own personality into it. They have entertained a lot of kids. A lot of kids tell me, "I didn't like books. But this is the first book I read by myself, and it turned me on to reading." I love that. That's rewarding. I think I added a successful strand to IFP. It was the most fun—to be part of the world of James Bond world, the James Bond family, and the Fleming family. I still am. I go to all the events. Actually, now writing this new book [*On His Majesty's Secret Service*], I'm back at the forefront of it.

I would never have known that going to see *Thunderball* when I was four or five years old, that I would be part of this world. I vividly remember seeing it for the first time. I remember going to the cinema and it being the most exciting thing in the world and James Bond being the coolest hero you can imagine. That amazing John Barry music has always been so much a part of my life. I would never have thought that one day I would write an official James Bond story. So it's been a childish delight. The pre-adolescent in me is enjoying this immensely.

SAMANTHA WEINBERG

Guardian Angel (2005)
Secret Servant (2006)
Final Fling (2008)

Short Stories
"For Your Eyes Only, James" (2006)
"Moneypenny's First Date with Bond" (2006)

Samantha Weinberg
Illustration by Pat Carbajal

Guardian Angel is the first book in your trilogy about Miss Moneypenny. Ian Fleming Publications had already expanded the Bond universe through Charlie Higson's Young Bond series, but the Moneypenny series is a distinct departure, moving the focus beyond Bond. How did that come about?
It was purely by chance. My agent was a lovely man called Gillon Aitken. Gillon had been approached by the Fleming Estate to represent them. They said, "Have you got any ideas of what we can do? How can we mix up the continuation novels?" Gillon happened to be coming to stay for the weekend. He said, "I've been thinking about it. What do you think of the idea of a Moneypenny *biography*?" I said, "I think it's great, but how about Moneypenny *diaries*? It was that instinctive. He went [approvingly], "Oh,

yeah. Would you really want to write them?" I said, "God, I'd kill to write them."

I thought about it a bit. I came up with a slightly crazy concept of trying to make the diaries appear real. We took it to the Flemings, and they liked the idea, and we went from there. That was exciting. Then, I wrote a proposal for the trilogy. We took it to some publishers, and they were all keen. It was a lovely experience.

Do you know if Ian Fleming Publications [IFP] was casting a wide net and approaching a lot of agents and asking if they had clients who might be interested?
I'm not certain, but I think they specifically went to Gillon. Charlie's Young Bond was right before me. They said, "Look, we've got Young Bond going. We'd like to broaden it further and also change the whole concept of continuation novels and move away from having the same people do them the whole time." They were possibly getting writers who were less involved in the Bond universe but had other writing skills of their own. For instance, Sebastian Faulks was a client of Gillon's.

Whose idea was the biography?
I think that was Gillon. I think they had the idea of broadening out the literary offering but he focused on Moneypenny and suggested the biography to me. I came up with the diary idea from that.

Of course, Pearson had previously published *James Bond: The Authorized Biography of 007*, so a Moneypenny diary is a logical step.
I really loved that book. So clever and funny. But for *The Moneypenny Diaries*, I loved the idea of looking at Bond's world through different eyes particularly looking at it through a woman's eyes. I also thought that there was more scope in a diary than a biography.

I always liked Moneypenny, even though she didn't appear much in Fleming's books. I had read all the books when I was younger and enjoyed her in the movies, particularly the older ones with Lois Maxwell. I thought that Moneypenny always had a twinkle in her eye. She was much more knowing than people think. Some people viewed her as an "older woman" who adored Bond, but I always thought that she had much more to her.

Most people's impression of Moneypenny is exclusively through the films and there's not much more to glean from Fleming's novels.

She has very, very, very few lines in the novels. I can't remember the exact number but there are very few. In fact, in the novels, she is a less-rounded character than in the movies. In the novels, she flutters her eyelids at Bond, and she's efficient. I think her character was more developed in the films than in the books.

In terms of building a character, you had a blank slate.
That was what was so great.

How did you begin?
I ignored the films and went back to Fleming's books. I read the books, analyzed them, and took pieces from them. I found plot points and characters and looked at their rhythms and chronologies. Then, I decided that I was going to insert Moneypenny into them.

I went and wrote a whole biography of Jane Moneypenny. This way I would get to know her. By the end of that, I felt I had developed a character, and then I felt that I knew her. Then, I was able to imagine how she would react in different situations.

Benson's final book came out in 2002 and your book was published in 2005. When did you meet IFP?
I would say at the end of 2003.

So there were roughly three years without Bond novels. However, it sounds like IFP was actively pursuing its publishing options shortly after Benson's tenure concluded.
The whole publishing process takes a bit of time. I went off to Cuba and had all sorts of fun doing things. [Book one is set against The Cuban Missile Crisis, and some of book two is set in Cuba.] It took quite a long time to set up the initial story. Each of the books didn't take long to write. However, the initial process of getting to know Jane Moneypenny and the different characters took some time to work out. I remember going away to Barcelona on my birthday with all the Bond books and reading them there. That would be November 2003. I had my second child in 2002, and I was taking quite a bit of time off. So I was ready for a new challenge. And this was a gift. God, it was such fun.

Who did you meet from IFP and the Estate?
I met with two members of the Estate, Lucy and Kate [Lucy Fleming and Kate Grimond], Ian Fleming's nieces [daughters of Fleming's brother, Peter]. They represented the family. I met with them and Corinne Turner, who manages Ian Fleming Publications. Then, we all met, and we all did

it together. Corinne filtered it and then took it to the rest of the Fleming Estate.

What was important to IFP?
I think they wanted to do justice to Ian Fleming, who is a really good writer. They wanted to reclaim the literary Ian Fleming and pay respect to his writing skills. They also wanted to expand the universe but in a way that did him and his books justice. They also wanted to hopefully bring people back to his books.

Benson drew from the movies, but that was his remit. Going back to the books was a different direction for IFP.
I don't know why they decided to do that. I think they wanted the books to be their own thing—separate from the movies. They also wanted to expand the universe and not exclusively be doing continuation novels. So they brought in Sebastian [Faulks] and Charlie [Higson] and brought all those kinds of people in. Anthony Horowitz's novels are the best—brilliant.

So you've got a blank slate for a character? Now what?
I had such fun. First of all, I read all the books. Then, I immersed myself in that period, I read quite a lot of history books about the 1960s and the 1950s. I did quite a lot of research into Fleming and read all the biographies of Fleming. I met a guy called [Colonel] David Smiley, who apparently was one of the people who Fleming drew upon to create the character of Bond. I don't know to what degree he was a spy. He was a lovely man, and his wife was rather wonderful. She had been brought up in Kenya. [Weinberg would place the young Moneypenny in Kenya.] My family's originally South African so I spent quite a lot of time in Africa. I liked the idea of someone who was outside of the English class system; I decided that Moneypenny wouldn't be a part of that. She would have to have had a pretty tough upbringing in terms of living in the elements, and she had to be resourceful and strong. Then, I built it from there.

    I could imagine Moneypenny, and then I filled in little bits of her life. Then, I got the idea of her dad disappearing. I was also trying to draw upon all sorts of things that were happening in the world at the time.

    I read all the Fleming books, and then I looked at the gap in the chronology—where Bond was between adventures and where I could realistically slip in an adventure. And he was feeling a little more vulnerable. It happened to coincide with the Cuban Missile Crisis. I wanted to mix real history with the Bond universe. I was playing with history, but I was also sort of playing with my mind quite a lot too.

Sometimes I got muddled with what was real and what was not. I've always wanted to go to Cuba. So that was an excuse to get on a plane and go. I also went to visit Colditz, Germany [where Moneypenny's father, Hugh, was held in a prison camp].

Did you ever consider setting your first story after Fleming's final Bond, *The Man with the Golden Gun*? Or a prequel to the first novel, *Casino Royale*?
I didn't because I liked the idea of overlapping real-world events with Bond. So no, I didn't consider it. I didn't want to do prequels or sequels. This story runs parallel to Fleming's.

The beauty of your books is how you drop into Fleming's stories and timeline, but then you create another parallel story that could have happened.
I took Fleming's books and decided that they were real and that they were the real truth of history. I tried to find ways that I could intersect between them.

You made it hard for yourself. A sequel or prequel would have been much less to keep track of.
I think maybe, with hindsight, I was too concerned about how the real Fleming fans would respond to it, particularly with the first book. I think I probably spent too much time with the footnotes. But it was so much fun trying to work it all out. I color-coded the three main different stories, which are: history, Fleming's story, and Moneypenny's story. I tried to make sure that each month of the diary had a bit of each of the stories. Colored codes made sure that the balance worked.

There's also Moneypenny's work life, her personal life, Bond's story, and the mystery of what happened to her father. There are a lot of threads.
I was trying to get her biography into the story without overdoing it. I hope I did it all lightly.

All those threads are what make *Guardian Angel* so ambitious. I love how Kate Westbrook is an academic and how she's pulling from different sources, as an academic might, to figure out the story.
That was a lot of fun, but sometimes my head would explode.

You gave Moneypenny the first name of Jane. Was there a backup

name?
No. I thought that if I were a parent with the surname of Moneypenny, then I would have called my daughter by the plainest name that I possibly could. My best friend's girl is named Jane, and I thought that Jane Moneypenny had a good ring to it. If she were Leticia Moneypenny it would be too much of a mouthful. It would be too mean to the poor girl. If you have a boring surname, then you can give your child an interesting name but not with the surname of Moneypenny. I also thought that Jane was a sensible name and she was a sensible, strong girl.

You wrote a bio for Moneypenny, and you wanted to make sure she was consistent with the books.
I stripped those books of every single physical detail but also all the emotional points. I took all the bits that I could.

Did you need to create a similar document for Bond?
Not the same document but I noted everything. I had spreadsheets about Bond. I read the books over and over. I also read a couple of books about Bond. I can't remember their names but they were nerdy books about Bond. I did as much research into Fleming's life as I did into Bond's.

Why was it so important to you to learn about Fleming?
I thought that I would put little bits about Fleming into the books. I thought that it would help build a picture of the world. Fleming's view of Bond was built on his own experiences. I went to see this amazing man named Peter Smithers, who used to work with Fleming during the war period. I went to see him in Switzerland, where he lived. Smithers had this sword thing that was disguised as a walking stick—it was one of the things that Fleming had. Smithers must have been 90 or something. He said, "I'd really like to return this to Fleming." So I took it back from him. A lot of Fleming's work with naval intelligence spilled over into Bond's work. Some of the crazy ideas that Fleming had went into the books. Moneypenny was in the office most of the time, whereas Bond wasn't. That type of research helped me build and expand that world.

Your story perfectly folds into Fleming's.
I was so lucky. It was lucky that when I was reading the Fleming books there were gaps in the chronology that happened to work with real historical events.

I had to research it because I wasn't living it the way Fleming did. Plus, he had such an extraordinary imagination that it seemed like he simply went down to Jamaica and dashed off the books. Once I understood the voice of the book, then the writing bit was fairly easy. The plotting took time to make sure all the stories meshed together. That was the thing that I loved, just trying to get my head around it. I used to skip to my office every day. But it was also a total mindfuck because I didn't know what was real and what was not. I was trying to meld my fiction with Fleming's history and with Jane's history. Sometimes, my head would ache, but I plotted it out.

When I initially heard the concept of the book, I didn't think Bond would be such a central figure. I assumed that he would always be slightly off-screen, as it were.
To try to draw Bond's world without Bond wouldn't have worked. I wanted to have a different view of him. He's such an amazing character. I was never going to do it without him. Part of the book is celebrating Bond as a character, but through Moneypenny's eyes and in a different way than we've seen him before.

What did you want to bring to the character of Bond?
I wanted to humanize him and bring vulnerability, which I think Fleming had in his books, certainly in *Casino Royale*. I think it's been lost in the films. In the novel *Casino Royale*, he has doubts about what he's doing. After *On Her Majesty's Secret Service* and at the beginning of *You Only Live Twice*, after he loses his wife, he seems much more real and less than this action man. I think Daniel Craig brought it back a bit. I hadn't read the Gardner or the Benson books, but I assume that they were influenced by the movies.

I am interested in people and characters, and I didn't want Moneypenny to be a subservient woman. I wanted her to be a strong person. That's why I gave her an African background. There were lots of women in the OSS [Office of Strategic Services] at the time. I read a couple of biographies of them, and they were amazing.

I also wanted to make Bond and Moneypenny's relationship complex, and I wanted her to be an equal. I had this idea that Bond was quite a typical man and that Moneypenny knew that he needed his ego fluffed every now and then. She knew what she was doing. She wasn't head over heels for him. He respected her for that.

It sounds like you blocked out the story for the first book but also had a good sense of where the second and third books were going.
For the first two books, I did to an extent. The third one was less blocked

out. For the second book, I knew that it was going to be about Philby and the Cuban Missile Crisis. But I didn't know that the ending was going to work. That ending only came to me as I was writing the third book. Then I went, "Whoa, yeah!" So there's a reveal [of what happened to Moneypenny]. It needed something to give a satisfying ending. I hope I found that.

Did you know who the mole was?
I knew who the mole was but not how I was going to use Bond [who has retired and now lives on the same remote island as Moneypenny]. That was a late addition. I didn't think about that at the beginning when I was writing the first book. But I was really happy with that. With the mole, I knew the mole wasn't Tanner. I knew that I needed a couple of misdirections and that I was going to seed it in the first one.

I'm so glad it wasn't your version of Tanner, who has such a loving and protective relationship with Jane.
[Laughing.] I'm so glad it wasn't Tanner, too. It couldn't have been Tanner. But I had to make everyone think it was Tanner.

Not only do we see Bond in the Sixties, but we see him in the mid-2000s when he goes by the name Randall "Randy" Macallan.
That came late in the process. It's a funny name. I liked Randall being "Randy." That was fun. Macallan is a Scottish name. I liked the idea of sending him to the Outer Hebrides [a chain of islands off of Scotland]. I went up there to the islands where he and Moneypenny lived. I didn't want them to be dead. I also didn't want him to be just hanging around the office. He would have retired by then.

I love the idea that they have a relationship. They don't live together. They have some sort of deep connection that is beyond the physical. I thought that was beautiful.
Thank you so much. I enjoyed writing that because I wanted to rebalance the relationship between Bond and Moneypenny and between male and female. I think I did that; I hope I did that. By the end, I wanted Bond to have so much respect for Moneypenny as this amazing woman. They had lived through so much, seen and suffered so much, and had suffered so many losses together. This was the relationship I could imagine them having in their sixties.

There is a big twist at the end of the second book. For all of book one and most of book two, we knew that Moneypenny was dead. We

didn't know that she was apparently murdered. This twist requires you to go back and reread them again but from a new perspective.
I wish I could say that I had totally planned that before the first one was written. But I hadn't. It suddenly clicked. She had to be dead; otherwise, the first book couldn't have been written [and Moneypenny's niece would not have received her aunt's secret diaries]. I'm not sure that I knew exactly how she died. I knew that it had to fit in with book one. It also had to be satisfying and it had to inform everything that happened. Moneypenny's death informs her character. You respect her as a person because of the way she died. You also understand her more as a character.

One of the challenges that you faced is including Moneypenny in the stories but not making her a fully accomplished secret agent. There would need to be a plausible reason for her to be embroiled in the missions.
I relied on real history. Once I got my head around Bond being a little more vulnerable and Moneypenny having to go save the day, then it was fine. I found bits from the Fleming chronology, and they worked with real historical events. I slotted in my story. Then I tried to work out ways Bond could mess up a bit and Moneypenny would go in and sort it out.

To promote the second novel, you also wrote two Moneypenny short stories—"For Your Eyes Only, James" and "Moneypenny's First Date with Bond." They seem to operate differently than your novels and serve a different function.
They did. They were to get people to read the books. They were only fun little things. They were much more lighthearted.

They don't follow the structure or the conceit of the novels being diaries. They are much more traditional short stories.
The diaries work in the books because you have a full immersion in the world. Those short stories were intended for people who are going to read a couple of thousand-word stories. Also, to go through all the backstory…to write about the Moneypenny that I knew from the books, would require too much backstory for people to recognize Moneypenny. I still hoped that she would behave the way that she would have in the books. They were still light-hearted fun. A little bit of titillation to publicize the books.

Let's talk about pseudonyms. Kingsley Amis used one for *Colonel*

Sun, **and Arthur Calder-Marshall used one for** ***The Adventures of James Bond Junior 003½.*** **What was the reason for using one here?**
I had come up with this conceit that the diaries were real and that Moneypenny's niece, Kate Westbrook, was a real person. If I had put my name on it, then you could just look up who I was. We couldn't suspend disbelief even for a second. I also wanted Kate to be an academic so that she could dig into history. I had to use an alias.

How did you pick "Kate Westbrook?"
The village I live in is called Westbrook, and my sister is called Kate. The books were my first attempt at fiction, and I think that it was helped by the fact that I'm a non-fiction writer. I approached it as non-fiction. I regarded the books as non-fiction and that they were real. This was the real world.

You reached out to Lois Maxwell, who created the character for the movies.
I spoke with her, and she gave me insights and anecdotes. Lois was wonderful. She was in Australia. It was not too long before she passed away. She was delightful and lovely. She decided that Moneypenny and Bond had a one-night stand and that they decided it wasn't going to work. That's how she played it. That was why they could have this flirty relationship. It was based on that.

I think Bond fans would like to think that there's a fraternity between all the Bond authors.
No, not really. Although I did quite a lot of events together, mainly with Charlie Higson. I got invited to the new movie and book launches. So I've met them all. I also did an event with Kim [Sherwood], Anthony Horowitz, and Charlie. We answered questions at the Crime Literary Festival. I think everyone operates in their sphere and we meet occasionally but it's nice to meet.

This book is about "continuation novels." What do you think of the term?
I don't think the books are continuation novels because I'm not continuing. I'm filling in the gaps. I see it more as belonging to a part of the Bond universe. I think of it more as an enrichment of something that already exists. It's seeing something from a different angle. I don't see it as a spin-off because I think spin-offs sound a bit tacky. I think it's somewhere in between. It's neither a spin-off nor a continuation novel. Just a sidestep. A sidestep. I like that.

Over time, do you find that your novels are being discovered?
Not that I know of. Upon release, the books were welcomed by Bond fans, particularly Fleming Bond fans. I meet people from time to time who read them but know nothing about Fleming's world. However, I don't think they're particularly selling at the moment. At the moment, they're gracefully lying down. Occasionally, someone will find one in a second-hand bookshop. It's a shame because I think they were fun.

I hope this book shines a spotlight on them.
There have been some wonderful ones. I think mine are a bit different. I think Charlie's brilliant and his are a bit different. My kids grew up reading his books because they were the right age at the time. They loved them. I think Anthony has done a really good job too.

I'm not certain that your books were completely understood upon their release. I feel like you and Charlie Higson must hear a lot of some version of, "I thought your book wasn't going to be any good but…"
I did. I don't know if Charlie has but I certainly heard that. When they first came out, I went down a lot of rabbit holes on Bond forums. The initial reaction was [adopting the voice of a skeptical fan], "Oh my God, how could they [Ian Fleming Publications] do that? They only want to make a lot of money." Once the books came out, pretty universally, the literary Bond fans were kind and nice about them.

The series is called The Moneypenny Diaries and each book has a different subtitle, *Guardian Angel*, *Secret Servant*, *Final Fling*. In America, there were no subtitles for *Guardian Angel*.
The books didn't sell well in America and, in fact, they didn't even publish the second two there. I don't know why it didn't work in America. It took me a long time to come up with all the different titles. I did consider other options, but I can't remember what they are now.

These days, the Bond continuation novels seem to do a little better in the UK than in the US. Of course, Bond is a UK character, like Sherlock Holmes and even the Doctor from Doctor Who. There is certainly more press for Bond in the UK.
That's interesting because I know there are a lot of literary Bond fans in America. I don't know how the other books sell in America, but certainly, The Moneypenny Diaries didn't. Which is a shame. But that's how it goes. I mainly wrote those books for the joy of writing them. I wasn't

writing them thinking, "I'm going to make my fortune." Instead, the minute I heard the idea I thought, "That's got to be the most fun thing that any writer could ever do." And it was.

How long did it take to write the first draft?
The actual writing process took about five or six months. I don't do a typical first draft. I redraft as I'm writing. As I went along, I made a lot of changes. Once I'm done with it, I find it hard to pull them apart and start again. I'm really bad in that way. My husband is a film editor, and he said, "Can't you try this? Can't you try that?" My answer is, "No, I can't. This is how it is." By the time I got to the third one, I don't think my editor made a single change. By that time, I was familiar with it.

What type of notes would you get from IFP?
Once we talked through the concept at the beginning, they left it up to me. I don't remember a single editorial comment, change, or advice." They said, "This is your thing." They were amazing all the way through.

You established that Jane Moneypenny wrote 40-plus diaries. I feel like one of them must have contained other adventures.
[Laughing.] I'm sure that there are lots of other adventures. For me, it was always going to be a trilogy. I waved goodbye while I was still loving it. I didn't feel like I was scratching around for stories. Once I wrote about her death, I couldn't go back. I couldn't just fill in different gaps or periods of her life. That was a period of my life. It felt like a complete thing.

The goal was always to have the last one published in 2008 because that was Fleming's centenary year, and a lot was going on. Henry Chancellor wrote a guide to Fleming [*James Bond: The Man and His World*]. We ended up going on the Queen Mary across to New York. Lucy Fleming was there and Kate. We had a Bond-theme crossing, and Henry was there. There was a Bond quiz, and Lucy and I did a reading. She's an actress, and she read Moneypenny, and I read Kate Westbrook. We had another charity evening where Joanna Lumley [*On Her Majesty's Secret Service*] read Moneypenny, and I read Kate Westbrook at the gallery in London. It was a joyous experience, and IFP was wonderful to work with. They couldn't have been better. I occasionally bump into the Flemings. I feel lucky and fortunate to have done it. But I'm not someone who looks back over my shoulder. I loved it. But I don't think I would want to be someone who keeps churning out the same thing over and over.

Last question. What was your goal for the book, and do you think you met it?

I wanted to make Moneypenny a real person, a strong person. I think I succeeded in that. She wasn't fleshed out either in the books or in the movies, although she was more fleshed out in the movies by Lois. I didn't want Moneypenny to be a Bond woman. That was my primary purpose. There was a bit of a feminist slant to it. The flip side of that was to give Bond more vulnerability. Those two sides needed to come together. In order to "up" Moneypenny, I needed to slightly "down" Bond's masculinity to give Moneypenny the agency that she had. Those were the character goals.

Where I failed is that the books satisfied people who knew more about the Bond world more than others coming in cold. They probably thought, "I haven't read any of the Bond books, and I'm not interested in Moneypenny."

I think the first cover of the book looks a little bit like "Chic-lit." The content didn't match the cover. The English cover had a pink ribbon on it. But the hardback cover was good. I do think they were hard books to sell. The more macho Bond fans thought that they wouldn't want to read books about Moneypenny, and women thought, "I've never read any of the Fleming books." So The Moneypenny Diaries fell in the middle. I was hoping that they would appeal to everyone as stories in their own right. I couldn't imagine that there was anyone who had never heard of Bond and Moneypenny.

I think people were turned off by the heavy footnotes in the first book. I probably didn't need to have them, but they were such fun to write. I'd done the research, and that's where the humor came in. The humor was more in the footnotes than in the books. But they were off-putting to some people, So I wish I hadn't thought about the Bond fans quite as much in my mind when I was writing the first book.

I wanted to tell satisfying stories. I wanted to have fun doing it. I also wanted to go to places, and I got to do that too. I went to Cuba, Kyiv, Moscow, Berlin, Jamaica, and Scotland. I was so lucky. I am a non-fiction writer, and I ended up taking the midnight train from Moscow to St. Petersburg. I certainly achieved the "fun" one. I hope I turned Moneypenny into a full person.

SEBASTIAN FAULKS

Devil May Care (2008)

Sebastian Faulks
Illustration by Pat Carbajal

Before your 2008 *Devil May Care*, there hadn't been a new adult Bond novel since Raymond Benson's 2002 book. How did you get involved?

My literary agent was called Gillon Aitken, who happened to be the agent employed by Ian Fleming Publications, as well. In 2007, he rang me up one day and said, "2008 would be the centenary of Fleming's birth; Ian Fleming's family and Ian Fleming Publications Limited asked if you would like to write a Bond novel." Gillon was surprised by this request...I was surprised by this request because I don't write thrillers. I had not expressed any great interest in James Bond. So we were both amused and bewildered. Then, we talked about what it might mean. Gillon felt that the family was likely to put a lot behind this.

    I didn't know a great deal about the family. I'm not one of those people who is interested in writers' lives. I seldom read their biographies. I'm only really interested in the novels, the stories, the books, and the characters themselves. However, I did a little bit of research, and I discovered the Flemings were from Dundee [Scotland]. They were [tea] merchants who sold sandbags to both sides in the American Civil War. Like a lot of Scot merchants, they made a ton of money in the Far East in

Hong Kong. They, actually, Robert Fleming, started a bank, which had been sold to Chase Manhattan for some unbelievable sum of money, making all the living Flemings astonishingly rich. [In 2000, Robert Fleming & Co. was sold to Chase Manhattan Bank for more than $7 billion.]

I did know that Ian Fleming had been married to a woman who rather despised his novels and was rather unkind to him about them. He also had a reputation as being a rather troubled man. I didn't want to go into all that and it didn't seem at all relevant. That was as much background as I wanted to know.

I wanted to look at the character and see whether there was anything I could do with it. So although I initially said no, I have this terrible habit of not being able to resist a challenge. I don't think that the Ian Fleming Publications people knew that about me. It's not something that I knew about myself, particularly. It turns out that I simply can't resist it. The more I thought about it, the sillier it seemed, and the more I was drawn to the idea. I said, "I'll go and have a chat with them."

I went to talk with Corinne Turner, who runs Ian Fleming Publications, another colleague of hers, Matthew Fleming, and one of Ian's nieces, Kate Grimond. Kate is the daughter of Peter Fleming, his brother. I got on very well with them. They were very nice. I had met Kate before because she happened to live quite near me in London, and she was friends with some friends of mine.

I asked, "Do you want me to write a contemporary one? Because I don't want to do that. And secondly, what are the constraints?" They said, "You can set it wherever you like. There are no constraints." I said, "I'm not a great expert on James Bond." They said, "That's fine." I said, "After Sean Connery, I lost interest in the films." I was born in 1953. I was young when Connery was at his peak. It was glamorous and exciting for a 12-year-old. When they got to Pierce Brosnan, I was grown, and he looked like a knitwear model. By then, I wasn't that interested in them. I hadn't seen many of the recent Bond films. They said, "That's not a problem." I said, "I'm not really into gadgets." They said, "That's alright."

I tried to raise lots and lots of objections. But they kept on saying, "No, that's fine. You can do whatever you like." I said, "I don't want to mess this up. There's only one way I can do that. I'll write an outline of a story, and I'll give it to you. If you don't like it, that's fine. We won't progress with it. I don't want to waste your time, and I don't waste my time." They said, "Good idea." They said that it would be entirely based on the books, not on the films. I said, "Fine."

I then read the books. I had read some of the books when I was maybe 12 or 13. I think I'd read maybe three of them. I started at the beginning with *Casino Royale* and read them chronologically. I was surprised by the fact that they did basically work. The way in which they worked was a striking thing to me. You felt this hero was in jeopardy. I'm not a big thriller fan. I don't enjoy the rigmarole, the setup, and all the tropes of thriller writing. I no longer find them exciting. I'm much more interested in a book, which is about a young girl's sentimental education than whether the bad guys can get the bullion out of Moscow before the ship blows up. It's simply that the younger sentimental education is more exciting to me.

There were moments in Fleming's books—in *Dr. No*, *Casino Royale*, *Live and Let Die*—when you feared for James Bond's safety. You were not sure he was going to get out of this alive. I thought that was clever. I also thought that was the essence of why the books were exciting and why they were thrilling. Of course, Fleming works hard not to show you what he's doing. The fact is that James Bond wears these soft shoes and handmade shirts, has a tiny gun, and is pitted against not only the evil empire of SMERSH but also SPECTRE. So he's basically against not only the whole might of totalitarian Russia but also against the world of criminal conspiracy. But he's just one guy in his soft shoes. No wonder you feel anxious on his behalf.

Moonraker is the most extraordinary book. Really, it's just two scenes [the card game and the car chase]. The car chase takes place not somewhere exotic but in a sleepy seaside town with a golf course, where Fleming used to play. But it's exciting. It just is.

I then read a little bit about the background of them. One understands that when they were being published in the late 1950s, the United Kingdom was completely impoverished by World War II. Russia, which, along with the United States, had won the war with us. Now, they were our enemy. There was also food rationing. It was a grim place. Suddenly, here was this guy with his fancy cigarettes, nice clothes, and fast cars who was also having a lot of sex. In theory, people in Britain in the 1950s were not having a lot of sex. Of course, they were, suggesting otherwise is nonsense. But they were not openly having a lot of pre-marital or extramarital sex. The fact that Bond did, while he was somehow protecting the United Kingdom meant that the readers at the time extended to him not only a license to kill but a license to have sex with lots of women without disapproving of him. It was like a perk he earned by saving this country.

As you went through the books, what did you discover?
As I went through the books, I began to see that the books became less pure and less exciting. I felt that Fleming slightly lost interest. I also felt that he became influenced by the films of his books. The books became slightly sillier. They became slightly Baroque. The women started having names like Pussy Galore or Kissy Suzuki [in the seventh and eleventh novels]. You think that he's no longer taking this seriously. Frankly, fair enough.

The other thing you notice James Bond does not work for MI6. He works for a different organization. Sometimes, he will ask M, "What is MI6 doing about this?" and he will get some reply. It's quite annoying in the films that he now apparently works for MI6 and so on. [In *Carte Blanche*, Deaver has Bond working for the Overseas Development Group.]

The other thing you notice is that he's not a spy. He doesn't do any spying. But it's a basic understanding that Bond is a spy who works for MI6. That's wrong on both counts. He's an international troubleshooter. He's a policeman who breaks up cartels. Occasionally, Fleming wonders if he's supposed to be working for an intelligence organization, then why is he acting like Interpol? So Bond will ask, "Why are we into this?" Usually, the answer is one line, "The government's worried." The novels shifted out of spying and into crime. Spying provides a bit of cover.

You have all the background. Now, how do you apply that to your work?
Having read the books, I needed to do two things. One, I needed to find an area of the world that Fleming hadn't written about. That was quite easy because he didn't write about the Middle East. He wasn't interested in the Middle East at all.

Secondly, I needed to find a big, dangerous, threatening, horrible thing for the villain to be involved in. Fleming had written about drugs a little bit in one of the short stories ["Risico," which concerned heroin]. He hadn't had a big main character in one of the novels involved in drugs. So I was already a little bit there. Interestingly, *Dr. No* seems to deal with selling bird guano, which seems, in retrospect, not that sinister.

Having got that in place, I tried to write what would be the next book in Fleming's series. As it turned out, that would have been set in 1967. I remember 1967 because I was fourteen and that was the summer of love. Like everyone else, I bought a flowery shirt.

How did you decide on the setting?
It's mostly set in the Middle East. Iran was a good place for me partly because in the 1960s, Iran was pre-revolutionary. It was under the Shah. It was not a hardline Muslim state. The Shah's police would go around and tear the scarves off women in Tehran because they wanted to change the prevailing impression of Iran being peasanty and backward-looking. It gave a bad impression of how sophisticated the country Persia, as it was then called, was. I happened to know British people who worked in Tehran in the 1960s, largely for British Petroleum, and they found it to be a sophisticated, quite exciting, Westernized place.

Of course, the Americans were interested in it. The CIA, along with British intelligence, staged this coup to install the Shah after they deposed the Persian ruler, Mohammad Mosaddegh. It fits a lot of things for me. There had been a lot of intelligence activity. The other great thing about the location was that there is the Caspian Sea between Persia and Russia. I also wanted the countries where Bond operated to still be relevant, menacing, and have resonance for people today. Obviously, Russia and Iran both had that.

What about the characters you surround Bond with?
As for the girl, I thought, "Let's double down on that." But let's not let's not make them like the poor girl in *Dr. No* whose ambition is to be a prostitute in Miami. We can do better than that. So it gave me great pleasure to make the main female rather better educated and better informed than Bond himself. You don't want to overdo that. Bond is your hero, but there was some comedy to be had there.

I liked the American Felix Leiter, the American CIA agent, so I thought I'd bring him in. I like the French agent, René Mathis, whom he occasionally has dealings with. I thought I better have a bit of hardware, some vehicle. But I didn't know what and I didn't want to go over the top on that. So it was everything I liked and none of the boring stuff I hoped for. And none of the silly names and none of the silliness of the films. I wanted it to be pure.

Then you went to outline?
Then I wrote the outline of the plot. I thought I would include all the things I like about Fleming and I would leave out all the stuff I didn't like. The plot had lots of double-crosses and action and so on. I sent it to the Fleming's and said, "This is my idea. Is this approach OK?" They said, "It sounds great. There's one thing, though. You have this shootout in the caviar factory." I said, "Yeah, I like that." They said, "Unfortunately,

they've already done that in one of the films." Although that was disappointing, I was also encouraged by it. It seemed to me I was thinking like a Bond writer.

I had to find something else. And then, by great good chance, as I was Googling about the Caspian Sea, suddenly up on my screen came this thing saying, "Caspian Sea monster." What the hell is that? It turns out that it's this monstrous hybrid vehicle, which is part plane and part ship. It had been invented at that time. I couldn't believe my luck. I worked that in and it became quite a big part of the story. The Caspian Sea connects northern Iran to the belly of Russia, which happened to also be close to where the main Russian nuclear program was being developed. Everything was falling into my lap.

Do you recall how many pages your outline was?
It would have been about three.

Now, they have approved the outline. What happens next?
At this point, we did some negotiation about the contract and the deal and how much money they might pay. Gillon, my agent, went off to sell the book in London and America. I want to be quite honest that money was a consideration for me. My last novel, *Human Traces,* is a book set in the 19th century about the early days of psychiatry. It sold surprisingly well but we're not talking great riches here. Writing, as you know, is not particularly well rewarded. I somehow neglected to start a pension fund. I thought maybe Oh-Oh-Seven could give me a helping hand here.

Anyway, the book got shown somehow to a guy called Steve [Stephen] Rubin, who was then running Doubleday in New York.[5] He was excited by it. We went to see him, and he bought the American and Canadian rights. We sold the rights in London to Penguin for really a lot of money. However, the deal was shared 50/50 between me and the Fleming family, which seemed to me entirely right. There would be no book without them, and there would have been no book without me. So 50/50 is absolutely fair. The Flemings were extremely reasonable and decent people to deal with.

The story is agreed upon and the contract is done. Now, it's time to write the book.
I didn't want to get into Fleming's life, or his personality, or his character, or his marriages, or anything like that. He had rather fortunately written an article called "How to Write a Thriller," which was published in a magazine.[6] I did read that. It was helpful. He said that, once you've got the plot clear in your head…it took him six weeks to write a James Bond

novel once he got it clear in his head. I thought, "Well, let's do it six weeks." So I gave myself six weeks, and I did it in six weeks. It was quite hard work. But the whole point of it was to keep the momentum and the speed going. I didn't write it, unfortunately, in a house in Jamaica, with lots of dry martinis in the evening and snorkeling and bikini-clad women. Instead, I wrote it in rather gray London.

I did enjoy writing it. I enjoyed trying to reproduce what was so good about the early books—the sense of jeopardy and excitement—a purity. I also equally enjoyed the slight spin I was putting on it. For instance, the female characters were considerably more emancipated. I was able to sketch out the political background a tiny bit more than Fleming did. I included a little bit about the Algerian War of Independence. It's only adding two or three lines. You don't want to do anything that's going to slow the story down. But I enjoyed all that.

I enjoyed him meeting René Mathis in Paris and Mathis persuading him to drink some wine, which he never drinks. Reading all of Fleming's books had given me terrible indigestion because he only ever drinks spirits or champagne and Benzedrine. The idea of all those vodka martinis, scotch, champagne, and Benzedrine. [Moans.] So Mathis persuades him to drink some wine. He says, "It's not too bad, we can handle that." It was immensely fun to do it.

Then you hand in your manuscript.
It was edited in England by a guy called Alex Clark. He was young, enthusiastic, a rather boyish, enthusiastic editor.

What was it like to publicize the book?
It turns out that Penguin had a big publicity budget, and we had a lot of fun planning the publicity for the book. It included getting a naval destroyer to come up the Thames. They had to stop the shipping in the Thames while this Royal Navy ship [the *HMS Exeter*] came up. Admittedly, it was only for an hour. Then a helicopter flew off it. The idea was to highlight Fleming's connection to the Royal Navy for whom he worked during World War II. This attracted some negative comments in *The Times*. Something to do with our security and how dare they, but the writer was quite light-hearted. It wasn't a big deal.

Penguin threw a lot of money at the publicity. I didn't have to do a great deal, but I did take part that day. They had a model [Tuuli Shipster] in a red leather catsuit, with a transparent briefcase carrying the book; she was brought aboard the ship from a helicopter. The press was there in huge numbers. It was a visual occasion. There was an enormous number of photographs. There were a lot of interviews that day with a lot of foreign journalists, one of whom was French and didn't speak English. So I had to do the interview in French, which, luckily, I can speak. It was pretty good fun. Sometimes when you have a book out, there's a long grind of publicity over four or five weeks traveling around bookshops, events, and so on. It was intense, but it was over pretty quickly.

The publicity paid off. The book sold very well.
The book went to number one in the *Sunday Times* bestseller list in London. It was there for five weeks. It was the fastest-selling hardback Penguin has ever published [since the *Harry Potter* phenomenon]. That success reflected the immense amount of money they spent on publicizing it, Frankly, one likes to think people enjoyed the story as well. But the publishers are generally averse to spending money on publicity because they think the best publicity is word of mouth. They are right but they would say that because word of mouth costs them absolutely nothing. This showed what putting money into publicity can do for a book

The hardback sold a large amount, something like 350,000 copies. The paperback sold something like 75,000 copies. That's a complete inversion of what normally happens. Normally, paperbacks sell at least five times more than hardbacks. In this case, it sold one-fifth. That is entirely due to the money they spent on it. It was also sold in 35 other countries or something. Some of whom paid quite a lot, and some of whom paid $2,000, or something like that. Financially, it was a big success.

People liked it. There were a couple of slightly sneery reviews from people who felt that they possessed "The Sacred Flame of Bond," and I shouldn't have been allowed near it. But mostly, the reception was extremely positive. It was great fun. I would do it again.

Given your literary background, you were an unexpected choice to write a Bond book.
Some people said, "You're a serious writer. You've written about war, madness, and serious things. Why are you messing around with this?" I said, "I take my books seriously, and they are still there. I like having fun as well. I don't take myself seriously." I think I've always had that distinction or tried to keep that distinction in writing. Last night, we did an event in the Cathedral in London for the 30th anniversary of the publication of *Birdsong*. It was my fourth novel, and it was set during World War I. The event was incredibly solemn and moving. Two actors read from the book, and people in the audience wept. Then afterward, we

all went to the pub and had a huge laugh. Anyway, the whole thing was a very positive experience.

While you were brainstorming, did you have any major ideas that you thought might work but then discarded? Maybe about the villain's plot or the setting.
No, no, I didn't start the story until I got the setting and the bad thing that the villain does. I'm not particularly well-traveled myself. However, I've been to India a lot, America a lot, Europe a lot, and Russia. I haven't been to South America, and I've only been to Africa a couple of times. So it wasn't as if I had a whole deck of cards with different countries on them. "Oh, I can set this one in Bolivia, or Colombia, or Peru." I didn't have that.

One thing I did want to do was to make the sex scenes less violent and maybe a bit more emotional. But that didn't work. That didn't work at all. It became rather queasy making Bond think about the woman's feelings. It was all wrong. It was all out of character. So I ditched all that, and I wrote a rough-and-tumble exchange.

Along those lines, did you find that you had to pull back on his internal life more than you anticipated?
Yes, and I did find that slightly problematic. Normally, in a book that I'm writing, the big development of the action would be some reveal about that character. It could be about their past, that they've met this new person before, or that their mother died last week. Normally, when you have a big plot development, you then have a pause in the story. You let the information sink in. This is the time that you feed the reader information that would otherwise slow things down. Now, you want to slow things down. You want to give them a bit about the character's childhood or description of the house or whatever it might be. When I did that with Bond, it didn't work at all. It made him sound indecisive. It made him sound silly. So I stopped giving him these moments of reflection. Instead, he had to do something else. He's an active character.

In some ways, he's not a great literary character. He's a hero of thrillers. There's a certain integrity in that because you know that there were certain things you can't do with him. That proves, shall we say, that he has some coherence to his character.

What else do you remember about working with the Flemings?
It became clear to me how protective they felt of Bond. It was Ian Fleming that they revered the most. Not Robert, who started the bank, or Peter,

who was a writer or adventurer. Not anyone else. It was quite strange…the fact they revered this man. They were keen that the book should do well and that the life of the character should go on for a while. At the same time, they were giving me this freedom.

I met Barbara Broccoli and Michael Wilson. Barbara is a sophisticated and humorous person, but she takes Bond seriously. I had to negotiate a serious path, and to some extent, be respectful. I didn't altogether share the reverence, shall we say?

Your first Bond effort was a short story that you wrote in 2002 for the radio program *The Write Stuff*. It's called "Bond Goes to Sainsbury's" and in it, Bond goes to the grocery store. Did that brief effort and light-hearted work inform your writing of *Devil May Care* or is that merely a funny coincidence?

It was a funny thing. On this program, you'd have an author of the week, [and all the panelists would write a parody story in the author's voice and style]. You would always be given the subject of the parody beforehand. It was usually something incongruous. One thing you never see James Bond doing is going shopping. So it seemed that would be a funny thing to write about. But I suppose it made me look at the books. So I had been looking at the books before the commission came.

When you're writing a parody of someone's book, you look at the style. You look at the length of the sentences and the way they are put together. To that extent, maybe that helped. I knew that Fleming had worked as a journalist for writers. His style is largely quite journalistic. I'd also worked as a journalist; you write short sentences; you don't use adverbs; you use few adjectives. It's factual and fast. The idea is that the guy on the commuter train in the morning has to get off at the station when he's halfway through the story. But he still has gotten the gist of what's going on. I suppose I'd thought about his sentences a bit.

When you published the story in your book *Pistache*, you changed the ending. In the original, Bond tells Moneypenny that she has a license to till. In the revised version, it ends with Bond buying M&M candy for his boss M.

I'd forgotten that. You've done more research than me.

Did you read any of the continuation novels?

I didn't read the Amis book. I didn't read any of the continuations. I thought they would confuse me.

What other unexplored ideas did you have?
At first thought that I would do what Kingsley Amis had done, and use a pseudonym or *nome de plume*. Originally, it was *Colonel Sun* by Robert Markham. Then later editions let it be known that it was Kingsley Amis. I said, "Let's do that." They didn't want that. They wanted my name on it. No pseudonyms, no *nome de plume*. It was a battle I lost. I think, fair enough. It was what they wanted to do, and it was fine.

Do you remember the name you suggested for your pseudonym?
Yes, William Lawless. William being the name of our elder son; Lawless is my mother's maiden name. But it also sounded pretty good.

Did you suggest any titles?
I proposed *Today a King* as the title. It's from an old French proverb, 'Today a king, tomorrow nothing.' Everyone at Penguin hated it. Someone in marketing or publicity came up with *Devil May Care*. I never knew who. I didn't love it but I thought it was fine.

In an interview, you said that the book is 80% Fleming and 20% Faulks. What part is you?
I was probably talking about the style. When you're writing a parody of someone, what you want to do is write 120% of them. You exaggerate their characteristics. That's where the humor is. I think I said it was 80% Ian Fleming meaning…that my style was 80% up to his. I felt that if I got any closer, there was a danger that it would turn into a parody.

When the book begins, we find Bond between missions. He wonders if he's lost his edge. It's a relatively quiet moment before the plot kicks off. I imagined that moment was a part that you enjoyed writing.
I did. I was obliged to start there because I was following Fleming's chronology of the story. In the last book [*The Man with the Golden Gun*], Bond ended up being badly beaten and shot by Scaramanga. I felt that I had to give him time to recover.

Of course, there is the pretty obvious trope of the gunslinger who's asked back for one last go. The other night, I watched the film, *The Eiger Sanction* (1975) with Clint Eastwood, where he's an assassin who has been called back for one last hit. It's corny, but it has a bit of jeopardy to it, too. Is he going to be fit enough? Is he going to be good enough? In it, Clint has to do a lot of climbing exercises to get fit enough to go up the

Eiger. I did enjoy that. I put Bond in Rome, which I could do fairly easily. I did enjoy that. I knew that there was going to be a lot of action thereafter.

What place does *Devil May Care* have as part of your body of work? Does it stand alongside the other books or is it somehow different?
It is and it isn't. *Pistache* [the book of parodies] has little jokes and some of it is in verse. It's not the same as *Human Traces* or *Birdsong*. But the Bond book is on the shelf. I wrote another continuation novel after Bond, a P.G. Wodehouse [*Jeeves and the Wedding Bells*, 2013]. That was more difficult to do because his style was much harder to catch. But I'm happy for it to be there. I have another book coming out, and the Bond book is listed on the "By the Same Author" page.

What do you make of continuation novels?
I've never read one. Not Bond or Jane Austen or anyone. I've never read a continuation novel. I think that Jane Austen fans want to linger in that world really. As far as the Bond books are concerned, in my own experience, lots of people seem to love the idea of 'Bond Rides Again,' the idea of him being back in the time when he was created. Lots of young people have come up to me and they're excited by the whole thing. They are young, nineteen or twenty-year-old boys. Some girls but mostly boys. To them, Bond is exciting. That's not a good answer, but I don't know the answer.

Did you ever have an instinct to return to Bond? You mentioned that your first contract included an option for a second.
There may have been an option for a second one. But I never intended to write a second one, no. Everything I could ever think or imagine or thought of Bond was in the book. My tank is completely empty.

Before your book came out in 2008, there hadn't been a new Bond novel since 2002. Did you feel any sense of pressure to start a new series, even if other writers were picking up where you left off?
I wasn't aware of it at the time. I was pleased that they asked William Boyd to do one. He's someone whose writing I like. I admire him. When someone is slightly sneery about me doing it, I say, "Kingsley Amis did it. William Boyd has done it." I didn't know that they were going to try to reboot the entire thing...I got the centenary and all the money behind it, which made all the difference. I did feel that I got the best gig.

JEFFERY DEAVER

Carte Blache (2013)

Jeffery Deaver
Illustration by Pat Carbajal

What is your James Bond origin story?
Some years ago, I wrote a book called *Garden of Beasts* (2004). It's my only historical thriller, and it's set in Berlin in 1936. It's about an American mob hitman who's given the option of being executed at Sing Sing [prison in New York] or going to Germany under the cover of the '36 Olympics to assassinate a rearmament czar who is working for Hitler. It's a fictional story. I wanted to create a multi-dimensional character who was on a collision course with my hero, Paul Schumann. I won't belabor the point, but it was typical of one of my books, going back and forth with big surprises. My assassin is a bad guy, so maybe the villain is a good guy. In the end, it turns out the Nazi he was trying to shoot hated the Nazis, and he wanted the Republic back.

Suffice it to say that it won the Steel Dagger Award for the best spy novel of the year from the Crime Writers Association in England. That award is presented by the Ian Fleming Estate. In accepting the remarks, I said what an honor it was because I was influenced by Fleming's books...not the movies...the books. I was born in 1950 and began reading Fleming at a young age. The first Bond book came out in 53. So it wasn't quite contemporaneous, but I picked up the timeline pretty soon. I was reading the books at eight or nine.

Being a scholar of Fleming, of course, the novels were pretty tame. He never swears, and all the romantic scenes were largely off-camera, so to speak. The violence was understated. James Bond had a certain element of glamor to him. He was also a shirtsleeve assassin. Meaning his job was to kill people, which he did with efficiency. After having taken a life, he kind of slumped into a depression. We don't see that in the movies, but we see it in the books.

I found him to be a captivating hero, a multi-dimensional character. He was alluring. There was glamour in the books—brand names, living a good life, driving fast cars, and so forth. I fell in love with Fleming.

What I told you were essentially the remarks I gave at the award ceremony. Not only did I thank the CWA (Crime Writers Association), but I also thanked the Fleming Estate for the award, and I spoke about how much of an influence Fleming had on my writing. Time goes by. Then I got a call from my agent, who said, "Jeff, would you be interested in writing the next continuation novel?" I debated for three seconds and said, "Yes." I was elated. We moved on from there. Agents talked to agents, of course. That's how it came about.

Did you have any concerns or initial ideas about which direction to take your story?
Talk about hubris but I did say, "For me to do this properly, I need the Estate to agree to three things." I wanted the book to be contemporary and modern-day; I wanted younger readers—to the extent that there are still younger readers—to experience a Bond story the way I had experienced a Bond story. He was a young veteran of the Royal Navy, serving in Afghanistan, who then moved to the Secret Service. That was oddly parallel to *Carte Blanche*, even though at the time there was no Secret Service, at least not officially. The Secret Service didn't officially exist until the cover was blown in the 1960s. I wanted the excitement that I felt about a young Bond being involved in all sorts of wonderful plots, tracking down villains. I wanted younger readers to experience that as well.

I haven't read many of my fellow continuation writers, Raymond Benson being an exception. Raymond is a friend of mine, so I think I read one or two of his books. I understand that some of the writers set their books in the 1950s or 1960s and made them period pieces. I wanted to make it contemporary so that I could avoid any speed bumps for the reader at any cost.

A speed bump is anything that takes the reader out of the story. Bond screeching to a halt in his Bentley, not an Aston Martin, is a speed bump. Feeding coins into a phone so that he can talk to headquarters is a speed bump. It can work if you subsume yourself and your imagination into the story, but there still can be that millisecond of "Hm, oh, ok, now I get it." I didn't want that to happen.

I wanted to be up to date and have the benefit of airplanes, cell phones with encryption, WhatsApp, and so forth. I wanted everything that we have nowadays so that the story would go smoothly in the reader's mind. So that's number one; I want to set it in the present day.

Number two, I had to write a Deaver book. By that, I mean that Fleming was a fairly linear storyteller. We meet the good guy and the bad guy right up front, and they are on a collision course. I would buy them for 25 cents—the Signet paperbacks—and I'd read them in one sitting. They weren't long, and I love that storytelling, but that's not what I do. *Casino Royale* had a big twist at the end [with Vesper Lynd betraying Bond]. That turned out to be a surprise, but everything else was pretty straightforward. That's not what I do.

I have surprise endings…plural. And many, many internal reversals and shifting points of view. Fleming's books were often told from a single point of view, putting aside one or two short stories and of course, *The Spy Who Loved Me* was from someone else's point of view. Anyway, I wanted a fast-paced, twisty-turny story that takes place over a few days. We weren't going to have all that travel time on the Orient Express, although *From Russia with Love* is my favorite Fleming book. Just bang, bang, bang, surprise, surprise, surprise, mistaken identities, people who are not what they seem to be. It's not a linear story at all. The Estate said, "No, that's fine."

So, two out of three [conditions] were good. The third one I didn't know about. I said, "I'll write an outline. I work from extensive outlines. If you approve of the outline and the general schematic of the story, then I'll write the book. I don't submit pages. I'll send you the manuscript when it's done. You can reject the outline, and you don't have to pay me a penny, but I cannot have anybody looking over my shoulder. I'll certainly work with editors. I have no problem with that. But, during the initial writing process, I cannot make changes because that's not productive.

I tell my writing students that if they're in a writer's group, then quit because otherwise, the story will go off in many different directions. Write the book and when the book is done, then give it to somebody you trust. Ideally, someone who has some experience in the world you're writing about, whether it's thriller writing or professional editing. Listen to their comments. Keep in mind that everything they say may or may not be helpful. Neil Gaiman said that when somebody tells you something in your book doesn't work, they're almost always right...when they tell you how to fix it, they're almost always wrong. Anyway, the Estate said yes to all three things, and I was delighted, or, as I got into the British mentality, chuffed. We went from there.

Can you tell me more about this initial phase of writing the outline?
I wrote the outline of *Carte Blanche*, which was 100 pages. That's a relatively short outline for me. Although, in fairness, the margins are small because I jot notes on the right side. So, let's say it's a 75-page outline from start to finish. That took about five months. The outline went to the Estate, and they made a few changes. Then, I wrote the book itself in about two months. I do a book a year, but I was also working on other books at the time.

What were your interactions with the Estate and Ian Fleming Publications like?
I had great fun with Corrine Turner and the Fleming Family. There were social events and press briefings. I'll be honest with you and say that one of the fun things about this was that it's hard to get publicity. I've written 50 novels, and I've had three movies and TV shows done. In terms of accomplishments, although not skilled accomplishments, that puts me on a higher level among writers. It's still almost impossible to get me on TV in America. In England, it's a little bit easier. Generally, they don't care about writers; they care about sports figures and reality stars.

We did the release in London with the Royal Marines abseiling from the roof of London's St Pancras station, 100 feet from the ground. He was holding a copy of the book, and I was thinking, "Please don't die. Please don't injure yourself." But those guys know what they're doing.

I was lucky because I love to do public speaking and I try to make my speeches kind of funny. I'm there to entertain the audience, and it allowed me to do that. Part of that was being with the Fleming family, Corrine, and all the people from IFP. None of the continuation novels have been turned into films. So I didn't meet with the Broccolis or anybody from Eon.

What is your connection to the Bond films?

I have a great reverence for the entire Bond franchise but the recent movies are not my cup of tea. I love the early ones, particularly *From Russia with Love*…it was dark and gritty. The quips were kept to a minimum; the gadgets were kept to a minimum. It was Grant versus Bond. Robert Shaw was a wonderful villain and we loved Kerim Bey, who gets knifed; and who does not love Rosa Klebb, but at your peril.

There are dark and gritty books like Len Deighton's *The Ipcress File* and le Carré's *Tinker, Tailor, Soldier, Spy,* but they appeal to a much smaller audience. Bond is big. Bond is a superstar. Bond is Marvel Comics. I think that intrudes on emotional engagement. A Michael Bay film, a Transformers film, or a superhero film often lack emotional resonance, which is what this business is about. I still reread the books and they still hold up. That's my connection with the stories themselves.

Who is your Bond?

Fleming's Bond wanted to be married. He wanted to settle down. It didn't work out with Tracy but not for wanting to try. He was not satisfied with the serial affairs. My Bond is the same way. He falls for an MI6 agent [intelligence analyst Ophelia Maidenstone] at the beginning. They're both single; she's broken off a bad engagement. Bond and she go to a restaurant, and they're talking, and it's time for a non-gratuitous sex scene. She's saying my flat is right across the way, let's go there. He sees where her engagement ring had recently been on her finger. Bond's thinking, I could do that. But Bond is also thinking, "She's not over that guy. I can't do this." I got a lot of flak for that. Some people said, "That's not what Bond would have done." Well, that's what the original Bond would have done, and that's what my Bond would have done. Bond has a conscience and heart.

Could you talk about those five months of finding the story and determining what Bond story you wanted to tell?

It was going to be a Deaver book. However, it was a Deaver book set upon a Fleming template. What's the Fleming template? Geopolitics, travel, a super bad guy, set pieces, and Bond's panache and smarts. That was always in the back of my mind. I looked at something that would appeal to Fleming fans but something that Fleming had not done. For instance, Fleming had not written about the Middle East. So I thought that was an opportunity. Maybe some of the continuation authors set stories there, but Fleming did not. Remember, I'm taking out the movies and the other continuation authors and only going back to Fleming.

I only write about places that I've been to. That's a rule. I've been to Dubai a few times. So I decided to set one of Bond's travels there. I set the climax of the story in Cape Town, South Africa, as I've been there a number of times. Of course, the book is also set in England, which I've been to a number of times, and Serbia. That's the general template.

The villain has to have some philosophy of being bad. Blofeld wanted world domination, and Fleming had SPECTRE and a criminal enterprise, but I didn't want to do that so much as having a non-state actor, who was more in it for himself. Severan Hydt is a villain obsessed with this concept of entropy—of the world slowly ending—entropy in our professions and our infrastructures. He's obsessed with aging. His lover is not a young thing. She's a woman who is getting older, and that is what turns him on. I set it up so that he's the *apparent* villain, but he's not the *main* villain. The real villain is Felicity Willing, the woman who Bond has an affair with. I set the clues that pointed to her so that a perceptive reader could figure it out.

Then, we come to the big surprise ending. Which is what? It's all about food insecurity. One Sudanese warlord playing against another Sudanese warlord. She was supporting one of them. What do we have today, 13 years later? Sudanese warlords fighting it out.

I came up with those ideas and I wrote them on Post-it notes. It's an eight-hour-a-day job to get the outline right.

The Bond in your book hasn't yet been on the adventures depicted in Fleming's novels. He's in his early 30s, and he's been on the job for only a couple of years.
Yes, he's fairly new. Bond's career is ahead of him. In my book and in my world, he has just started. He's in the Royal Navy and he's a recent veteran of Afghanistan.

We see his first meeting with M at the club, and M says, "We need you for this new division." So, I created a new division. You might know this story, but MI6 denied their existence until they finally got outed by somebody who said, "No, the Secret Service does not commit targeted assassinations." It was like, "Oops! I just admitted that there was a secret service." It was more subtle than that. MI5 is similar to the FBI and MI6 is like the CIA.

M tells Bond, "We have a new division. I need someone like you who's smart, who's a patriot, and who is willing to do what needs to be done." M lets it go at that. Bond says, "What's the remit, sir?" M replies, "*Carte Blanche*. Do whatever you want." "Does that mean assassinations?" "Yes, it probably does."

Bond's parents play an unexpected role in the book. First, he believes that his father was a spy and possibly a traitor. Then it's revealed that his mother was the spy.

That was a popular subplot. I put in all the clues about Bond's parents when they died. The first time it's mentioned, it's an offhand comment. They died in a climbing accident. It's a traumatic experience for Bond, but it's also glossed over in the original books. I thought, let's run with that a little bit. So, what do I do? I made his mother a spy. Now, that didn't contradict anything Fleming had said about Bond's mother. It adds facts. I didn't change the facts. You can't do that.

I also resurrected one aspect that Fleming had said. He wrote that a young Bond had gotten himself into trouble at Eton with a housemaid. It was maybe consensual, but he was young, under eighteen. There's some age disparity there. I thought there was a story there. I concocted a story that Bond had beaten the crap out of an upperclassman who was attacking this woman. So she was saved. But the older boy started a rumor about Bond and the maid. So that was in there too. I like to think that Fleming would be smiling, knowing that nowadays we couldn't play his original version but that Deaver found a way to save him.

Then I started going over the outline, staring at it and going back and forth, thinking, "This will work, but that won't work. I need a character here." I needed to introduce Felix Leiter at some point. So where does he come in? Well, you can't have him walk on stage. So you need to be it a set-piece or a surprise where we think there's a bad guy, but Bond and Leiter both know who each other is; it's the reader who is surprised.

I made sure those conventions made it in. I got the outline and the pacing right. The book took place over a short period of time and even with the traveling you had to be credible about it. They didn't have time travel, so you had to take into account that it takes 13 hours to travel from London to South Africa for example.

I know you wanted to please Bond fans with the book, but *Carte Blanche* seems like it was written for someone who has never read a Bond book. You don't take it for granted that your reader knows Bond, the supporting characters, or the world. You set it all up. No pre-existing knowledge is required.

Exactly right. I wrote it for the 12-year-old. By that, I mean I wrote it for the 12- to 14-year-old male or female. Bond is an alluring man. He's a romantic figure. But it's an adventure story. I'm not sure what the demographics are. Maybe 60–40 male–female.

This book is for somebody who never knew the books. I wanted them to experience this hero. Someone who is gritty but sophisticated. A man with tastes who knows the best wines and beers. I've toured Franschhoek and Stellenbosch in South Africa. I like my wine. I was able to let Bond sample those wines and know something about them. He likes his champagne, and yet he's not pretentious. The Bond of the books could skew that way a little bit. He could be a bit of a snob, but people who know these things sometimes are. My Bond knew what he wanted. I wanted readers to sit down and think, "I like this guy. He's not the movie Bond, but he's someone I would like to follow."

The book Bond is different from the movie Bond. How did that impact your writing?
Audiences know Bond through the movies and through Sean Connery, George Lazenby, and Daniel Craig and think that they are interesting characters. Take Q, which is, of course, not a person in the book, but it's a department within the Secret Service. It's headed by any number of people. For the movie fan, Bond calls up Q and gets all these gadgets which coincidentally come in handy later in the story. That's unlike my telling of the Q experience, where we don't even meet the head until halfway through the book. Bond calls up [Sanu Hirani], and he says, "I've got this problem." The head of Q says, "Let me think. I've got a solution. So a messenger delivers the device to Bond in the field. That's how spies work. If they get a laser-cutting watch in the first scene, then the audience is simply waiting until he can use the laser-cutting watch. That's a movie gimmick.

There were story threads that were not wrapped up at the end of the book, particularly as it relates to the mystery of who killed his parents and why.
I will tell you that we talked about a sequel. We talked about doing a second one. If there was going to be a sequel, that would be the crux of it. Fleming's short stories are a little more personal than the novels. The short stories are smaller and less geo-political. I'm not sure the parent mystery would have sustained the entire novel by itself. It could have played a core role.

I anticipated that the mystery would have led Bond, who is a detective in his own right, to lead to something more geo-political. He would have had to follow the lead of the steel bullet [found near Bond's parents' dead bodies]. That was the clue, and it was a Russian bullet. How can you lose by making the Russians the bad guys? That would have propelled him into the second story. That would have been the springboard. Then there would be the inevitable, "Mom, oh God, what did you do here? You were working for the Chinese." There would be a lot of back and forth. I'm not saying that it will never happen, but my plate is pretty full at the moment.

Why didn't it come to pass?
Of course, I don't own the copyright to the story [Ian Fleming Publications does]. I've never written anything that I don't own the copyright and that includes the 90 short stories, 50 novels, articles, non-fiction books, and songs that I've written. I was delighted to cede the copyright in this case. I was well compensated, of course. But it was time for me to get back to doing what I do. I have fans who are not Bond fans who want my Lincoln Rhyme character [a quadriplegic forensic criminalist] or Katherine Dance [a special agent who is an expert in interrogation and kinesics], and I have some new characters in mind.

It was an extremely positive experience, and the family was generous. The folks in the publication's operations were wonderful folks and we had a lot of fun together. So it was a constructive experience and we wanted to get a good product out there. I hope we grabbed some readers who went on to read the next book in the series. Although, I don't know where we are now and who's doing the new one.

What's the hard part about writing Bond?
The ideas come quickly. The ideas are not the problem. The difficulty is in the execution. Although, I'll say doing an outline is tough work. I enjoy getting all the pieces organized. If you have an outline, you can write the end of the story at the beginning of writing or whatever part you want. You need an outline, or you're driving a car that hasn't been built. An outline will tell you that this is not a book that should be written. It's better to figure that out before you've written 200 pages of prose. Or when you get to the sixth or seventh Post-it notes up on your board, you can look at it and say, "This isn't going anywhere." Then you throw out those Post-It notes. If you don't do that, you have to throw out those 200 pages of well-written prose. Everybody can write well-written prose if they set their mind to it. It may not be David Foster Wallace's style, but it'll be functional. There are a lot of thrillers out there, genre fiction, where it's a functional style, and they make millions of dollars.

You can throw out those 200 pages, or you can commit the sin of all times and fill the middle with cliches, or get to the end, and there's no big surprise. We owe our readers more than that. We owe them more than clichés and give-me-a-break moments where the hero's phone happens to lose reception at a critical moment. If you want to do that, then the villain can parasail past the cell phone tower and pour honey on top of the antenna. Now, that's impossible and maybe not credible, but it's better than the confidence of a cell phone not working at a critical moment. We owe the readers more than that. We owe our readers everything.

Did you have working titles before you decided on the final title?
I have written 50 novels and 90 short stories, and 99.9% of those titles are my creations. There have been a couple of possible titles for other novels that have not worked for various reasons. Sometimes, the title might conflict with another title, but the one I could not come up with was the title for the James Bond book. I probably submitted 40 titles. But none of them quite worked. My agent had read the book, and she said, "How about *Carte Blanche*?" And she nailed it.

Do you happen to remember any of the ones that you submitted?
Sadly, I don't. I think "fire" figured in some of them, and "dirt" figured in some of them because of the entropy angle with the villain.

Do you recall any moments where IFP [Ian Fleming Publications] made specific suggestions on how to depict Bond?
There may have been a bit of line editing, but it was minimal. There is one suggestion that comes to mind. I needed to get Bond some money. I initially said that Bond's parents or his uncle or aunt had died and left him a big trust. Their comment on that was, "No. James Bond is not a trust fund baby." I think it was okay for me to give him an uncle who passed away and left him the car. But that was a valid comment. "We don't want him to be spoiled."

In Fleming's books, Bond drove the Bentley GT primarily. Once, he drove an Aston Martin because the Bentley had crashed, and he needed to drive a pool car. I don't know what the economics are like in England, but I suspect that you cannot go to a government agency, and they give you an Aston Martin DB7 as a pool car.

I gave Bond a Bentley, and I took a lot of flak for that. They asked, "When doesn't he drive an Aston Martin." I said, "In the original books, Bond didn't have an Aston Martin." They said, "He did." "Well, he drove one in *Goldfinger*, but I think it got blown up in a crash too."

They gave me a Bentley to drive. The *Top Gear* TV show in Australia gave me one to drive. I drive fast. I've driven sports cars; I've driven 150 miles an hour. I have no problem driving fast, but get me to a track. I don't know what a Bentley GT costs to drive, probably $300,000 to $400,000. I don't want to drive through the streets of Auckland and if I scratch a wheel, it's $15,000. So they showed up at the Auckland Hotel and handed me the keys. For insurance reasons, nobody could drive with me. They gave me directions and a GPS to get to a track. I've never been so nervous in my life, but I made it, and I drove it on the track. It was great. It was the right-hand drive, which made me a little cautious. I didn't have to shift, it was an automatic. Beautiful car. But how does Bond, a civil servant, afford a car like that?

You don't title your chapters. Fleming and most continuation authors name them, but you had 72 chapters, so I could understand why.
That's intentional. I want my books to be immersive experiences. I want you to buy into the story from page one and race through the book in one sitting, even if the book is 120,000 words. My books are shorter to read than it takes to watch a Netflix or Hulu series. Novelists compete against more passive entertainment. It's easier to sit on your ass and flip channels than it is to read a book. As I say, I want the reader to be consumed from page one. That means eliminating all self-consciousness. Chapter titles are self-consciousness. They are another speed bump. When you read a chapter title, you might stop and think, "Oh, that's cute. What does that mean?" But if you pause to figure that out, then I have to get you back into the story. Most of my chapters end on high notes. I don't want there to be that little glitch in the reader's attention.

What did you want to achieve with your book?
I like to tell a good story. I don't have Dan Brown or James Patterson's 50 million readers around the world. I probably have a couple of million readers. The readers I have are completely devoted. They know that they are going to get a Deaver book that grabs them on the first page, has lots of twists and turns, and has a big surprise ending. All of my books have multiple surprising endings.

They'll also learn something interesting and a little esoteric. In *Carte Blanche*, they learned about using food as a weapon. [Felicity Willing, the managing director of the charity International Organization Against Hunger, can provide or withhold food to change the power dynamic of a region.] I didn't know about that before. We always hear about the problem of hunger and lack of food. I learned that there was a ton of food already going to Africa, but it was going to certain places where certain people wanted it to go. I felt a responsibility to the Fleming fans, but my true loyalty is to the Deaver fans. I thought mixing the two was great.

This question is a little "meta." Broadly speaking, these books are called continuation novels because the author is continuing the story and setting the books after Fleming's final book. But with *Carte Blanche*, you didn't continue anything. You took the character and put him in a new timeline, one that was largely separate from Fleming's.
You're absolutely right there. "Continuation novel" is a handy shorthand and its *sui generis* ["of its own kind"]. But no, it's not a continuation at all. Frankly, I think it's the start of something that, if anybody else wanted, could be continued. I thought that would be great.

Your instinct was to write a story that didn't follow Fleming's last novel.
If my agent had posed that question to the Estate, they might have wanted a Bond novel set in 1967. Lyndon B. Johnson is in the White House, and the Vietnam War is ramping up. England is having problems in the Caribbean. The Cold War was hot and heavy. The Estate might have wanted that and if they had, I would have said, "Let me think about it. There's probably something that I can do."

It's interesting that you didn't get any pushback from Ian Fleming Publications about setting *Carte Blanche* in the modern era. I say that because the books immediately before and after yours are period. Your book is an outlier.
I wasn't quite sure how they were going to respond. My pitch is, imagine it's 1953 all over again and *Casino Royale* just came out. There's this idea of a singular hero, a war hero from the same conflict. It's the same geographic conflict. He is ingenious, sophisticated, and brave but he has a dark side to him. Let me sit down and write that. Let me write a story that modern readers will appreciate. It's not going to be Graham Greene, who I love. Bond was pre-John le Carré. I heard an anecdote that George Smiley was an antidote to Bond because Smiley is what intelligence is all about.

I wanted to create the knight errant. Instead of going against dragons, he's going to go up against the Russians or the Soviet Union or against international criminal conspiracies. That's what I had in mind. I think that the Estate appreciated that.

I don't look at sales figures because I have a clear idea of what I want to do. I'm not going to adjust my writing, or my storytelling based on whether this does well or that does well now. The idea that I could step into the shoes of Fleming in 1952 and put my *imprimatur* on that character was exciting to me. But in terms of "continuation" and the Estate, they bought into it, and they were happy with it.

For these books to work, they have to honor Fleming's work, but the continuation author has to bring themselves to it.
Carte Balance was a Deaver novel populated by James Bond. Otherwise, you have a pastiche. I remember reading a Fleming takeoff in the 1960s [*Bond Strikes Camp* by Cyril Connelly]. I was probably 13 or 14. It was a funny book, and it was a takeoff of the Bond novels. Or look at the first *Casino Royale* movie with David Niven, that was [almost like a] musical.

Raymond Benson and Jeffery Deaver, Mysterious Bookshop, 2014
Courtesy of Gary J. Firuta

Can you talk about the marketing?
They made a limited edition book with a bullet hole in it. It was a limited edition *Carte Blanche* with a hole drilled into the front jacket halfway through and a real slug—numbered, mind you—stuck in the hole. We also did an event with the Royal Marines sailing down the Thames.

It almost seems like they are trying to bestow Bond-like qualities on the continuation authors.

There was talk of me parachuting out of a helicopter or lowering me, in a Bentley, from a helicopter into St. Pancras railway station. It's an old station in London, and it's now used for events. I said no to that. Dead authors sell books, but only once.

WILLIAM BOYD

Solo (2013)

Short Stories
"William Boyd Interviews James Bond" (2013)
"William Boyd Q&A with James Bond" (2013)

William Boyd
Illustration by Pat Carbajal

How did you come to write the James Bond continuation novel *Solo*?

The offer came out of the blue. You can't audition for it. My agent, Jonny Geller, rang me up. He represents the Fleming Family and their attempt to monetize the legacy of Ian Fleming. He said, "Would you be interested in writing a continuation Bond?" After one second, I said, "Yes."

      The reasons for my immediate yes were that I know much about Fleming; I know people who knew Fleming—one of his friends mentored me when I started out publishing; and I have written about Ian Fleming quite a lot. Fleming was a deeply complicated guy. I even used Ian as a character in one of my novels [*Any Human Heart*, 2002]…I wonder if that is why the Fleming family asked me. It seemed apt in a way.

I also instantly accepted because I've written two spy novels [*Waiting for Sunrise* and *Restless*] myself. *Waiting for Sunrise* took place in World War I, and *Restless* in World War II. So I thought, "Here's my Cold War novel."

In addition, I know Sebastian Faulks quite well. I knew that Sebastian had written what might be called the second series or second season of continuation novels. I never expected that I would be approached. When I said yes, the whole process took over.

What happens after you say yes?
I had a meeting with the Fleming family representatives. I had vaguely known some of the members of the Fleming family. I had questions for them, and they had questions for me. I wanted to find out what the parameters of the job were. If they had conditions, I would have withdrawn. They said, "You have total freedom. You just have to respect the genre." That's what I wanted to hear. The only other condition was that I had to do a detailed outline of the book and submit it. That way, I don't hand in the manuscript with Bond having a leg amputated halfway through. I think we had a meeting then. Then, they read the finished book, and that was it.

Who was at that initial meeting?
Lucy Fleming was there and Fergus Fleming [Fleming's nephew who is also a writer and chairman of Ian Fleming Publications]. I reviewed one of his books well, I'm glad to say. [Boyd reviewed Fleming's *The Sword and the Cross* (2003) for *The Times*.] Corrine Turner from IFP [managing director], who runs the whole business, was also there, along with probably four or five representatives of the Fleming family, but it was very amenable. It wasn't a cross-examination. I suppose that they wanted to see how serious I was about the job. And I had those questions for them. It was pretty brief and very genial.

From your perspective, you wanted to make sure you had creative freedom.
From my point of view, why ask people like Sebastian Faulks or me to write these books if you don't give those authors total freedom to run with it? I thought it was a wonderful gift. Here's this mythic figure, and I'm allowed to add a new chapter to his life.

The book you write [as a continuation author] is sold as a 50/50 split between you and the Fleming family. That's how they monetize it, and that's made clear before you go to work. So having had that meeting, having satisfied myself, and having satisfied the Fleming family that I was a responsible person who was going to do the job, I went to work.

Describe that work.
I started to think about the novel I would write. I reread all of the Fleming novels and short stories in chronological order, with pen in hand. I had read the Bond novels as a teenager but I'm not a huge fan of the films. Obviously, you ignore the movies and concentrate on the literary legacy. I spent some weeks reading them all. Some of them are good. Some of them are indifferent. For some of them, you can tell that it was like getting blood out of a stone. I knew about Fleming's life. I know how difficult he found it was to write the later novels, in particular. Then I wondered about what story I could write, where I could take Bond, and what I would do in my novel that would be different and satisfy my literary ambitions.

How many pages was the outline that you gave them?
It was probably 10 to 12 pages. They wanted something detailed. They didn't want the back of an envelope stuff. They wanted the narrative. So I evolved the narrative and wrote a detailed outline. So we had another meeting after that, or, at least, I got notes back from them. I think there was a consultation afterward. I think they were happy with it. I don't remember any corrections or suggestions. It was a substantial outline of the book that I intended to write.

You followed Sebastian Faulks and Jeffery Deaver. Faulks set his novel in 1967 and Deaver set his in modern times. Yours was 1969. How did that come about?
I read Sebastian's novel when it came out because he is a friend of mine. However, there are no references to the previous continuation novels in mine. It's like a blank sheet of paper. Having reread all the novels, I thought it would be interesting to posit a Bond at age 45. In my rereading, I realized that's when Double-O agents are meant to retire.

Some decisions were pertinent to me. I had just written a novel [*Trio*, 2020] that was set in 1968, and I didn't want to do that again. Also, I live in Chelsea [London], and Fleming gave Bond an address in Chelsea. It's about 400 yards away from my house. So there's that curious connection. I wrote this article in the *Times Literary Supplement* about finding his address ["The Spies Who Lived Here: How I Found James Bond's Precise Address," July 2020]. I identified the flat where Bond lives in Wellington Square.[7]

Of course, 1969 was the height of swinging London. Kings Road was in Chelsea, where all the shops and cool kids were hanging out. I thought it would be funny to have this 45-year-old spy living in the heart of swinging London. I took Bond up Kings Road and put him in a café [Café Picasso] that existed in 1969 and that was still open at the time of the writing. It's gone now. It was these little things that made me focus on the date.

William Boyd and Sebastian Faulks at *Solo* book event, 2013
Courtesy of Gary J. Firuta

You placed his mission in Africa.
There's never been a Bond novel set in Africa. At the end of *Diamonds Are Forever*, Bond goes to Africa and kills a few people in a helicopter. I was born in Africa, and I grew up there. I thought that would be an interesting setting. It all began to evolve.

I had my time, my London locations as determined by Ian Fleming. Then, I thought, I'll send Bond off to a nasty African Civil War, which is closely based on the civil war that I witnessed as a teenager in the Nigerian-Biafran War from 1967 to 1970. I was drawing on my autobiography but also trying to give my Bond story angles that were different and that had to do with me rather than with the genre, the man, and the myth.

My other ambition was to present a portrait of the quote-unquote "man" James Bond in middle age, 45 years old, that would speak to a reader who had never read a James Bond novel but had heard the name and knew what type of man he was. I had this ambition to create a portrait of James Bond drawn exclusively by Fleming.

Was it called *Solo* at the time?
No, there was no title. Titles are important for me in all my novels. I spent

a long time thinking about one. Sometimes, they come easily, and sometimes, I run through dozens. I hadn't come up with the title at the time. So I referred to it as The Bond Novel. But in the back of my mind, I was constantly thinking of potential titles.

Do you recall any alternate titles?
I was thinking of calling it *Dark Imaginings*—a James Bond novel with a quote from William Wordsworth. I lifted something out of that, but it wasn't right. I think *Solo* might have been suggested among a series of titles by Jonathan Cape, the publisher. I thought, "Bingo, that's it." So we went for it. Of course, it's the perfect title for the novel because Bond is alone and without gadgets and weapons. He's going rogue as well. So I had no title until the very end.

The first line of the novel is "James Bond was dreaming." It's a great opening line. It's evocative; it gets into Bond's interior life, and you're setting up his past and his time in the war.
That line came very early in the ways that are part of the mystery of writing fiction. It came into my head. What triggered it was half a dozen references scattered throughout Fleming's novels about Bond's World War II combat experience. Maybe only four or five. It's odd because they are almost like throwaway lines. "He hadn't heard that noise since the Ardennes Offensive." Hang on, was Bond in the Ardennes in 1944? So it was another opportunity to take something from Fleming and Bond's experience in World War II as a young soldier. I thought that might be a good place to start.

Previously, I reviewed a book called *Ian Fleming's Commandos* [subtitled *The Story of the Legendary 30 Assault Unit*] by a man called Nicholas Rankin. It's about Fleming's experience in the Naval Intelligence Division, where he created this Commando unit, particularly after D-Day, where they would gather up German secrets that might be useful. I thought, "Perfect! Bond is one of Fleming's commandos." I had authorization from Fleming himself because of all the references to World War II.

I was also working under the assumption that, as Fleming had said in *You Only Live Twice*, Bond was born in 1924, so he's a 19-year-old young officer in Ian Fleming's Commandos. There were a lot of nice overlaps there. So how do you get that in? I thought, "Let's start with him dreaming about World War II and how he stared death in the face for the first time." It all came together neatly.

It's also a good way to get into Bond's inner life. You're not requiring Bond to be introspective.
Yes, and I had given myself this challenge to only set the action of the novel through Bond's eyes. In *From Russia with Love*, Bond doesn't appear until page 70 or so, let alone *The Spy Who Loved Me*, which was the worst James Bond novel. Fleming was not a natural writer, and he found it difficult. He would jump from one point of view to another…from Bond to M's or Blofeld's point of view…or whatever.

I'm a great believer in structure and keeping your point of view consistent. I thought, "I'm only going to tell the story through Bond's eyes." Of course, you're right. You're in his head. You're immediately in his dream life, and in the first paragraph, you're in his point of view, and it doesn't let up until the last sentence. It's Bond's point of view throughout. I think that makes the novel slightly different from Fleming's novels.

Can you talk more about determining the novel's point of view?
The novel is told entirely from Bond's point of view—all of *Solo* is seen through Bond's eyes. By the end of the novel, I had hoped that readers would have a real sense of James Bond, the individual with all of his problems. He's a functioning alcoholic, he's a nervous flier, he vomits when he sees carnage; he doesn't like women who paint their fingernails. He was an avid reader. Fleming said that Bond's flat was "book-lined." I thought that was interesting. Fleming provided all these details in a throw-away manner. As I reread the books, I noted all that stuff down. It became the raw material for my portrait. I gathered it all up to create a portrait of James Bond in his middle 40s.

Bond has a military background, but we don't normally see that part of his character. But in your book, he uses his military experience to lead an army.
Yes, exactly. If we agree that he had combat experience in World War II, then when he's in Zanzarim, in the middle of a war, he can rely on his experience and his training. So that initial decision—or lucky find—that Bond had seen combat played perfectly into my nasty little African Civil War.

***Solo* opens with Bond's 45 birthday and he's feeling it.**
I think that there are certain birthdays when it begins to kick in. Turning 40, for example, is catastrophic in anybody's life. Maybe it's the beginning of middle age. There's another line that I like when he's in bed

with a movie star, and she looks at his body and says, "You've got more scars than a gladiator." He has been through the mill.

He smokes 60 cigarettes a day and drinks two bottles of vodka a day, like Ian Fleming—Fleming was a bit of a drunk, and he gave Bond all of his habits and tastes. Fleming was also interested in women's couture, so Bond is interested in women's couture. Fleming was a bit of a dandy and so Bond cared about what kind of cotton his polo shirt was made from, what kind of marmalade he spread on his toast, and what coffee he brewed in the morning. He gave these tastes to Bond. I felt that was something else I could exploit in this portrait of Bond that I was painting.

Tell me about creating your villain, the mercenary Kobus Breed.
When you say yes to the job, you have to respect the genre. You need to have stuff in it about cars, food, and drink. Bond has to have at least two love affairs. There has to be a serious villain, these are the components and the tropes of a Bond novel. Don't take the job if you're not going to create a serious antagonist for Bond. It's that simple. Determining what kind of villain is part of the novel writing process.

When I was thinking about what villain would be a good antagonist for Bond, I was thinking about the worst South African mercenaries who were involved in the Nigerian Civil War. I was in my late teens during the war. I was never in any danger, but it completely transformed the way that I thought about conflict and warfare. You'd be stopped at roadblocks by drunken soldiers and have an AK47 waved at you. I was strip-searched, down to my underpants, in the Lagos Airport before they realized I was not a threat.

I used to stay at this hotel near the Lagos Airport, which was full of mercenary pilots who flew the Nigerian MiG-15s. I searched my memory and recalled the atmosphere in that hotel. I thought that a brutal South African mercenary would be a good antagonist for Bond.

Then I thought of who he might have an affair with and so on. I didn't have to hand in the outline for many weeks after I got the job. I could go away and think about it. I concocted, dreamt, and researched the novel that I wanted to write. Of course, I put in a lot of ideas that interested me because why ask me to write a continuation Bond, unless it included my thoughts? A lot of what went in were notions that had been parts of film projects that were going to be set in Africa but collapsed. I had all these ideas swirling around in my head. So I saw a way of recycling them into my Bond. Of course, it had to be compelling, exciting, and have many twists and turns, and suspense and shocks.

I drew not only upon my own experience in Nigeria but also ideas that I had for other novels, movies, or television series that would be relevant but that I hadn't had the opportunity to finalize or thoroughly explore.

There are some hard-hitting passages, such as when Bond does his long walk through the jungle and comes across the starving children. It was almost as if you were testing the limits of what could be poured into a Bond book.
I wanted it to be a serious book. Look at the Fleming novels. The good ones are the most realistic. The silly ones veer off into non-sensical plots that Fleming would dream up when he was writing them in Jamaica. I wanted to write a grounded, gritty, serious novel. I wanted to remove Bond from gadgetry and the *deux ex machina* machines that arrive in the nick of time.

I put Bond in the jungle. He doesn't have a gun. He's starving. He has to walk to safety. It was based on the Biafran War, where a million people, mainly civilians, died from starvation. It was one of those crazy surrealist wars. I put in all that stuff about the Nigerian Army, who wouldn't march unless they had a beer, and the Afghan army, who wouldn't go into battle unless the Fetish priests made them invincible. There was all that madness of war in West Africa that I witnessed from the sidelines that went into making Bond's experience as realistic and non-silly as possible.

That also applies to the second half of the book, rooted in the historical situation in Washington, DC, at that time. After the death of Martin Luther King, massive riots made the capital of the United States one of the most dangerous cities on the planet. That was all included to make it, as they say, as granular and as realistic as possible.

I was trying to get away from the absurd silly Bond which is particularly prevalent in the movie version. The early Bond novels are realistic. I think my favorite is *From Russia with Love. From Russia with Love* is a proper spy novel; it's realistic and rooted in the world. Then Fleming's imagination began to fall short and he started inventing monsters who dreamt of world domination. I think my motivation was to make it as absolutely real, visceral, and tangible as possible.

On the flip side of that, I also think the novel is funny, sometimes darkly. M tells Bond to make the villain a "less effective soldier" which is a sly way of saying eliminate him. Elsewhere he thinks that someone's mustache isn't doing them "any favors." Or talking to a

hotel clerk, Bond ingratiates himself by talking "as men do."
I describe myself as a serious comic novelist. I see the world through a comic lens. For example, when he goes to the film set, he pretends to be a representative from Equity [the actor's union] to get into the trailer of Bryce Fitzjohn [an actress]. I've written a lot of movies, so I know film sets. I liked the idea of putting James Bond on a film set. There is wry humor about Bond as well. Where have you seen a vinaigrette recipe in a James Bond novel? That's from Fleming, as well, who put a recipe for scrambled eggs in one of his short stories ["007 in New York"].

I thought if Fleming had done it, I would have the license to do the same. So there is absurdist humor lurking beneath the novel. That's my voice. I wrote it in my voice. I didn't want to write a pastiche of Fleming. It's the reason that *Solo* sits on the shelf with all my other novels. I'm proud of it. I had a lot of fun writing it, but I took it seriously. Because it's a realistic novel, it stands up.

It was published in 2013, and I'm still getting letters and emails about it. In fact, my novel triggered an article about James Bond's World War II experience. This guy tracked down all the references to Bond's experience in World War II, and that had been sparked by my novel.

I think it's being reassessed within the canon of the continuation novels. I feel pleased about that and that all my hard work is still being rewarded. The book was a real attempt to make him and the situation a living, breathing, three-dimensional character. I wanted to make the book plausible and authentic and not fantastical or drifting into pantomime, as it can do in Fleming.

Excuse me for bringing this up, but your comment about making Bond human made me think about something. In *Solo*, Bond's on a stakeout, and he's consumed too much American coffee, nature calls, so he takes care of those needs. Now, he's worried that he's missed his mark. It was a little surprising to read it, but it's a human moment.
Right, what happens is a real spy goes on a stakeout and nods off or is distracted. He's a living, breathing man on the job. He's bored rigid but he has to keep looking. You ask yourself, what's the reality of the situation? Whatever novel I am writing, I ask myself the same question, "How do I render that moment in a way that will resonate with the reader?" So it's a genuine William Boyd novel even though it's about James Bond.

How long did it take to write the first draft?

It was quite a quick job by my standards. I got the commission in early 2012 and the book was published in September 2013. So it probably took me four or five months to write the first draft. That's fast for me but it's like any novel. You do all the research and background detail, and you block out the narrative, which I was going to do anyway. If you're happy with the shape of the story you want to tell, then you apply yourself day after day until the book gets written. It was quite probably one of the fastest novels I've written. However, my earlier novels were written at high speed because I had illimitable reserves of energy. In this case, I knew when I had to deliver it and when it had to be published.

Do you remember any incidents where you and IFP had a creative difference of opinion on how Bond was depicted?
Because I reread all the novels and took notes, I'm pretty sure that I knew more about James Bond than they did. So when they queried certain things like Bond's drinking or fear of flying, I could quote Fleming, chapter and verse, back. The one area where we disagreed was that they felt I made the Bond and M relationship too close. They felt that it was a strictly professional relationship between a boss and an operative. I countered by quoting examples where, in various novels, Bond goes to M's house. I felt strongly that M was a father figure to Bond. Remember, Bond is an orphan and his father and mother died in a climbing accident when he was eleven years old. But their comment wasn't an instruction.

There was one particular scene that they felt was slightly wrong. Bond has nearly been killed in Africa, and he's recovering from his wounds in a hospital near Edinburgh. M pays an unofficial visit to him in the hospital and gives him half a bottle of whisky. That gesture and the fact that M had come to visit him provokes, in Bond, an emotion and affection for his boss. I made it quite explicit that it was a filial, paternal relationship. The Fleming Family said, "We don't think that's true." I adulterated it and took out the words "father" and "son."

I still think that in that scene, an Englishman of a certain era would have found it hard to express emotion. I still think Bond harbors unexpressed affection for M, who has been so important in Bond's life. We don't know what M is actually thinking because you only see it from Bond's point of view. That was the only time that the Flemings were able to get me to make a minor change because I shot all their other objections down in flames. I still think they're wrong, but I wasn't going to go to the wall for this. I just turned down the volume slightly in that scene.

I read it again the other day for some reason, and it is an emotional encounter between the two of them. M sent Bond to this war, and Bond nearly died after being shot three times in the body. Does M feel guilty? Bond tries to articulate this, and you can sense the emotion. That's all subtext, not overt.

But that's the only area where we disagreed. We had a very good working relationship, and it continues. I still get invitations, and Corrine and I communicate. That's the only time we disagreed with my interpretation of Fleming—but I still think I'm right. [Laughs.]

Functionally, are IFP and the Estate one entity?
I don't see any separation between the family and the Estate. My impression is that the Fleming Family set up IFP as a way of ring-fencing and monetizing the legacy. As you know, Fleming sold the film rights to Cubby Broccoli and Harry Saltzman in perpetuity because he was terrified of his tax bill. So there's a complete gulf and schism between the movies and the books. The books have fed off the success of the films, but the films have gotten further and further away…to the point that the films have nothing to do with the books, apart from Bond, M, and Moneypenny. I think that the Fleming Family, or at least the two members I know, are very much hands-on, and Corinne is there to run the business.

Who are the continuation novels for? Are they for Bond purists or the wider audience?
There's no doubt that the global success of the Bond movies has benefited the sales of Fleming's novels. The fan base is enormous, and it's deeply pedantic. When I chose a Jensen Interceptor as Bond's car, I had the most extraordinary communications with people saying, "Bond would never drive a Jensen Interceptor because it has an American engine." Of course, I could counter that Fleming had an American car, so why couldn't Bond?

Suddenly, I was aware of this community of people who are obsessed with Bond and everything to do with Bond. However, I don't think the books are primarily for them. I think they are for people who have enjoyed a couple of films and are curious to read something. If something is made for film or television, it sends people back to books. If you have an adaptation of *Pride and Prejudice* on television, suddenly Jane Austen is number one on the best seller's list. Reading, as opposed to watching, also engages a different form of pleasure. I suspect that all the people who love Bond and all the Bond myths are going to be drawn to reading a continuation novel. Certainly, that applies to *Solo,* which has been sold in 40 counties.

There's a funny phenomenon in that I have worked with three of the actors who have played James Bond: Connery, Brosnan, and Craig. Daniel Craig was in two of my films. Years after playing Bond, they are still mobbed. I saw Pierce Brosnan a couple of years ago when he was shooting a movie in London. He was in another one of my films, and that's how I got to know him. He said that he was on the embankment of the Thames in London, and this bus stopped. Eighty Japanese tourists got off the bus and ran to him, screaming, "James Bond! James Bond!" And his last Bond film was decades ago.

The same with Daniel Craig who is globally famous. He cannot go anywhere. He was hiking in the Atlas Mountains in Morocco and walked into a village. All the kids ran out screaming, "James Bond!" Bond is a massive phenomenon, and the books tap into that quite broadly. They are not aimed at only a single audience. The books are for people who see the O-O-Seven symbol and think, "That would be a good thing to read on the plane." They're directed at Bond lovers around the world.

You wrote two short stories—"William Boyd Interviews James Bond" and "William Boyd's Q&A with James Bond." In them, you go back in time and interview Bond. How did they come about?
When a book comes out, you're always asked to write articles. I'm such a James Bond expert that I could go on quiz shows about James Bond. I have all this odd arcane information about him. The interview and Bond from A to Zed were written as part of the book promotion. They also allowed me to exercise and aerate all this weird information I happened to have. It was a fun thought experiment. It was, "Here I am, William Boyd interviewing James Bond." You have to laugh.

Did anything surprise you about the experience of writing a Bond novel?
I don't think so. It's a William Boyd novel that features James Bond. I had written spy novels before. I've written many pieces of journalism about spying, and I'm steeped in that world of espionage. I knew that when you're writing a spy novel it's got to be exciting, it's got to be baffling. There's got to be twists and turns. At the end of my novel, Bond realizes that he has found someone that he could be with. But if he stays with her, he will put her in harm's way. He walks away from something that might have consoled him in his middle age. The last paragraph of *Solo* is something that I took great pains over to get the mood and tone right. But I would do that for the last paragraph of any novel.

I learned a lot about Bond and his world and about Fleming's struggles to write them. Although I knew a lot about Fleming before I came into it. My novels are narrative-driven, anyway. I often import genre elements to give them that motor force. So I learned a lot about the details of Bond and his life, but I didn't learn anything about how to write a spy novel. As I said, I had been there and done that.

You leave Bond in 1969. As a thought experiment, did you think about picking up the next one with Bond in 1970?
I asked my agent, Jonny Geller if I would be asked to do another. He said, "Well, it's not impossible." I said, "I did not want to do another one. This is the only one I'll do." Some years after *Solo*, I was asked to write a Raymond Chandler continuation novel, and I turned it down. I'll never do it again. Anthony Horowitz has done three Bonds and Sherlock Homes [*The House of Silk: A Sherlock Holmes Novel*, 2012 and *Moriarty*, 2014]; Sebastian has done PG Woodhouse [*Jeeves and the Wedding Bells*, 2013]. I won't—"never say never—I won't do another one."

Writing Bond was a wonderful opportunity. It came at a perfect time in my writing life. I had finished a novel, and I was fascinated by Fleming. But I didn't even consider doing another because I closed that door. And sure enough, they didn't ask me to write another one. So it wasn't something that I had even posited the vaguest notion. I signed off after *Solo*.

Given that the experience was positive, why didn't you consider writing another?
I think it's because I've got so many things on the go anyway; I'm not a jobbing novelist; I'm not looking for another payday. I write films, television series, theater, and journalism, and I'm incredibly busy. The gap that allowed me to write the Bond novel was perfect. But if I was going to write, say, a Raymond Chandler continuation, that's going to eat up a year of my life. It would stop me from doing the three other things I want to do. I think if I was harder up and desperate, I might have been saying, "Hey, I've got a great idea for a sequel." [Laughs.] But in fact, not writing another one has more to do with my program and my ambitions for the work that I'm generating myself. I'm the kind who multitasks and has many irons in the fire. I don't want to be distracted. I say no, lots of times, in fact, for other offers for precisely that reason.

More than the story itself, I like the way you tell it. I like your voice.

Thank you very much, Mark. It's exactly what I wanted to achieve. I wanted it to be another novel that I'd written rather than a well-paid job.

Looking back at this experience, what are your thoughts?
It was great fun, but I took it seriously. The measure of that is that I see this Bond novel as completely part of my canon of work. I don't see it as a job that I dashed off and disowned. I own that novel. I'm proud of it. In the vast world of the James Bond myth, I think it earns its keep. More to the point, it's written in my voice, and it's my point of view. It's my take on it. I'm glad that I was given this opportunity. I seized it with both hands, used it, and benefited from it in all sorts of ways. All in all, it was a really great experience.

STEVE COLE

Shoot to Kill (2014)
Heads You Die (2016)
Strike Lightning (2016)
Red Nemesis (2017)

Steve Cole
Illustration by Pat Carbajal

How did you come to write a new series of Young Bond novels?
The short answer is that I was contacted by my agent back in December 2012. Weirdly, my first encounter with Bond in print was finding a copy of the *James Bond and Moonraker* novelization [by Christopher Wood] in the bargain bin of a bookstore in my town. I was only eight or nine or something. I didn't have a lot of pocket money back then, but we bought it because my Mom was such a huge Roger Moore fan. We had so many photos of Roger Moore around the house that I used to think he was my dad at one point. There were more photos of him than my actual father.

I remember reading the novelization, and it couldn't have been more different from Fleming's *Moonraker*. At the time, I assumed that the books were based on the films, not the other way around. The first Bond film I saw at the cinema—in fact, the first time I went to the cinema—was with my friend, Sean, to see *For Your Eyes Only*. I vividly remember seeing it in the gigantic 2,000-seater cinema that we used to have back then before home video destroyed it all.

Then when *A View to a Kill* came out, I knew it was based on Fleming's short story. I had learned about that in the library, but I couldn't figure out how they could make an entire movie out of a short story. I read the short story at the library, and I realized that it was nothing like the film. I still remember being shocked. The story had Bond losing his wallet and his virginity at the age of sixteen. I remember thinking that Fleming's Bond was world-weary and seemed like a real person. He was not the suave, unflappable Superman that Roger Moore was portraying. I had also read some of *Colonel Sun,* that massive, dust-jacketed hardback version in the library.

At this point, I would have been about fourteen or so. I started to read all of Fleming's novels to see how they differed from the films that I'd seen. Then I read the books that I hadn't seen. I remember the absolute shock of realizing that *The Spy Who Loved Me* movie was so different from what I read in print. I wasn't impressed with that one. It wasn't the Bond that I had expected. Then when *GoldenEye* came out, I realized that they weren't using the books anymore. Instead, they were referencing Fleming himself [and the name of his estate in Jamaica]. Before that, at least, they were using the [book] titles. But at that point, it moved away from Fleming.

I had also read Charlie Higson's Young Bond because I was working in children's fiction anyway. I was interested to see what he had done with it, and I enjoyed that. But it was a total surprise when I was approached to write Young Bond. It's because I had worked with Red Fox, part of Random House's Children's books. Random House has published a lot of my work.

Charlie Higson and Steve Cole
Photo Courtesy of Mark O'Connell, Catching Bullets

I'd written a couple of thrillers (*Tripwire*, 2010 and *Deathwing*, 2011) with a real-life bomb disposal expert, Major Chris Hunter. That was set a few years into the future, and it was about a teenage bomb disposal expert, Felix Smith. He was a kid, but he had tradecraft. He had nerve and he got caught up in adventures. He was also underestimated because he was a teen, but he was self-reliant and clear-thinking. He was able to visualize an objective, fix his sights on it, and achieve it. I think there were similarities there. Perhaps, Ian Fleming Publications saw how Bond could work out. They asked me if I would be interested in having a go.

What was your reaction to being asked?
I didn't say yes straightaway. I said, "Well, I need to think about it." Then, I thought about it for about three-quarters of a second and said, "Yeah, all right. I'll have a go with that." Once you've been offered something like that, it's difficult to turn it down...*then*, you'd have to stay quiet, see someone else get it, and then they'd get to talk about it. Plus, why would I want to turn it down? Although it was a little bit intimidating.

While I'd worked with Random House before, I hadn't worked with Ian Fleming Publications. They wanted to see how I would approach Bond and how I would want to map out the four titles. It was always conceived as a mini-series of four books with a story arc stretching across all four of them. I had to come up with a treatment of roughly what would happen and what would be the storyline. I worked out the first book in depth, and I wrote the first three chapters. It was a sample to show what I would do with it. I was happy to do it because they were charming and courteous to me.

They also sent me a full matching set of Fleming's novels. It was the latest ones that were out at the time. That was exciting because I had a smattering of different old paperbacks from different imprints and different times, which I still have. It was nice to have a matching set on the shelf and to reread them and be reminded of the way Fleming wrote. Of course, I reviewed Charlie's books as well. I wanted to honor what's gone before, but you also want to try to push your agenda and assert your own point of view on it. At the same time, I had to work out what my view was!

How did you discover your point of view?
I had to work it out...what *was* my view of it? That was the bit that took the longest, I think. I remember thinking that this was the sixth Young Bond novel and that the sixth James Bond novel (*Dr. No*) was the first

one they made into a movie. I thought, why don't I send Bond off to Hollywood? I thought that [symmetry] might appeal to proper James Bond aficionados. It also gave me a way into what I wanted to do.

I then had to answer the question, how feasible would it be for Bond to go to Los Angeles in the 1930s? This period pre-dates the commercial jet age, but, of course, the airship was popular in about 1934. With the circles that Bond moves in, it seemed to me to make sense. The pieces started to fall into place. Once I made that initial creative choice, I had to go in and meet the Flemings at their private bank in Piccadilly and discuss the situation.

What was the meeting with the Flemings like?
It was slightly nerve-wracking because, as well as being a big fan of Ian Fleming, I was more specifically a fan of Lucy Fleming [who is also an actress]. I thought she was fantastic in the *Survivors* show in the 1970s. She was also in an *Avengers* episode. I've always fancied her, I have to say. Before meeting her, I told myself, "Play it cool. Play it cool." As soon as I was introduced, I said [brightening], "Hello, Lucy Fleming. I promise not to ask you any questions about Terrence Dudley and *Survivors*." "You were a fan?" "Yes, I am a fan. I'm sorry." They were all very kind and courteous.

There was a buffet there. At first, I thought, "I'll get some lunch here." But the interrogations started almost immediately. They would say, "Do you think there are maybe too many characters in this storyline, and Bond won't be given the chance to shine?" I would reply, "I think the characters are there to help tell the story, and they will all bring out different facets of Bond's character. I think there's enough room there for Bond to have space." And they'd say, "But do you think there are maybe too many characters in the outline? There won't be enough space for Bond to shine?" So I said, "I'm gonna tell you what. I can maybe take out one of those characters." "Oh, would you? That'd be a good idea." [Laughs.]

They were gently but very firmly prescriptive in certain things that they saw. In the end, I think they were absolutely right. What I had done in the first book, *Shoot to Kill*, was to surround Bond with a ton of characters. This way, I didn't have to fully commit to what I was going to do with him.

Who was at this initial meeting?
Lucy Fleming, Corrine Turner from IFP [Ian Fleming Publications], Josephine Lane, the editor at the time, Jonny Geller, IFP's agent, Diggory

Laycock [Lucy Fleming's son], who is quite high-up in it. I think Diggory Laycock rose to prominence during my time. From that first meeting, I perceived Fergus had stepped back, and Diggory had stepped up. Diggory gave the speeches at the book events. Kate [Fleming] wasn't there, but it was a bunch of them. We were all around this big, old table. I could imagine that if I said something wrong, they'd press a button, and my chair would tip over, and I'd fall into the vat of sharks behind me. There was a sense of that.

It was interesting to see Fleming's relationship with Bond. They are all tremendously well-off just from the bank. Bond and *Chitty-Chitty-Bang-Bang* are sort of birthright that they get to enjoy and play with. They take the responsibility of looking after the heritage and the ongoing adventures of Fleming's characters seriously. I enjoyed their attention and their clear passion for it.

After we talked through everything, they said that they were going to discuss and think about it. When the word came through from the UK that I got the gig, and I'd be writing Young Bond, I was in Manhattan. Looking out over the whole of midtown from the hotel I thought, "This is one of those moments you remember. This seems like a Bondish place to be."

How did you figure out how to get a handle on the character?
Initially, I found it quite hard to get a handle on what I wanted to do with him. I knew what Charlie had done with Bond, but Charlie pushed him through some pretty heavy shit. It was a matter of *trying out* how we'll go forward. I thought the more characters he has around him, the more we can see how he deals with different people, different temperaments, and different views. We could explore all that together, and I'll find out more about him as I go. In the end, I did trim that down.

Part of my arc over the four books was to put fewer and fewer characters around him. In the first one, *Shoot to Kill*, there are several friends, but by the time you reach the fourth one, *Red Nemesis*, it's only him and the Bond girl. It's the two of them against everything. The arc was that he went from being surrounded by friends to being isolated and pushed down this path further than Charlie had pushed him into becoming what we all know he will become.

That's the unique thing about this series about a teen. Normally, when you're writing a book, you don't know what the central character will be like as an adult. As a writer, it's outside our purview. We don't care about it. But with Young Bond, we all know what's waiting for him. It's a tragic case about this teenage boy who is denied a proper childhood.

He's forced down the road to becoming a weapon for his country. So it was interesting to shine some light on those key moments along the way.

Beyond limiting the number of characters who surrounded Bond, what else did Ian Fleming Publications request?
It was established early on that it would be a direct continuation of Charlie's books. It wasn't going to jump ahead in time. It was also always tied to Fleming's Bond. We had some biographic detail from the obit in *You Only Live Twice* and various reminiscences from Fleming's book. But Ian Fleming Publications weren't prescriptive in terms of what they wanted me to do with the series. They were interested to see my take on it…what I would do with it…and how I saw Bond.

I saw potential in Bond's early childhood and his parents' deaths. It's interesting to see how the Daniel Craig films also reflected some of that. It was looking back to his childhood times and trying to create an "everything I know is a lie" moment.

I was originally going to have someone claiming to be his father. That would have occurred in the last book. Bond isn't sure if he could trust this person at first, but he's slowly won over. Of course, it is an imposter. That was the plan. We decided that it would be stronger if it was almost a message from beyond the grave. This way, there is a promise of a mystery that Bond has to solve on his own rather than pairing him with an adult, which lessens his own impact.

I was keen to put Bond through the wringer as never before and test him psychologically and emotionally. It was the fact that his father had actually been murdered [as revealed in *Red Nemesis*] rather than having died in an accident [as implied in *You Only Live Twice*]. We had this character, Mimic, who can precisely imitate someone's voice. Through Mimic, I was able to replay Bond's dad's last moments from beyond the grave. That was a good triggering event for Bond.

Originally, I wanted to put Mimic in as early as the second book. Somewhere, there's a draft of *Heads You Die*, which had Mimic in it, but the character didn't fit properly there. I wanted him in *Strike Lighting*, as well but he did not quite fit into that either. I was glad that we found a story that worked for him. I was keen to use Mimic.

You can tell a good Bond story by the quality of his enemies. I thought that it was nice to have a nod to that slightly outlandish and fantastic, but at the same time, to be plausible. Especially a villain that's his age. Someone who is on his level but who can test his agency. There was no directive other than we wanted it to appeal to not only teens, but to the wider Bond fan. There's plenty to enjoy in Charlie's books. I had to find a way of making these books different.

It seems challenging to not only follow Fleming but also to continue an established series.
Shoot to Kill was the trickiest one to write. It took months. I was always thinking about the story. I remember saying to my editor, Ruth Mills, at Random House, "I'm not sure how much of Charlie to take to it." Ruth said, "We'd quite like to see what Steve Cole brings to James Bond. You can write it as you would write it." That was the confidence boost I needed to take elements of what had gone before but to try to do it my way.

If you try to impersonate someone, it's always going to be watered down. I wanted to be faithful to Charlie's books but not be a direct follow-on. There seemed to be little point in doing a watered-down version of Charlie's books. For better or worse, I needed to find an identity of my own with them.

There is a nod to the Fleming style with the almost forensic detail of brand names, meals, and technology. Those things are great fun to research and write. So it was a demanding job. I look back on it with pride and pleasure.

There is a six-year gap between Higson's last book in 2008 and your first book in 2014. Yours didn't immediately follow his. Perhaps, it's not necessary to consider Young Bond as a 9-book series; maybe they can be viewed as two different series with the same character.
I was keen that my book would be a set that you didn't need any foreknowledge to read. As you say, many years had passed since Charlie's books, and while they all stayed in print, there wasn't a big push for them. With the new books, I knew there would be a big push for the first book in the new Bonds.

Charlie had neatly finished things off in his last book, By Royal Command, by giving us a great explanation of why Bond was kicked out of Eton. *By Royal Command* is my favorite of Charlie's novels. I knew that when I took over, I didn't want to start him off at Fettes College in Edinburgh. We know from the obit that's where he went. However, if we did that, it would seem like I was repeating *SilverFin* [which spends more than half the book setting up Bond's life in this strange, new environment]. I thought that we would start off the book with him later in his tenure there. But Ian Fleming Publications was keen that he didn't age too quickly.

They were mindful, I suspect, that, at age sixteen, he was going to be losing his virginity. Plus, by keeping him younger, we could avoid the whole sex thing, which can be problematic for a younger audience, or any audience, one hopes. It also meant we could avoid the perceived misogyny associated with some of the movies as well because the cinematic Bond's attitudes toward women date from a different era.

By operating before that age, we could portray the females around Bond as equals, and he's happy in that relationship. He might know that women around him find him attractive, but he's not actively working to exploit that for anything. The women save him as much as he saves them. That's true with Fleming as well. Fleming did the same thing. Bond is not always galloping in as the white knight and saving the day. He is often helped and rescued. He loses his heart to them as well. He is heartbroken at times. I think the movies set up a perception of Bond that wasn't quite the case in Fleming's books. From the movies, people perceive Bond one way, but when you come to Fleming, it's quite different.

You put Young Bond in a progressive school that wasn't established in Fleming's obituary.
When I was researching, I realized how much time we had to allow him to catch the end of the term at this progressive school. Certainly, Aunt Charmian seemed the sort who would be interested in that. I was reading about these establishments, which were quite in vogue at that time. I think that if things had been different for Bond, then he would have done quite well in an environment like that, which is slightly less orthodox. It also allowed me to put him in a school where you have the opposite sex. You couldn't do that at Eton or Fettes [a boys-only school]. This different co-educational environment allowed me to establish a different mood and tone from Charlie's books. There was freedom in no uniforms. It provided an instant point of contrast to the ritual of Eton.

Of course, I hauled him off to America anyway to get him somewhere else. I had given him a character with dwarfism as a companion. That was to bring out a different side of Bond and pair him with someone humorous because Bond is a serious young man of course. I also put in the characters of my choosing rather than inherited ones. From that point, it was easy for me to get a fix on it and start over. Years later, in the third book, *Strike Lightning*, I brought back Perry, and Charmian had a bit more to do. But that was fine because, by then, my series was halfway through my cycle. I wasn't trying to pretend Charlie's hadn't happened. Eton was a big part of Bond's development.

How many pages was the outline that you gave them?
It was a detailed piece. It was probably about 7,000 words. When we go from an outline to the manuscript, we tend to expand by a factor of 10. So 7,000 words would go up to a 70,000-word novel. It was detailed, pretty much scene by scene. I did that for the three remaining books as well. I was keen to not dumb it down. I wanted to maintain that Fleming edge.

I worked with another editor at Ian Fleming Publications, who was brought in on for *Strike Lightning* and *Red Nemesis* as well. We would have wonderful meetings in the gin bar around the corner from *IFP* in Golden Square called Graphic. We would drink this spectacular gin and tonic while writing our notes. At the end of the afternoon, we'd invite Jo Lane from IFP to come and hear what we'd got. We would discuss it with her. We knew if we were onto a good thing because she would pick up our bar bill. That was always good. That was nice. That was fun working on that.

Can you describe your research for *Shoot to Kill*?
There was a lot of research into the Hollywood movie industry, which at that time, was hit hard by strikes and labor relations. The studio bosses were doing shady deals to make sure that their people were working and if they weren't getting the big payouts, they would start encouraging workers to go on strike.

Originally, I had a character who was a technician at one of the motion picture studios who was on strike. He was being threatened and extorted by one of the gangsters when they got the evidence against the bad guy. Eventually, he gets killed. That survived the outline. After the first draft, they decided that they wanted it to be simplified for the younger audience.

I did have to compromise on certain things. It was a task that I handled readily and put a lot of work into. It was Bond, so it was worth the effort. This was a project that I knew that I would enjoy and that I would commit to for a number of years for four books, for four pretty major chunky books.

The McGuffin of *Shoot to Kill* is a snuff film. The book is not necessarily aimed at young kids.
I was keen to keep it hard-hitting. It's not kid-friendly in many ways, but kids today have access to so many graphic videos on social media. Kids today see scenes of police brutality, arrests, and all sorts of horrible things. Teens have access to this like never before.

Because I set it in the 1930s, I was worried that it would turn off some modern readers. I wanted to show them that there are undercurrents in the 1930s that are a pretty worrying mirror to what we're living in now. That includes the rise of totalitarian regimes, right-wing feelings, or power blocks who are looking to isolate and make war. Of course, the big enemy of the UK in the 1930s was the Soviet Union. Here we are today, dealing with similar things going on. I was trying to show that there are 21st-century parallels even if the technology was different. It existed in a way that might surprise them.

That big chunky reel of film was also a good way to establish the technology and remind readers of the time. I wanted to show that he didn't have a phone, he couldn't use a computer, and he couldn't find out where he was by checking his GPS. He doesn't have any of that, but he does have his wits, the occasional blunt object, and a small set of allies. It was all quite deliberate.

It allowed me to do a huge amount of research, which I love. I can spend a whole day researching without actually writing, but still feel good about myself. At the end of the day, I was like, "I got a lot done today." I was watching old Pathé newsreels, checking something out, and making notes. It's useful to immerse yourself in that world. 90% of that research will never make it onto the page, but if you can picture it in your head, then maybe your reader can picture it in theirs. That's the point you have to get to. It feels like nothing's happening for a long time, but you're educating yourself and building up that world within you, so you can start writing.

Did your experience writing *Shoot to Kill* impact your approach to your second novel, *Heads You Die*?

I learned about my handle on Young Bond. More specifically, I think I now had the confidence to pare down the number of characters around him. I also realized that it was time to take him out of the concrete chunks [big cities in the UK or Hollywood] and put him into rainforests. Originally, I was going to set the story in the Amazon and draw upon Fleming's brother's accounts of his own Amazon expedition. I thought that would be interesting. It would also be sticking with Fleming although a different Fleming. I can see why Ian Fleming was jealous of his brother and why he wanted to be an author himself. He must have been livid with his brother to have these incredible adventures and go where few white people had ever gone before.

The first draft of *Heads You Die,* or *Hellstriker*, as it was called then, was very different. We had some creative differences. The synopsis was approved, but after getting the first draft, they wanted to make changes that were quite major to the second half of the book. I ended up saying, "I can't change the second half without also changing the first half." I went back and pretty much rewrote the whole thing from scratch. It definitely benefited the book, which is my favorite of the four.

The plot with the poisoned money had been floating around my head for years and years. This was an opportunity to use it. Originally, it was going to be a thriller, printing the poison on London subway tickets. So everyone would pick up their tickets and come into contact with the poison that way. But putting the poison on the money seemed like an interesting twist. I was looking into counterfeiting and how banknotes were made at the time. Scolopendra [the villainous biologist] had this expert knowledge of nature in South America and these unexplored areas and undiscovered creatures. It all fits in quite well. Moving into Cuba and the surrounding islands gave it more of an edge.

In terms of style, I think it pretty much kept it the same. I brought Nazis into it. I wanted to do more with the political situation in the world at that time so I used the Nazis in South America.

Hellstriker seems like a great title for a Bond book.
I quite like it.

For *Heads You Die*, what was the nature of the creative disputes? I should add that in any creative endeavor, it's quite common for two different parties to have different ideas and approaches to the best way to achieve the common goal.
Yes, right. It was nothing huge. Ian Fleming Publications felt that it would be stronger if we kept the action more focused. I had branched off. Maybe they were also concerned that Charlie Higson's *Hurricane Gold* had already done the jungle territory and fire ants. Maybe they felt that it would be treading the same ground.

Originally, the plotline was slightly more fantastic. Particularly in terms of the villain's lair. The villain's lair in the jungle was kept secret by this massive natural tree canopy over the top of it. It was hidden so no one could spot it from above if they were flying over. In addition to the counterfeiting, there was also an auction for various unfriendly powers, and of course the Nazis were there. I think they were thinking that it was going a little bit fantastical. So we reined it back in and focused on the action. That's when I chose to give Bond the poison so that it gives him a much stronger through-note to achieve resolution and it keeps the action on him.

Before that, they were worried that Bond was caught up in this massive pre-war, Nazi adventure in the blazing jungle. I think at one point, the Germans tried to seize the place from Scolopendra. At the time, he was known as Lobo, the wolf. It was all quite different. It became more focused and more tightly plotted with the rewrite. I still have memories of it being the best of times and the worst of times. Overall, it was a good one. It informed my approach to the last couple of books. I made sure that what I was doing was okayed in advance. Before Heads You Die had been tentatively okayed, it was decided that maybe it was going too far. I could be wrong about that, but that was my understanding. It was never a big deal. It's just one of those things and some books get rewritten more than others.

Is that why there was a two-year gap between the first and second novels? Or was that always part of the schedule?
I recall that with *Shoot to Kill*, first we had a hardback and then the paperback followed. Originally, we were going to a hardback for *Heads You Die* and then a paperback. Then I think we decided that we would concentrate on the schedule by going into paperback with limited edition hardbacks alongside. They were planning to come out with them every six months after *Heads You Die*. For that to happen, you have to have a bit of extra time between *Heads You Die* and *Shoot to Kill*. So that's why we did that.

How long did it take to write each book?
Months. I would say that the first book, *Shoot to Kill*, took me about eight months, on and off, to write. That's longer than any of the books of that length that I'd written before. Of course, that's spread over gaps between rewrites and everything. *Heads You Die* took about five or six months. The last two books involved less rewriting. I was much happier with the style. Then, they would take about two and a half months, so it accelerated.

The way it worked was that first, Ian Fleming Publications would contract you and then it would go to Penguin Random House. Penguin had acquired Random House even before book one. Before that, Penguin published the first lot of Young Bonds, but they weren't so keen on continuing it. I felt that this could be problematic. So you do three drafts for IFP and when they were happy it goes to Penguin Random House. But, of course, for Penguin Random House, this was a fresh draft, and they would want changes. Sometimes those changes would push it close to how it was in the first draft. In a way, you're a servant of two masters.

I tried to be mindful of that. The first few drafts were my time to make it right and make sure that the Board of Ian Fleming Publications was happy with what we had got. Then, I would deal with Penguin Random who would make more nuts and bolts types of edits. Then, we'd make sure that the Flemings were happy with that, while at the same time, making sure that Penguin Random was happy.

Were there any changes in approach between books two and three?
Heads You Die was to be the last appearance of Queensmarsh, Bond's pistol. I had planned to have him use this rough pistol that would come to signify a part of his character. By *Red Nemesis*, the final book, he would put away Queensmarsh, much like he puts away other childish things. Maybe then, he'd use a real gun. That was my wish, but one of the Flemings didn't like it. So Queensmarsh, alas, was no more. I wasn't allowed to refer to it anymore for the last couple of books. [Good-natured laugh.] So Queensmarsh vanishes from the zeitgeist, at that point.

What was the creative inspiration for *Strike Lightning*?
I wanted to do a Steampunk-Bond type of thing. I thought that would be quite an interesting thing to do. It was a genre that Bond hadn't done before, and it betrays my interests. I imagined [Marvel's] Iron Man suit as if it was conceived with 1930s electronics. I was looking into some of the automated stuff that they had in the 1930s. The Russians were already looking at the idea of automating certain parts of warfare. They already had a remote control tank.

Fleming introduced some fantastic ideas like the giant squid in *Dr. No* and psychic powers are apparently real in *Live and Let Die*. I wanted to push the bounds of extreme possibilities. If you look at the movies, we've had invisible cars and technology that do things that are beyond the scope of what's possible in our own lives. I thought it might upset some Bond purists but that it might excite some teens who don't know so much about it.

I also wanted to explore Bond's school situation, which had to be different from his time at Eton. I was lucky enough to have support from Fettes College. They had warmly invited me along to explore the place and see the buildings Bond would have moved through. Even today, it is similar to his time. The dorms or houses are still there. They've been upgraded, and the shower situation is much better. I couldn't have asked for more. They showed me loads of stuff in the archives from the years

Bond would have been there. They gave me a special badge for Bond's house, the one we thought he would have gone to had he been there. Getting to see and add these real things was great.

Better than that, they brought in a bunch of old Fettes, the old students who would have been boys at the schools in the mid-1930s. They all came into the library and sat down and talked to me about their experience of being there and being teenagers at Fettes. That was glorious. You can't get that level of detail anywhere else. Just to be able to speak to these guys. They couldn't remember what they had done that morning or the week before, but their memories of being students at Fettes were as fresh as a daisy. I found it moving.

They didn't mind the beating that they got when they had done something wrong or naughty. It was the unjust beating—when someone would beat them because they could—that still stuck with them. It was about the lack of respect they felt. I could see there was still a little shared anger and also resilience when they spoke about the injustice there, all those decades later. You realize that even though it was peacetime, some of the boys were forged in fire at some of these austere institutions. Certainly, a lot of the stuff ended up in Bond's experience when I was writing it. I went there a couple of times, and it was exciting to work with their archivist and their PR people and explore that era of Bond's life. It gave it a different edge.

I was also fascinated by some of the interesting cars at the time like a Czech car called the Tatra. It was a thing of the future, and it seemed like a very Bond thing to put in there.

I always knew that book three would be my back-to-school story. When we started *Strike Lightning*, he'd been in school for about a term and a half. He's used to living at Fettes, and we don't have to worry about him establishing himself there. When we pick up, he's been there for a while. So, we don't have the conflict like in *SilverFin*.

Strike Lightning was a chance to explore the extreme possibilities of the time. That one was more fun, but it was more European. I was able to go and explore in person and sit across from the Hague and the area. I was able to get a sense of where Bond would be roaming around with his friends, Perry and Kitty Drift.

Kitty Drift is a fun name for a Bond woman.
It's a great name, isn't it? Originally, she was going to be called Bethany Peaks. Then I found out about this stretch of railway in the Northeast called Kitty's Drift. I thought that Kitty Drift was such a good Bond Girl name. So Bethany Peaks was no more, and Kitty Drift got there in her

place. I enjoyed writing her. She was based on someone I knew to a degree. It was nice to bring her along.

Talk about the apparent villain, Hepworth Maximilian Blade.
You also get a villain in the classic Fleming-Bond-thing. They're scarred, and the external scar often reflects some inner scar or evil. It is someone who has Stone Man Syndrome, which is a horrifying real-life condition. The twist is that he's not evil. He's just misshapen and ugly.

You use Aunt Charmian differently than Higson does. Higson's Charmian is unflagging and supportive. Yours still loves Bond but she doubts him too. By design, it seems that you wanted to isolate Bond more.
As you say, I wanted to isolate Bond for a bit to increase his self-reliance. It's no coincidence that Perry gets put out of action by being injured. Bond can no longer rely on Perry either. It was part of that program of pushing Bond along. I was thinking, realistically, no matter how loving or supportive people are, when they are faced with a story like that from Fettes, Charmian would wonder, "James, is this really the case?" I wanted it to be slightly shocking.

    It's a way of using a character differently from how she has been used before. I didn't want Bond to be too present there. It gives Bond that extra boost to prove himself to Aunt Charmian and get her back on track. It becomes a positive push for him. I also wanted to show that not everyone has your back the entire time. There will be times when people find it harder to support you. During those times, what are you going to do? Are you going to roll over and take it, or are you going to do something about it? Bond is one of those people who will always do something about it. Of course, it ends with Bond strapped into a mechanical fighting suit and having these gladiator duels with the Nazis, which is something that Bond would do. I did enjoy writing that one.

Writing Bond is not for the faint of heart.
We are talking about the writing process and how long they take to write. For every one of these books, I would be up for 30 to 33 hours straight. Literally, starting in the morning, stopping for meals, and working through the evening and all through the night, through the next morning. Then, getting to lunchtime the next day and finally finishing it. I was getting about 8,000 to 11,000 words and then crashing because I was living it with him. I found it incredibly focusing.

For the only time in my professional career, I did write some lines of *Shoot to Kill* in my sleep. It was quite something. I woke up with a start, and I realized I'd written three lines toward the climax, where the villain pulls off his glove, revealing three perfectly manicured female fingernails, and rakes them across Bond's face. For a minute, I thought, "That's brilliant." But then I realized, no it's not. It makes absolutely no sense at all. What the hell is going on? [Laughs.]

Writing *Strike Lightning, in particular,* was quite epic…11,000 words in one sitting. So I came back to write the final stuff, the epilogue, after I had some sleep. It's not my favorite book in the series, but I enjoyed writing it.

In your final Young Bond, *Red Nemesis*, you make Bond's dad a spy. Can you talk about your thinking behind that decision?
That came from wanting to do more with Bond's past. I also wanted to suggest that there's nothing about this boy's life that is ordinary. So why should his parents be ordinary? From Fleming, we knew that his dad worked for Vickers. As a journalist, Fleming covered the case in the Soviet Union, where some of the Vickers' staff were suspected of being spies.

Vickers' staff would be good spies. In their business, they were making and selling armaments on enemy soil, as well as gathering intelligence. It seems likely that Bond's dad, while not being an active spy, would certainly have been able to collate information that he would have been able to feed back [to a British intelligence agency]. It didn't seem to me to be an outlandish plot twist to have Bond's dad involved in something like that.

You thought of Bond's dad as more an asset than a full-fledged spy.
Exactly. In Charlie's book, we know that there is an interest in Bond as an asset from his master at Eton. In real life, that's where these people were recruited from. Given that, it seemed plausible that his dad could be used as an asset. From there, they could see that Bond was going to outshine the father in suitability for the role.

I set up the character of Adam Elmhurst in *Shoot to Kill* as the proto-father figure for the orphaned Bond. I brought him back for *Red Nemesis* to betray Bond. That seemed to be emotionally satisfying for the arc that I set Bond on.

I also wanted to set up a mystery for both Bond and modern kid readers to solve. It couldn't be too easy, too arcane, or too obscure. I wanted it to be feasible. I used clues that would be familiar to a boy in the

1930s but still make it easy to guess for a modern audience. It took a while to come up with a suitable solution, but it was a real riot writing *Red Nemesis*.

I got the assistance of an expert on the history of the Opera House. He was useful with that. I did a lot of research. I remember being so excited one day about finding out the actual flight that Bond would have taken to the Soviet Union and where he would have stopped over. I think the flight times were there, and even in-flight menus for the three or four stops it would take to get there. I remember thinking, "Pay dirt." It was so great to be able to get the details and put them in.

As a reader, I always love the feeling I get when I'm actually in the place. I was reading a lot of contemporaneous stuff like *The Master and Margarita* [by Soviet writer Mikhail Bulgakov]. It's a fantastic novel set in 1930s Moscow. There were details in it that inspired me. For instance, they were building the tube system through Moscow at that time. It wasn't that many years since Lenin's Tomb had been there. It's not only a matter of visiting the place and describing it. You also have to transplant yourself back in time. You have to visit it through the literature of the times and the films of the times. You have to use the different media accounts and documents of the past. You have to hunt them down. It took a lot of work, but it was definitely rewarding.

Did Ian Fleming Publications have a reaction to using Bond's dad in that way?

It was right there in the initial outline. They always knew that we were heading there. In that initial document, I killed Perry. He was going to die. The idea was to leave Bond even more isolated and have him make poor decisions. In the end, it felt like too much, and it felt like there was no need for it. I didn't want a Bond in mourning for the entire book. I was also going to kill Charmian at one point.

[Shocked.] You would have killed Charmian?

I think that she would have been hit by a car and killed. They don't know if it's a hit-and-run incident or if it was murder. It feeds into Bond's paranoia. He's quite upset, and her murder is the reason Bond becomes more trusting of the Amherst character and turns to him. But it felt too big, and it would cast too much of a shadow over Bond and the rest of the book.

I compare it to *Star Wars: A New Hope* where Luke goes home and finds the charred corpses of his Aunt Beru and Uncle Owen. Then, there's a lovely bit of John Williams music as he looks over the sunset.

That's it. We will never get back to that again. Luke never mourns them at all. He doesn't talk about them or mention them again. It's like, you heartless bastard. He's just wandering off around the universe. We just get on with the Space Cowboys. But they died for you, man. Mourning for them for the entire story would be a different type of movie and would sabotage the whole thing.

A death like that feels to me like a benchmark in the emotional intelligence of your readership. With a younger audience, you don't have to linger on the sad stuff. I felt with Bond, it wasn't feasible to kill off people so close to him without affecting him and costing him in that way. It would also impact the mystery and the adventure. Instead, it would be, "I'm still thinking of Charmian, and I'm still upset and sad." So I let Charmian and Perry live. I was under no pressure to spare them. It was something that we discussed. They were happy to have me do it if it suited the story. When it didn't, there was no need to kill them off.

At the end of the story, Mimic imitates Bond's father's voice, moments before he was killed. Mimic is doing it to torture Bond, but perversely, it allows Bond a few last moments with his dad.
Mimic is using his father's voice against Bond but, as you say, it also gives Bond insight into those last moments of his dad's life. It's the impact of hearing your dad one last time. Especially in those days when mementos would have been fewer and fewer. Bond doesn't have that much from his father.

It goes back to Bond discovering the note from his dad to him. It's like the note was inviting him on this adventure. There was a sense of unfinished business and a sense of loss. It also gave him a closer appreciation and a better understanding of who his father was and what he was doing. There was also this idea that maybe his father was spying for the wrong side. It fired Bond up, and he thought, "I'm going to prove them all wrong." It was also putting Bond in an emotionally unbalanced position so that he could make some mistakes that would come back to haunt him. I enjoyed writing that because it made it meatier.

It drives Bond to the point that I was working toward over all four books. It's his question, "Would I be able to take a life in the final analysis? Am I that person?" There's a sense of him being aware that, from his experiences, he's becoming more and more of a weapon. A weapon that can be wielded by his country, which is what happens when he's an adult. The question became, how far do we start to push him on that track?

There is more of that track ahead of him. At the end of your four-book series, he's still at Fettes.
I was aware that another author might do another Young Bond series at some point, and that author might have their own stuff that they wanted to do with the same character. I didn't want to have all the fun of getting him right to that place. I wanted to leave him that much closer.

At the end of *Red Nemesis*, Bond seems to be on the verge of deciding if he's going to be used as a tool for the government. Where do you think he is in that?
I think he's not made up his mind yet. The details aren't decided. The future will decide them for him. In the final scene, he buries the backpack that came from his father. It's like a portion of the past has been put to rest. But he's keeping certain stuff from it. It leaves the audience wondering.

We have the advantage of knowing what Bond doesn't. We know his future. However, he does know that he can do what he has to do. He knows that he's finished his father's business, and that's enough for now. He can get back to being a kid and finishing school. We know that he's going to lie about his age and join the Navy a little early. We know the rest of it.

He's one of those kids who is fueled by the need for adventure and danger. He's a hugely damaged individual. Poor bastard. Bond's life is not something you'd want for your children. It is exciting escapism. And Bond has always provided that, whatever his age.

When you handed in your final manuscript, you knew it was all over. What were you feeling?
I was aware that while it's a huge privilege to write, Bond is the type of project that can completely subsume and consume your life. There is a huge love for the character and genre. Each book required the same four or five drafts. I was also writing books for younger readers and there were other things I wanted to do. Bond is one of those things that I did. It was hard work. I was always thinking that when I look back on the experience it was going to be one of the coolest assignments of my professional career. I thought, don't ever try to stick at it longer than it needed to be. It can just be that thing.

When I left, Ian Fleming Publications and the publisher took me out for dinner, and they gave me this lovely artwork of the characters that I brought to it. It was the characters and an illustration of myself in the middle of The Veil, Scolopendra, Hugo, and Boudicca ["Boody" Pryce from *Shoot to Kill*]. It was very nice of them to give me a little memento of my time there. It was a lovely closure.

I still get invited along. I was invited to the London Library [in 2023] for the seventieth [anniversary of *Casino Royale*] event that they put on. It was great to catch up with Charlie there. Once you've written for them, you are part of the Bond family. We all get the invites. It's nice to catch up with them years on.

It's always a pleasure to see Corrine [Turner]. Much of the team has changed since I was there. But it's always lovely to go back and still be a part of that. I always knew that those four books would be my shot at Bond, which is why I worked hard to make them count.

The four books were always the understanding up front. I didn't think we were going to do it anymore but they accelerated the program [of how quickly each book was going to be published]. That became a bit of a headache. It meant that it was over faster than I would have preferred. It was an amazing ride, but it is grueling at times. Hugely rewarding as well. So the books are there in the records. It's a little footnote in the life of James Bond. I'm privileged to have got to script those.

For fun, did you ever consider what a fifth Steve Cole Young Bond book would be? Would it be more Fettes or would you have gone further into Bond's future?

I wanted to do a novel about Young Bond's war years. Some sort of miniseries set during his time as the war breaks out. They've gone on to do it in the comics. [*James Bond Origin* (2018–2019) is a twelve-issue comic book series that explores Bond's time in World War II.] I think it's a shame because that's what I wanted to do. I wouldn't want to go back to Young Bond, but I would like to do a slightly less Young Bond.

When you mentioned the War Years to Ian Fleming Publications, what was their reaction?

I think it was something that they were already thinking of exploring, although not necessarily in novel form, at least not initially. As custodians of the character on his whole timeline, it was something that they were already thinking about. I don't think I was the only one who would want to write it. It would be really good fun to do but I think they already were making inroads there.

Any other fun ideas?

I've always joked that I wanted to do Old Bond…retired and decrepit and infirm. He realizes, "I used to be saving the world." Maybe he's dragged into one last adventure. Like Hercule Poirot [in Agatha Christie's *Curtain: Poirot's Last Case*, 1975]. I love my take on Young Bond. I love the character and love to explore different facets of him. But that idea was only for fun. I never had any serious plans for a fifth adventure.

Did you ever broach the topic of Old Bond with Ian Fleming Publications?
I don't think I did. I think I mentioned the wartime thing to them. As for Old Bond, I was being facetious but the more I think about it, I like the idea. It hasn't been done. You'd be slightly hamstrung because where would you set it? Bond has become a character that you can flit about within different periods, and he tends to broadly stay the same age. Where would you place his last days? Would it be in the 2040s or something in an extrapolated sci-fi future? You can't shove him into his retirement in the 1970s or 1980s with Fleming's timeline. But it's fun speculation.

With these continuation novels, you can place Bond anywhere on the timeline, including shifting him to the future. At what point does it stop being true to the character?
I think that there are traits that Bond always has, even if they mean less to him as he gets older. I think there is an argument for someone distilling all the continuation novels into one timeline, and he's lived them all. Even if some of the adventures might be the result of his fever, and aging head. Maybe some of them didn't happen as he remembers them happening. I think there's fun to be had with Bond as an unreliable narrator. As we know, he went through brainwashing and the treatments he went through to betray his country in *The Man with the Golden Gun*. I think you could tell a really good novel with Bond in his last years.

I was recently in this place in North Wales called Portmeirion, where *The Prisoner* is set. I like the idea of a retired secret agent who knows too much and who is incarcerated in this artificial community. There's also a mystery of why he resigned. I think the Bond version of *The Prisoner*'s Village would be a lot sexier.

Who are the continuation novels for—Bond purists or the casual fan?
I think it's a combination. It's also for fans of the continuation authors. Because the continuation authors always bring their fans to it, whether it's Boyd or Horowitz or whomever. Inevitably it's for Bond fans who have a special interest in it. Then there's also the more casual reader of

thrillers who liked the sound of a Bond story set in the 1960s. The stories themselves appeal to readers who enjoy books in the spy genre.

I think that the first purpose of continuation novels is that they should entertain as broad a readership as possible. I think that we're looking for something that works for a general readership. That's preferable to making it so insular and aimed only at readers who are already experts on Bond's world. I think the most successful ones are the ones that cast the net wider while remaining authentic and maintaining the voice. Generally, the authors that Ian Fleming Publications uses have affection for the original novels. I think that's why the hit rate is generally good.

The books should also include nods to the committed fan so that they can say, "I picked up on that reference." In *Shoot to Kill*, the first chapter title is "You Asked for It." That was the initial American title for *Casino Royale*. It's a way of saying, "I'm down for this, and I appreciate the importance of what I'm doing." I've written a lot of novels and Doctor Who is another fandom that can be divided but passionate. You want to do something that hasn't been done before whilst still ticking the boxes that ensure it stays true to Bond.

We've been talking for the last 90 minutes. My impression of you is that you're personable, self-effacing, and funny. Did you get to bring all aspects of your personality to Young Bond?
I don't think so. Because at the end of the day, while I enjoyed Bond, I can't relate to his character, to his politics, patriotism, and, frankly, bravery. Those things are not me. The Doctor from Doctor Who is a slightly more maverick and anti-authoritarian figure. [Cole has written over a dozen Doctor Who novels.] They are poles apart, even though they both change their faces quite regularly and flit about in different times. Some arguments can be made about Bond being a Time Lord.

It goes back to what I was saying about different characters bringing out different facets of Bond. A bully is going to bring out one bit. Percy will bring out something else. A female character will bring out yet another thing. That's like all of us. For me, Bond brought out my serious side. I did try to keep the plots colorful enough and broad enough. As I said, I touched upon how *Strike Lightning* had some sci-fi elements there. So it allowed me to explore a part of myself that I haven't expressed so much in fiction. It was hugely rewarding as a result.

ANTHONY HOROWITZ

Part One

Trigger Mortis Trigger Mortis (2015)
Forever and a Day (2018)
With a Mind to Kill (2022)

Anthony Horowitz
Illustration by Pat Carbajal

How did you prepare to write *Trigger Mortis*? Did you start by rereading Fleming?[8]

Yes, I had to reread the whole lot. I had previously read Fleming's books many times throughout my life. They've been part of my genetic makeup for as long as I can remember. But, in order to do the job, I had to read them in a different way than I had before. I had to read them *technically*. I had to look at how Fleming achieved what he did. I had to see what Fleming's mannerisms and tropes were so that I could exactly imitate what he had done before.

Were you also looking for any characters or plots that you could

use for your novel?
A launching point. Unlike the other franchise writers who had come before me, I was given an original short story by Fleming called "Murder on Wheels," a treatment for a television series, which I used as a springboard to leap into this world. I was looking for clues in the novels and "Murder on Wheels" that revealed what makes Fleming's writing so idiosyncratic and special.

I had to ask myself why this character has survived so long, why the books are so good and are there clues and secrets inside of them. I wanted to isolate those secrets—they could be phrases or a couple of words that hinted to me how he wrote—so I could then imitate them. In fact, I have my notebook in front of me now as I'm sitting here and I'm looking at all the different things that I wrote down.

Would you mind sharing them?
In no particular order. "The herb garden…smiled up at him," which is a line out of *Thunderball*. Fleming takes inanimate objects and animates them. He makes them seem real, and he makes them seem like participants in the story. He does it all the time. Above that [and also from *Thunderball*], I've got "a room-shaped room with furniture-shaped furniture." That's classic Fleming writing. It's absolute deadpan but there's a smile in there somewhere. It's cold-blooded and yet somehow so exactly right.

[Continues reading.] "Do you want to drink solid or soft?" someone says. That's Fleming. Here's another one, "The men laughed various kinds of laughs." That is out of *Thunderball*. It's that same trick he used with the furniture, and it's so Fleming. There are lots and lots of them in my notebook…about fifty or sixty. That's how I began.

You were soaking up his style and the way he uses language.
His language, his style, and the little tropes that he uses time and time again.

What about his sentence length?
Absolutely. If you read the books carefully, you'll see that the modulation of the sentences is cleverly done. If you look at the opening of *Casino Royale* or *Goldfinger*, the sentences are considered to be *Weltschmerz* [world ache], which is a part of Fleming's style, this tiredness with the world. The sentences are long, but they're well-modulated. They're ever so slightly elegant.

Anthony Horowitz at the London launch for *Trigger Mortis*
at Waterstones Piccadilly, 2015
Courtesy of Mark O'Connell, Catching Bullets

Look at the opening sentence to *Trigger Mortis*—"It was that moment in the day when the world has had enough." It gets you into that *Weltschmerz* feeling. The world is incidentally being personalized…that's one of his styles.

Then there's a second style, which is his action style, which I kept in mind while writing the car chase in my book. When I wrote that section, I went to the nearest chase scene I could find in Fleming, which was the sleigh run in *On Her Majesty's Secret Service*. It's fast, and it's speedy. Suddenly, the sentences become incredibly short. Sometimes, just a few words, and they jump around. So, instead of using a forward-flowing narrative, you're going in and out of Bond's head; you're going where he is. The camera is outside him when he's speeding down the hill, but then suddenly, you're right in his thoughts, thinking, "Hang on, damn you. Don't let go." It's staccato, punctuated writing that adds to the tension and excitement.

Did you look at the novels to help answer the question, where do we find Bond? How do I reintroduce Bond in this book, what should his opening scene be?
They vary. Some of the books open straight with the action. Sometimes, it's the blubbery arms of the good life that wrap themselves around him, and he's in stasis and waiting for something to happen. In my case, it was clear that the book was going to start two weeks after *Goldfinger,* and, therefore, I knew exactly where I was going to be both within the canon and within his life…between missions seemed like the best place to begin. Some of Fleming's books take you into the action faster.

London launch for *Trigger Mortis* at Waterstones Piccadilly, 2015
Courtesy of Mark O'Connell, Catching Bullets

When did you come up with that idea?
As soon as I got the job, I decided that for me and for my Bond it had to be within Fleming's world. It had to be inside the canon of his books. For me, the best James Bond novels are the early ones—*Live and Let Die* (1954), *Moonraker* (1955), *Diamonds Are Forever* (1956), *From Russia, with Love* (1957), *Dr. No* (1958), and *Goldfinger* (1959). They are the golden period of about 1954 to 1959. Then, after that, you get short stories, you get *Thunderball* (1961), and *The Spy Who Loved Me* (1962), which even Fleming himself said was a mistake.

I love all the books. I'm not criticizing them, but for me, the great ones are the first six or seven, which is what you'd expect. It seemed critical to me that any new Bond novel should take place within those parameters and in that time period. I simply looked at when he might have had a rest.

I'm looking at my notebook now. *Goldfinger* takes place in April to June 1957, and then there's a little gap, and we don't know what he's up to until May 1958, which is when [the short story] "From a View to a Kill" (1959) takes place. So there you've got the time period for Bond to have another mission.

That moment in time also immediately allowed me to think, what happened to the girl from the last novel? By and large, when the books end, the relationships end. Tiffany Case is referred to as having had an affair with Bond that lasted a little bit longer in the book and ended unhappily. It seemed an interesting thing to look at that first and to see what happened next.

We know that Bond is going to end the relationship from the

previous novel. But how would he do it and, more importantly, what would he be feeling?
Well, yes and no. One has to be careful when you use the word *feeling* and ask, what is Bond *feeling*? By and large, Fleming doesn't give us the soft center of Bond's emotions. One of the chapters in *Trigger Mortis* was criticized. I have a moment where Bond attacks a young man and then thinks, "This is a young guy trying to earn a living," so he decides not to kill him. But that isn't part of Bond's makeup, and there's a danger in over-humanizing him.

The reason he has survived as long as he has is that he is slightly on the edge of humanity. He's not somebody you want to sit down with to have dinner. He's not somebody who you will ever truly know. In that respect, he's a little bit like Sherlock Holmes. [In *The James Bond Dossier* (1965), a study of the Bond novels,] Kingsley Amis famously pointed out that Bond has few hobbies. He doesn't read literature, he doesn't go to the cinema, and he doesn't have any particular cultural awareness. He is a man with limited capacity in terms of his humanity. There's a danger in trying to humanize Bond too much.

If I had written sequences in which he and Pussy Galore had been at each other's throats, it would've been a mistake. The way that the relationship ends is carefully controlled. It's ennui. He likes her more when she's in danger in America and when she's a gangster. When he comes back home, they're going out to dinners, to the theatre, or doing tourist things. That's not him.

You couldn't get too far into his emotional life, but was there anything that you figured that you could reveal about his character?
Thinking of Bond from Fleming's perspective, I thought to myself, where does Bond come from? He comes from two places. The first is World War II. Special executive and military intelligence, a world of secrecy. It's a world where nobody really knows anybody, where everybody observes fine lines of both rank and need-to-know. It's quite a cold and highly focused world. If you're in the SOE [Special Operations Executive] like Fleming was, you're not spending your time chatting about what you did the night before. That focus is very much a part of Bond.

I also think he harkens back to the nineteenth century to that type of Englishman, Kingsley Amis, identified as the Byronic hero [Romantic hero]. In modern terms, it's like Clint Eastwood in the Sergio Leone westerns. He's that same figure who comes from nowhere, who is going nowhere, but who affects everybody and saves everybody while he's in the room. Bond is in the tradition of that character. Sherlock Holmes would be equivalent; he's the only other British character in fiction who has had the same impact as Bond, and it's much the same thing. You don't know about their parents, you don't know about their childhood, their friends or anything like that. They are what they are. They come, and they go.

That opaque character is well suited for the movies because you can read into their faces whatever you want to.
You could also add that each movie's incarnation brings the spirit of his age to that part. That's what's been so clever about the franchise. Sean Connery, along with Daniel Craig, was closest to Ian Fleming's original Bond. But when you get into the seventies, everything gets a little bit softer and larkier. Roger Moore takes over and there's suddenly a completely different Bond. You're getting more jokes, more double entendres and the action is a little bit more camp. You get a reaction against that in the late eighties with Timothy Dalton trying to go back to the harder incarnation. However, the truth of the matter is that Bond always reflects the current society in which he operates. That's one of the clever things about the franchise…it keeps redefining itself. It isn't stuck in the fifties and Cold-War-Bond or Byronic-hero-Bond. It has done a Bond for each age.

You deliberately went back to the time period when you wanted to be within Fleming's canon. You're going against the grain of what you said has made the franchise so successful. Were you at all worried about not being reflective of our time?
Well, it's a good question, and the answer is that my job was to write an Ian Fleming pastiche, to write an homage to Ian Fleming. As far as I was concerned, it had to be set entirely in Ian Fleming's world.

Having said that, I could make a few little post-structural nudges toward the modern age. For example, there's a reference that smoking can give you cancer. I had to put that in because I'm a children's author, and I don't normally write books in which characters smoke. I also give Bond an openly homosexual friend named Charlie Duggan. I did that in order to tease out the latent homophobia in some of the books. There's also a slight feminist smile there in both the creation of Jeopardy Lane and in the way Pussy Galore treats him [Galore leaves Bond for another woman]. In fact, all three women treat him quite roughly. Later in the book, there are references to America's expansion and how it leads to "carelessly trampling on [Korea's] culture."

These are all nodding to a modern audience who will not put up with some of the attitudes of the fifties. But outside of that, my job, as I saw it, had nothing to do with the films. The films and the books are two separate things. The films remain a huge global event. They are probably one of the most significant cultural events of our times. That's true all over the world.

The books, however, are nestled in an oasis in a remote place. I'm not sure how many people now go back and read the books and have an understanding of what Fleming created. What I've found is that the audience of people who wish to read a James Bond novel—either the originals or one of mine or someone else's—is minute compared to the number of people who go to see the films. So it never occurred to me to try to modernize, make it relevant, or to make it cinematic. My job was to live in the world of the books, as if the films had never been made.

I discovered Fleming after the films. Like many, I liked the movies, so I read his books. The Bond of the films has eclipsed the Bond of the novels. Why isn't there more interest in going back to the source material?

It's because we no longer live in a particularly literary world. The ratio of people who read compared to the number of people who play computer games, watch television, go to the cinema, or whatever is small. *Trigger Mortis* did well; it sold, I think, about a hundred and twenty thousand copies in hardcover and in e-format. Everyone is happy with the result of it. But the fact is that in audience terms [compared with the movies], that's relatively tiny. But I knew that before writing it. Even the decision to make the book as authentic as I tried to was not a commercial decision. Having said that, Jeffery Deaver tried to move Bond into the modern period with *Carte Blanche*. I'm not saying he failed, but I'm not sure that he satisfied either side of the equation.

Kingsley Amis wrote *Colonel Sun*, the first continuation novel. Then John Gardner picked up the torch.

I've read them all, of course. I know the Gardner novels.

When I first started reading Gardner, I didn't truly understand what a continuation novel was. Bond belonged to Fleming, and I didn't originally understand how another novelist could continue where Fleming left off. As much as I wanted to read more Bond novels, the notion of a continuation novel seemed foreign to me. These days, the idea has permeated throughout pop culture.

You're right; the whole word continuation novel has probably only entered the lexicon in the last ten years. It isn't only Bond, of course. It's a huge industry. From Jane Austin to Jeeves and Wooster to Agatha Christie, etc. I have always feared that there was a certain cynicism at the heart of this exercise. A mixture of slightly nervous publishers desperate for an instant bestseller and, in some cases—not with Fleming—an estate that might be trying to rekindle interest or to rekindle value from a trademark.

I have to emphasize that this has not been the case with the Fleming Estate. They have very good motives for wanting to continue with the books. It is a modern phenomenon, that's for sure. It was one which I had to think about twice before I accepted doing it. There were only two characters I would've ever done—Sherlock Holmes and James Bond. Holmes was the first one I did with *House of Silk* (2012) and *Moriarty* (2014). I was reading Sherlock Holmes when I was in my late teens, and he was very much a part of my life. I did Bond because there was no way I was going to turn it down.

Could you talk about working with the Fleming estate? Did they ever say Bond wouldn't do that or you shouldn't do that? I don't ask that in an authoritarian context where they're trying to arbitrarily limit your creative approach to the project. My question comes from an assumption of their love of the character and wanting to see him being treated in line with Fleming's conception.

On the other side of that equation is you have a writer who will not kowtow. I'm old and experienced enough to be quite arrogant in the way that I write. Generally speaking, I write what I want, and I don't like being told what to do. When I entered into this agreement, I was quite nervous, to be honest with you. I knew that the Fleming Estate was quite powerful and certainly would have the last say on matters. They could basically fire me. I did have great nerves.

When I wrote the Sherlock Holmes books, I made it a condition of writing that I would not meet the Doyle ancestors and I would take no notes from them. That was the condition on which I would do it. That did not hold true for Fleming because I wouldn't have gotten the job if I had insisted on conditions. I met with them, and I was quite nervous. I thought it was going to be a bad experience, that I would get a lot of notes that would cause arguments. However, they were terrific to work with; they were smart and sympathetic to what I wanted to do. We did have discussions, but they had great notes.

One of the members of the family was concerned about the title, *Trigger Mortis,* as being too jokey and also that it might not translate. In retrospect, that was quite a good note and maybe I chose the wrong title. The title of a James Bond novel is, without any question, the hardest thing to get right.

We discussed at some length whether Pussy Galore could come back; some members of the family didn't think it was a good idea. I had to hold my own on that one and say look, this is what I want to do. They voted on it, and the vote went my way. To give them that credit, they said fine, ok, go ahead.

There were other things in the books that I got wrong...I'll give you a good example of that. The origin of the name Jeopardy Lane was going to be that her parents had watched the television show *Jeopardy!* day in and day out; they liked it so much that they named their daughter after it. The estate pointed out to me that the program *Jeopardy!* started in the mid-sixties, and my book is set in 1957. So that wouldn't work.

Another example of a correction was in the original manuscript, I had Bond getting out of bed with Pussy Galore and going into the bathroom naked. I made a big point of the fact that Bond slept naked. They pointed out that Bond doesn't sleep naked; he wears what is called a bed jacket [or "pyjama-coat," as is established in the novel *Casino Royale*]. Now a bed jacket is probably the least sexy piece of clothing a man could put on. It's sort of a pajama jacket that comes down to the knees. I had to smile and take out the naked section because that wasn't accurate, and it wasn't true to Fleming. But I didn't specifically mention what he was wearing because he would have looked ridiculous.

So that was the type of thing we discussed when they got the first draft of the manuscript. I think they gave me about ten big notes and twenty small ones. I corrected about two-thirds of those notes, and for the other third, I argued and won.

That seems like a good give-and-take. Like a healthy collaboration.
It was a collaboration. They were also in charge. They could've said no. They could've said, do this, or you're off the job, but they never did. They never threatened me; they were always reasonable. They're smart.

When Raymond Benson took over from John Gardner, he had to come up with an outline on spec. Then he had to write the first four chapters on spec before they officially hired him.[9] He had to jump through a lot of hoops.
I didn't have that same experience. I produced an outline, and the outline was what I wrote. It ran about five or six pages. I went to my first meeting with them with the outline. Before they had even asked for one, I had

done it. The plot for the novel came quickly. Normally, plots take me a while but for the Bond novel, it fell into my lap almost at once.

Can you talk more about that meeting?
I had lunch with Corrine Turner, who works for the estate [as the Managing Director], and she gave me the once-over. I started talking about ideas with her. I came to the meeting with that treatment and a photograph. I submitted a photograph of a train station in New York, which is underneath the United Nations. It's a disused station, an Art Deco station, and it's beautiful. The American transit authority must be crazy not to open it to the public, but maybe there's a security issue. I was going to set the climax there, but as things turned out, it wasn't possible to do that. But that was how I presented the original idea. I was thinking visually. While the book has nothing to do with the films, nonetheless, the book has to have a modern pace, and it has to be visual. It has to be written for a modern audience.

We were talking about the interior life of the character, and you said that you don't want to get too deep. In a movie, the audience will impose their thoughts on what a character is thinking and feeling. The silent hero works particularly well. In a book, we expect to get inside a character's mind.
I don't think you do expect to go inside Bond's mind because where in the Fleming novels does that happen? Where do you ever see doubt, insecurity, or anything other than the occasional anger, self-anger, determination, ruthlessness, snobbery, and carnal desire? Where do you see, *am I doing the right thing,* his doubts or uncertainty? The rule was only to do what Fleming did and to do nothing that he didn't. With Bond, that works.

It works in the same way as it does with Holmes. I could write a Sherlock Holmes novel in which he bemoans his lack of sexual activity and that there are no women in his life. However, that would be anathema to anybody who loves these books. That's where I begin; I begin on the side of the uber fan. I'm not that interested in the public at large; I'm not interested in publishers. I tell you I *am* interested in the Estate because they are the uber-fans of all uber-fans. I'm beginning with the purists.

While I have taken exception to one or two things in some of the [other continuation] books and in one or two of the films, that's only as a purist. That is not to say that the books aren't wonderful, and the films aren't brilliant. As somebody who is attached intellectually, emotionally, and psychologically to this character that I was reading in my formative years, nothing should break the rules; nothing should break the spell.

The way you ended *Trigger Mortis* gave a sense that while Bond survived this mission, his luck would inevitably run out, and his mortality would catch up with him. Not today, but eventually.
When I pitched to the Estate, that paragraph was in my pitch; that last paragraph and those last three words, "But not today," were included. That sense of nothing is forever is so Fleming. Bond. It's an existential ending. That whole hard-edged rain coming down, another dead body, the endlessness of it. It felt right for the book. The end of *Moonraker* is a fairly bleak ending as he and Gala Brand go their own way. The books don't always end with a smile. They sometimes end up in a grey area, which is what I was aiming for.

What surprised you most about the experience?
I was unprepared for the way that being involved in James Bond puts you in a strange place. Things that you say innocently and trying to be helpful, as I am with you now, are misinterpreted. It can sometimes seem as if everybody is looking to hurt you. It was quite a painful experience in some ways. I was embroiled in rows that were certainly not intentionally of my own making, and I upset people. But as I've been talking to you, I've been careful to say nothing that can be misconstrued. So when you go back over this tape, you'll see that I have not criticized anybody and would not dream of it. But to give you an example, if I were to compare "James Bond Film A" with "James Bond Film B" and say I preferred B, a journalist would run a story about how much I disliked A and try and make something of it. That happened over and over again, and I was hounded. It was not a happy experience.

    The experience of writing the book, of working with the Estate, of doing serious interviews like this one, and of the response to the book, the critical response certainly, and more importantly still, the response from the Uber fans, has all been one hundred percent positive. In terms of what it did to me as a writer, it made me realize that there is a world out there that I don't necessarily want to be too much a part of. I'm happier with my head below the parapet, writing quietly, not in the bright spotlight. That was the worst of it.

    I found myself at a signing with William Boyd and Sebastian Faulks. I'm not quoting them, but they said they had experienced much the same thing. I apologized to them because somebody had written a piece that suggested I had criticized their books, which I had never done.

I've been talking to you about how Bond should be this, should be that, but I've carefully said, "That's as far as I'm concerned." But I'm not judging others. They said there's nothing to apologize for because we know, we've been there, we've been through this fiery hoop, and we know what it's like.

So you're now part of a small club of authors who have written Bond continuation novels.
Correct and I'm hugely proud to be part of that. I'm proud of everything I've done. I'm proud of Alex Rider, which came out of my love for Bond. But to be one of a small group of people in the world who have written a James Bond novel is a fantastic thing. Going back over the whole experience, although I might have been a little more circumspect and more careful when it came to publicity, there's nothing else I would have changed. I've heard writers say that this is the book I was born to write. It always sounds a little saccharine and horrible when I've heard it. But this is the book I was born to write, and I've written it.

ANTHONY HOROWITZ

Part Two

The following is my second interview with Horowitz. Before it began, I shared with him my belief that the continuation novels are as worthy of study and appreciation as Fleming's originals. He charmingly responded, "Do I agree with that? I wonder."

Before your Bond trilogy, Ian Fleming Publications would commission a single book by a well-known author. After writing only one Bond novel, Faulks, Deaver, and Boyd each moved on. The assumption was that you would follow suit. After *Trigger Mortis*, how did you come to write a second book?
I think the Estate discovered that changing the authors was not doing them as many favors as they thought it might. The trouble was that readers didn't know what they were going to get. There was no continuity. The books were set in different worlds. Sebastian Faulks was set in the correct period [in 1967, following *The Man with the Golden Gun*]. Jeffery Deaver's book, the middle one, was set in the present day. Boyd was set in the late sixties in Africa. You had three different voices, different periods, and different approaches. It was doing them a disservice. The success of *Tigger Mortis* and possibly a conversation in which I said that I would be interested in doing another one led them to the decision to ask me to come back.

The first line of your second book, *Forever and a Day*, is "So, 007 is dead." Is that the sentence that made you realize that you could write another book?
You've got it in one. Once I had that idea in my head I was committed to writing the book. I would not have written the second book if it hadn't been for that line popping into my head. When I was thinking about whether I even wanted to do a second book. I did have reservations. I wouldn't have done it if I didn't have a strong enough idea to make it worthwhile. Then it suddenly occurred to me, "So, 007 is dead." That implied to me that 007 was a number, not a man.

I thought it would be a great opening sentence and it would be a great opening chapter. That led me to the thought that I should do an origin story. It became the making of James Bond, his first mission, and how he got his number. Of course, there are clues in Ian Fleming's books and the two cases he mentions that earned Bond the Double-O. I looked at those again. I wondered, why two such different jobs? Fleming refers to the Stockholm silent kill. I wondered why was it silent? Who did he kill in Stockholm? What was that story? Those questions became catnip to me. I couldn't resist it.

It's a great opening line. I love the "So" before "007 is dead." It diffuses the weight of the shocking news and gives the reader a moment to get acclimated to the weight of the sentiment.
Those words fell into my head with the "comma" and with the "so" from the start. M, who says that line, would not say, "007 is dead." I think that it's such a terrible thing to happen, and it's such a big statement. You need to have a breath before you say it. That's what the "so" and the "comma" do.

As you say, *Forever and a Day* functions as an origin story. You address the formation of the Double-O section, and you explain why there are only three Double-O agents in the section and why Bond doesn't use an alias, as his cover has already been blown.
Having just taken on the mantle of Double-O Seven and because James Bond is such a great name, it seemed a bit foolish to call him Mark Hazard or whatever his alias might be. I dispensed with the secondary name and didn't do that as camouflage. It would have made it less interesting. I wanted to get into the story. After all, it takes four chapters before we get to Marseille to get us into the flow of things. I didn't want to waste any more time.

How did you come up with your master plot for your villain, Jean-Paul Scipio?
The book was, to a certain extent, guided by a desire to include a second extract from the television stories written by Ian Fleming. You will recall that in *Trigger Mortis* I had gone to the Nürburgring and Grand Prix motor racing. *Forever and a Day* was more difficult because the only story I found that I thought I could incorporate took place in a casino in France, next door to the sea. That directed me toward the south of France as a location for the book.

I began to think of what might be interesting in the south of France. I then began to think about Marseille, and drugs, which were huge at that time, and the influence of the mafia and the whole smuggling operation. One thing leads to another. That's how my mind works. You follow the clues to where they take you. You don't impose your own view on the book.

I must say, it was chosen for me. From that moment on everything began to fall into place, particularly with the creation of Jean-Paul Scipio. which I was particularly happy with. Not only him but also his translator. That's the gimmick you look for—like Goldfinger and Oddjob. In this instance, it's the other way around almost [and Scipio is the physically imposing figure]. I just love that.

What did you want to do with Madame Sixteen, who essentially teaches Bond the art of lovemaking?
He's a younger Bond, and he has had probably fewer women. In real life [in Fleming's novels], Bond was expelled from Eton for sleeping with one of the chambermaids even then. Presumably, he was a sexually active teenager and into his 20s. I wanted to color in some of the areas that Fleming alluded to. I also wanted to leave my mark on the books. That applied to his sexual prowess, too, and that Sixteen is, by far, the more confident lover with whom he's been. I love the moment when she says, "Don't grab me like a schoolboy." That line was the essence of the book. Other things as well, like the inscription on the gunmetal case [which reads Forever and a Day in all capital letters]. They were my way of putting my stamp on the Bond novels forever. It's my vanity.

There's one scene where she tells him to set the table. It's one of my favorite moments in all the continuation novels. It's a simple moment of domestic life. He realizes that he can't remember the last time someone asked him to lay a table.
It's nice of you to pick it up. I remember writing that moment. There are few moments in any of the books, either by Fleming or anybody else, where Bond is living a normal life. Because I knew how the book was going to end [with Madame Sixteen's death], I also wanted it to seem that this was a real relationship between a man and a woman. They don't just make love but have dinner together, they lay the table, they do the washing up, they make the bed, and they are having an ordinary life. This way, when she is taken from him, it is all the harder and all the more difficult.

Sixteen was, incidentally, based on a real person you might be interested in knowing. In the book, she's called Joanne Brochet. A lady bid in a charity auction and paid a large sum of money for the right to be the love interest in a Bond novel. The winner's name was Joanne Pike. I'm afraid you cannot have a Bond heroine called Pike. No, not really. So I translated it into French. So Pike became Brochet. In her youth, this lady worked with a syndicate gang ripping off casinos. Unbelievable. She was also stunningly attractive, and everything in that character is her.

What were your guiding principles in writing the books?
I will tell you a rule that I had when I was writing the books: I would ignore all the continuation novels. I only wanted Fleming. Fleming was my world, and I didn't want to interfere with anything that he had written.

After your second book, *Forever and a Day*, did you think that you were done with Bond, or did you anticipate that you would write a third?
This time it was slightly different. The second book was also very successful. It had wonderful reviews. What pleased me the most was that people like yourself, people who love the books, the literary Bond, and understand the world that Ian Fleming created, should never feel that I was an interloper or that I had damaged the myth or the legend. That was always my first consideration. After the first two books had been successful, it was almost as if, this time, the Estate just assumed that there would be a third.

I did have an idea in my head for a third book that made it seem right. That idea was based on probably my favorite three or four chapters in the entire canon, which are the opening of *The Man with the Golden Gun*. After those chapters it's not a terribly good book, I'm afraid. There's a lot after that doesn't work. Fleming was ill when he wrote it. But I think that the opening sequence, in which Bond comes back to London [and tries to kill M but, shortly after that, is sent on a new mission], is irresistible. The way it subverts his relationship with M, the way M uses him and fires him back at the enemy, is brilliantly done. Only Fleming could have written that.

I had an idea in my head that would be interesting and fun. It also occurred to me, in the same breath, that the three books would form a trilogy, although not quite done in the right order. The three books were a beginning, a middle, and an end.

There were many good, compelling reasons not to write a third Bond novel. A lot of people were advising me not to do it, particularly my wife. She knew how difficult it was and how much work doing these books involved. My agent also had other things he wanted me to do. But it felt right to have this extraordinary opportunity to do a whole trilogy—beginning, middle, and end.

How did you decide to set your book immediately after *The Man

***with the Golden Gun* and link the plot of your book to it? You could have conceivably set the book a few years later and put Bond on an unrelated mission.**

Of course, I could have. But the thing is, for me, the Bond novels have to exist at the correct time. Now, this is not a criticism of those who have chosen not to do that. It's everybody's choice and decision. To me, if you take Bond out of his timeline, you have lost half of what makes him a great spy. That's my personal view.

I didn't want to move it too far into the 1960s. It was going to take place in Russia anyway. I began to think, *The Man with the Golden Gun* ends [in early 1964 and starts in 1963], so we've got Khrushchev's Secret Speech [denouncing Stalinism and charting the new direction for the Soviet Union]. We've got this quite interesting world here. I thought, let's dive straight in, and let's keep going.

I also loved the fact that Ian Fleming died in 1964, around when 1963's *The Spy Who Came in from the Cold* was published. I think that the crossover bridge from Fleming to John le Carré is really interesting. I thought that it was time to pitch my book into that tiny frame of time where you are between two worlds. It's after Fleming is dead and before we go into the world of Smiley. It's going to be completely different. Don't forget le Carré did not particularly like the Bond novels. He was deliberately writing "the real spy world," as he saw it. As is the case with the second book, and I think this might be the case with continuation novels, the books tell you what to do.

Not only does *With a Mind to Kill* immediately follow the events of *Golden Gun*, but it also fills in the gap between Golden Gun and Fleming's previous novel, *You Only Live Twice*.

No, of course, that's right. Colonel Boris was a gift because he's mentioned in *The Man with the Golden Gun*. He's also mentioned him in *From Russia With Love*, which is interesting. This name obviously meant something to Fleming throughout his life. Boris is an enigma, a mystery. Just like the killing in Stockholm, I started to ask, who is this guy? What does he look like? What motivates him? What is his relationship with Bond? From that, I'm up and running.

You spend a page or two convincing the reader that Bond is under the villain's spell and that he will carry out the mission to assassinate Khrushchev. You firmly establish that Bond is unable to break free from mind control. There is no hope. Then you write,

"And yet." Then you explain how he breaks free. The change pivots on those two words. It all begins with "And yet."
That's a Fleming trope. It's a Fleming trick of taking him so far but then just putting in two or three words that pull it back again. I'm trying to imitate Fleming's voice as best I can.

In terms of your own rules, did you approach *With a Mind to Kill* in a different way than your first two?
Book three is the trickiest. It has more plot twists than any of the Fleming novels. In that respect, it's less like the Fleming novels. One thing you should understand is that by the time I got to the third one, I had nothing to lose. I knew it would be my last one. I knew that the first two books had been successful and that I was trusted with the world of Fleming. Therefore, I felt I could be less deferential and less worried about upsetting people. This time, I could do a bit more of my own thing. There is a chapter in that book which makes me happier than all the other chapters. It's as close to Fleming as you can get, but it's not something that he would have written. I think Fleming would have loved to have read it. It's the fight in the underground. Pretty much my favorite sentence is the last sentence of the chapter.

Do you recall it?
Let me get it. [Horowitz gets up and picks up a softcover edition of *With a Mind to Kill*.] It's pretty much the last sentence of the chapter. Here it is. "There's no need to worry, Comrade Colonel. I took care of it." That's from the chapter "Beneath the Chandeliers." That's quite a good Fleming chapter ending.

In *Forever and a Day*, during the murder in Stockholm, you use the phrase "dying by inches" to refer to the sheet that is slowly covered in blood as Bond's victim bleeds out. I like that, "dying by inches."
The next chapter is "The Human Element," which is, of course, a Fleming line. [Paraphrasing the line.] There's no need to worry, Colonel. I threw him under the train. I threw Zephyr under a train." It's so Bond. It's so cheeky. It's so funny. I love that line.

There's also a funny line in *Forever and a Day* when Bond meets his new secretary, and they talk about Pett Bottom, and Bond wonders if their entire relationship is going to be based on…
"…on obscure village names." Again that is quite in the mode of Fleming. When I wrote it, it reminded me of something in Fleming's writing. Even

now, I'm not even sure what. Bond doesn't make jokes. Bond never tells jokes. That would be a mistake. But there is laconic humor knocking about in all of the books. It's Fleming's particular taste. You see it with names like Pett Bottom and all the rest of it. It's very Bond, very Fleming.

With a Mind to Kill ends with the apparent death of Bond. Although you don't state it, you do imply that he might be shot down. It's something that you set up earlier in the book and the first two. All the books indicate that Bond's luck might run out one day.
Originally, when I was writing it, I saw that in the last chapter, Bond would be in a plane hurtling towards the ground. That was an image in my head. I would cut out [of the story] with the ground coming closer and closer. It would end before the plane hit. So you wouldn't know what happened.

It was the third book, and Bond is getting old. There's always been a problem with Bond getting old. The older he gets, the more introspective he becomes and the darker the books become and, therefore, the less enjoyable they are. I think Fleming had a problem with that in all the books after On Her Majesty's Secret Service. That sadness [after Tracy's death] never quite goes away. That's not why you read Bond. At the same time, I thought Bond should die at the end of the book. But I can't kill him.

I thought it was a big mistake to kill Bond in [No Time to Die]. He's not ours to kill. He's Fleming's creation. Therefore, Fleming is the only one who can make that decision or that choice. At the same time, Bond belongs to the whole world. So a writer like me can't come along and say, "Your hero is dead, guys." I was annoyed by that decision in that film. It's got a lot of great things in it, of course, like all of them. But I thought that was a mistake.

I went as close as I think you can to killing Bond. Of course, we don't know if the bullets were fired into his back or not. He could have walked over the line and made it to the other side of Checkpoint Charlie. Another continuation novelist can come along if they want to and pick him up on the other side of the line of Checkpoint Charlie and send him on his next adventure to wherever. That's their choice. However, I strongly believe that a continuation novelist does not have the right to kill the character.

Should we read your books in the published or chronological order?
I don't think it matters, but I'd say read With a Mind to Kill last. You can

twist around the order of the first two if you want to. It's a funny thought but if there was ever a box set of the three books, I think I probably would want to see them in the order of *Forever and a Day*, then *Trigger Mortis*, then *With a Mind to Kill*. I would put them chronologically [and not in order of publication].

What are your thoughts on the term "continuation novel?"
I will say straight away that I really dislike the phrase continuation novel. I've furiously written an introduction for *Colonel Sun,* and the first paragraph begins with how much I dislike continuation novels as a phrase. Then, there's an explanation as to why.

My gripe is that a continuation novel is much more than that. Your job isn't just to continue. It's a much more complicated and complex and more rewarding job than that. It's an act of imitation, yet it also has to be original. You have to live inside the world…yet you have to find ways to extend it. You have to balance this with the expectations of people who love the books but with a determination to do your own thing. The whole idea of a "continuation novel" slightly short changes what the book actually is.

The notion of a continuation novel was originally created quite cynically about 15 or 20 years ago. A publisher had the bright idea of taking a famous writer and pinning that famous writer to a famous character—Sherlock Holmes, Jeeves and Wooster, Agatha Christie's Poirot, Bond, whatever. And bingo, what happens? Money. You've made money. I find the words "continuation novel" carry something of that cynicism about it. I don't like the hint of cynicism. I think it shortchanges what I'm trying to do in the book.

I didn't do the Bond novels to make money. In fact, it's the opposite because I actually earn considerably less after I've shared profits with all the other people involved. It's a labor of love rather than money. I would only write a novel if I passionately loved the character I was writing about. I don't just do "continuation novels." Come to me tomorrow with whatever famous character you want me to write, and the answer is almost certain to be no.

Is there a better word?
No, it's a perfectly usable word. It's just not one that I particularly like to use. People talk about "cozy crime." I hate that expression. I never use it. Crime is never cozy. You murder someone, and it's horrible. I never talk about "Bond Girls" anymore. Now, it's pejorative. It suggests ownership. It's demeaning to the Pussy Galore and Tiffany Cases of this world.

That's just me. It's a personal preference. I'm not banging my fist and saying, "Never call my books continuation novels." Those are just words I don't use myself.

In the case of *Forever and a Day*, it's a misnomer because it takes place before *Casino Royale*, so you're not continuing anything.
[Laughs.] Right, it's not continuing anything. That's a very good point. But it's a continuation of Ian Fleming. That's really what we're talking about. You're writing it as if Ian Fleming hadn't died. But when you get to some of these continuation novels, they don't connect with Fleming at all. Not in their language, not in their setting. It doesn't make them bad books, but it doesn't make them continuation novels, either.

Bond purists have embraced your books, and even other Bond continuation authors that I've interviewed have praised your work. How come your books are so true to Fleming's spirit?
First of all, I am absolutely delighted by this question. How kind of you to ask it and it's a lovely thought you put in there. Why the books have succeeded is not really for me to say. But there might be one thing that makes me different from other continuation novels. Bond has been a huge part of my life. I'm not sure I would have been a writer without Bond.

When I was at school—ten or eleven years old, I was miserable as hell. I was at the worst school in the world, in a gray, drab environment with no decent food to eat…no nice weather. I can only remember fog and rain. No women. It was an all-boys school. I was beaten by sadistic teachers. I was utterly miserable. Then, my parents took me to see *Dr. No*.

The books saved my life, and therefore, my life is in them. It's not that I'm saying that the other continuation writers didn't have as much respect for Fleming as me or that they didn't love the books as much as me. I don't think that they have that 50-year devotion, all my life, to these books that I love. I have loved those books all my life. I've read them every decade of my life. It is the same as with Charles Dickens, Sherlock Holmes, Tintin, and a few other books—they are my heart.

You mentioned that your wife noted that writing a Bond novel is consuming for you. Can you talk about why it's challenging and the toll it takes?
The biggest challenge of the books is simply this—I write very much with immersion, with flow. I enter the world of the book, and I write it quickly.

Normally, I use a fountain pen. I don't like to use a typewriter. Although, funnily enough, with the Bond novels, I did type them straight into the computer. Why? Because Fleming did. I had to do it the same way as him but with a computer and not on a typewriter.

But when writing the Bond novels, I have to stop, start, stop, start. Whenever I get to something new, I have to stop and research it—whether it's what to eat, to drink, to wear, what car to drive a car, what fountain pen to use, the hotel room, the light, the floor, the carpet, what's outside the window, what people are wearing in the street, I have to go and research it. I have to find the answer somewhere. Although I surround myself with books and photographs and everything else in the period, it's still always stop, start, stop, start. That makes it difficult.

Plus, it's also the weight of expectations…of fear of what people are going to think of the book. It's the sense of being inside this temple, the temple of Fleming, and not wishing to make a fool of myself. There's a certain nervousness there as well.

Given the reception you were given, did that assuage those fears at all as you wrote the second and third ones?
Very much so. *Trigger Mortis* was the most difficult of the three simply because I was unaware that the world of the press and the media would be so ready to pounce on me or that it would be such a big deal. It's a bit like when a Bond song for a film is announced, and the whole world holds its breath. I wasn't prepared that I would have that much limelight and I don't like the limelight. I like to write quietly in my room.

I made mistakes. Particularly in relation to the publicity and comments about the films. I've lost all that fear now because it's behind me. I regret certain aspects of the *Trigger Mortis* launch, which was huge, and it was the most publicity I've ever had to handle. I got things wrong. I won't deny it. But like all Twitter storms, these things disappear. Those things don't last, and I'm doing other things now.

In the acknowledgments of *With a Mind to Kill* you write these are likely the last words on Bond that you'll ever write.
I'm not going to go back.

What was it like saying goodbye to writing Bond novels?
It was tough. I'm missing it more than I thought I would. I feel bereft. I made exactly the right decision. I know that if I'd written a fourth or fifth book—forgive me for saying it, just like John Gardner's—they would have gone off. I stopped at the right time. But it was hard to stop, especially

when you love something as much as I do. It goes back to the earlier question of yours; the books were a lifeline. I've let go. That doesn't feel comfortable.

Given everything you said, I know you'll reject this idea. But could you write a Bond novel that is set in modern times?
If it's the present day, James Bond would be 97 years old. What's he doing?

You can time-shift it.
The films do that well, and that's great. But that's not a novel. What people never seem to understand is that 90% of people who talk about James Bond have never read a James Bond novel. They are talking about the films. Now, I love the films. I love all of them, from Sean Connery to Roger Moore, all the way to Daniel Craig. They've been a big part of my life. But I'm not writing the films, and my books will never be filmed. I am happy to be living in the world of Fleming's books. That's it.

Fans sometimes talk about their interest in a book about Bond in his later years. The more I see that idea explored in popular culture with other beloved heroes, the more I think we don't need that Bond book.
That's correct. You're absolutely right. I've said earlier that Fleming himself had that difficulty with Bond. With that said, Bond is already having his doubts in *Casino Royale*. So it's perfectly reasonable for me to continue that thought in my novels. Read Kingsley Amis' book, *The James Bond Dossier*, and the section about how Bond is the dark knight. He's almost not a human being; he's also a legendary figure. He's like Clint Eastwood, The Man with No Name. He's the Dark Knight of the Byron poems. You don't have these guys looking in the mirror and worrying they're getting crow's feet around their eyes or getting a little bit of arthritis and being a bit slower on the draw. That does happen in the Bond novels. In *Thunderball*, Bond is in a pretty bad way and has to go off to Shrublands. There is mortality; he is not a Superman or a superhero. He is a human being. I think the secret of Bond is not to pretend that he is an ordinary human being, and not to focus on ordinary things. The exception is rare instances where, now and then, he might do something that you and I would do.

Like how he sets the table with Madame Sixteen. In our conversations, you've always been clear that you had a good

relationship with the Estate.
And it remains cordial to this day.

You had discussions with them about some of the particulars in Bond lore.
Yes, we had discussions. Never a dispute. There was a discussion about whether Bond sleeps naked.

You wanted him to sleep naked in *Trigger Mortis* and they said he wears pyjamas. After we initially spoke, I found an instance where Fleming indicates that Bond sleeps naked.
I recently noticed it, too. They were wrong. It's lovely to talk to someone who knows as much about the character as I do. I was reading something the other day in an original Fleming novel, and sure enough, he was naked. I thought, oh, gosh, they got it wrong from the start.

Along those lines, Deaver wanted a young Bond to live off a trust fund that his parents left him after their death. They said that Bond shouldn't be a trust fund kid, which seemed like a good note. But then, I noticed that in *Forever and a Day*, you had him initially living on a trust fund.
I remember writing that, but I'm surprised that they would have been worried about that since his parents had perished young, and he was still at Eton and having a fairly lavish lifestyle. There must have been money somewhere. So a trust fund of some sort seems sensible. I don't think I was tearing the envelope by suggesting that. But the Estate knows about as much as I do about what's going to sell and what's right and what's wrong or whether we should have Pussy Galore or not [as a character in *Trigger Mortis*]. They were nervous about that. But they took a vote, shall we have Pussy Galore in *Trigger Mortis*? If they voted against it, I might never have written any of the books.

When Bond goes into the public domain, how will that impact the character?
I wonder if that's true. Or I wonder if they found a way to protect "007" and the name "James Bond" as trademarks. I think there might be a way of protecting them as trademarks if nothing else. I think there is a greater danger to Bond that they killed him in the films. How are they going to get back from that? What is the solution going to be for that? Now, Amazon has taken over the character as well. They're going to exploit them in all sorts of different ways. There is a reality game show involving James

Bond [*007: Road to a Million*]. The Ian Fleming Estate has been clever in rigidly controlling the product. That's similar to the Hergé Estate with Tintin. Once you begin to let anybody do what they like, you will inevitably have a decline in standards. But that decline has already happened anyway. It happened the day Ian Fleming died.

Let's be honest about it. Nobody has ever written a James Bond novel as good as Ian Fleming. These other ones that exist—the ones you are studying—the continuation novels, are entertaining. Some of them are good; some of them are better than others; some of them are terrific. I always say this as self-defense, but they are irrelevant. It is Fleming's 14 books that matter. Just that. Those 14 books will last, I think, forever. No matter how many mistakes are made by other creators in the films, the original cannot be harmed.

KIM SHERWOOD

Double Or Nothing (2022)
A Spy Like Me (2024)

Kim Sherwood
Illustrations by Pat Carbajal

How did you come to write the Bond spin-off novel, *Double Or Nothing*?
You probably heard this from Anthony [Horowitz] and Charlie [Higson], who I know are such fans, but it was a lifelong dream to write Bond for me. I've always been a fan. All of my life I said to anybody who would listen, "One day, I want to write James Bond." It was just a matter of saying it to the right person, which is my agent.

　　She heard that the Flemings were looking for a new author. They'd been looking for a couple of years and hadn't found the right person. It's really important to them that you're a fan because this is their family legacy. They were keen to hand it on to a female writer in particular and hadn't been able to find the right person. My agent said to them, "I might have the author for you."

　　They liked my first novel, *Testament* [2018, about a woman who discovers the atrocities that her grandfather experienced in the Holocaust]. They invited me to send them some ideas. At that point, I was sending them Bond ideas. Then my agent said, "Do you have anything you can send them that demonstrates your love of Bond?" Anybody can say, "I'm a huge Bond fan, but do you have evidence?"

Luckily, my mum had kept a piece of homework I'd done. When I was about 14, our English teacher asked us to write about an author we admired. I made this booklet about Ian Fleming with illustrations and pull-out flaps. So I photocopied that and sent it to them. So this was quite literally a lifelong dream come true.

They liked my ideas. They invited me to lunch and said, "We'd love for you to do it. What we're after is an expansion of the Bond world. So bringing in these new Double-O characters, how would you go about that?" I went away, and I wrote them a pitch document, which, in essence, was my ideas of how I would do it. They liked those ideas, and it all took off from there. It was an unexpected, surreal turn of events. For a long time, it felt like a dream.

Who was at that lunch when they invited you to write a book? Corinne Turner?
It was Corinne [Turner] and Phoebe [Taylor], the editor of the time, who's no longer there, so now it's Simon Ward [Publishing Manager]. So it was the person who was in Simon's position. They were incredibly welcoming. They were saying, "We like your vision. We want your vision." That was a really encouraging place to be as an author. Because it felt like they were going to welcome me into the family. That's how they behave. They behave like it's family, and once you're in, you're very much in.

***Double Or Nothing* Book Launch, 2022**
Courtesy of Mark O'Connell, Catching Bullets

Generally speaking, after Ian Fleming Publications vets the author, the author has another meeting with the Fleming Estate.
That meeting with the Estate was very delayed because of the pandemic. The whole thing was agreed just before March 2020, which was when the UK went into lockdown. Then we had three lockdowns. It was only after that I went to meet with the family. By then, I'd pretty much written the whole book. We went for lunch. It was surreal because I had just had COVID. I was literally limping out of bed to go to this lunch because there was no way I was going to miss it. But I was out of it. God knows what I said.

Who from the family was there?
Diggory [Laycock] and Fergus Fleming.

During those meetings with the family, authors usually get critical information that helps them write the book. Yet, in your case, you had nearly finished it. Were you worried that they would have given you a piece of information that would have better served you before you started writing the book?
No, because they were brilliant and supportive through the pandemic. Over Zoom, I really felt like I got to know Corrine and Phoebe. I felt like I was being held. I also think it gave me creative freedom and permission because it was a secret that I was doing it. I wasn't allowed to tell anybody. I hadn't even met the Flemings yet. So the whole thing had that edge of not feeling real. I think that reduced how daunting it was. I was able to feel like I was just a kid again, pretending I was James Bond in my imagination. This was a fantasy. I think that gave me the freedom to write the book and take some creative risks that maybe I wouldn't have had I felt a bit more exposed while I was doing it.

Did they discuss the period and setting with you?
They said they wanted it to be contemporary. They wanted it to feel contemporary in terms of technology. They wanted it to have that cutting edge. They wanted it to feel gritty. They wanted a new character. How I did that was entirely up to me. Bond's status was entirely up to me.

What about style?
They wanted a fresh take. They said, "Don't try to write like Fleming. Write like you." That was freeing. I had a few different approaches to that. A big part of that for me was to go back and think about Fleming's prose. I first read Fleming when I was 12. And I read him repeatedly. He had a

really big influence on my style. I thought that I wouldn't try to imitate him. I can only write like me. But I explored his influences on me. I thought about how I could be conscious of that, raise it to the surface, and play with it explicitly. So there was a shared DNA between my style and his style because of how he influenced me when I was growing up.

Where is that shared DNA with Fleming in *Double Or Nothing*?
I thought about point of view. I use a third-person omniscient point of view, which I take from him. I also thought a lot about his imagery. Fleming has this visual, vivid style with uncanny imagery. Particularly, he uses similes that dehumanize and make strange and relate to the human body or animals or burnt meat. It's this visceral style of writing. I'm image-led as a writer. I tried to meet him there and bring in some imagery that wouldn't necessarily occur to me. For example, I don't have at all his background in deep-sea diving and fishing. But I brought in quite a few nautical images to try to cross over to that. So those two things—style and point of view. I felt like those were the ways that I could connect with his writing.

I think of a couple of examples of your nautical imagery that connect with Fleming. You write that the villain's boat looks like a mirrored whale as it is cutting through the water. Elsewhere, you say that the boat is alive with spines. What about some examples of how you are dissimilar to Fleming?
Good question. Fleming lets himself go; lets himself have quite long wordy descriptions, towards the beginning of his books. That's when things are going right for Bond...before he is in too much jeopardy. You see that particularly when Bond gets to a new place. Other than that, Fleming tends to have quite controlled prose and uses quite short, terse sentences. I will go into short sentences when I'm moving into action, but I do love a run-on sentence. I love my lengthier descriptions and scenes that are more about bringing out the place as a character. I suppose I give more words to that than he does. Perhaps he's more economical than me. As my English teacher put it, I'm verbose as a writer. [We both laugh.] I think that's probably the main difference. He wrote these books in three months, and he wrote quite short word counts, whereas I'm writing a book a year, which still feels quick to me, but it's longer than three months. I have a bit more space in there.

How many words is *Double Or Nothing*?
96,000 words, I believe.

Double Or Nothing Book Launch, 2022
Courtesy of Mark O'Connell, Catching Bullets

Did any of your ideas from the initial Bond-focused pitch make it into the book?
Not into *Double Or Nothing*, no. But some things have been bubbling over in my mind for the books to come. But not into that first one.

You indicated that Ian Fleming Publications left Bond's status up to you. Sounds like they were open to where Bond was in his life and how you would incorporate him into the book. When did the hook become "Bond is missing"?
That was really early on. That was what was really exciting about this opportunity to bring in new Double-O agents. It also felt like a real challenge as a writer because Bond commands attention on the page and the screen. Where he goes, your eye is drawn. That's where you look. That's where the spotlight goes. That makes it hard to introduce new characters and say to the readers, "Hey, look at these new heroes." Bond is in the way.

I thought, "What do I do about that?" My solution was to bake those challenges meta-fictionally into the story and have Bond vanish from the beginning. We have these new Double-Os trying to find him, and, in a way, that reflects the readers' eye, who are also trying to find him. I also hope that it redirects the spotlight. It moves him into shadows and opens up the spotlight, which these new heroes can step into.

What I hoped would happen is that there would be a transfer of sympathy. These new heroes care deeply about Bond and want to find him. Bond cares about them. As the reader, we care about Bond, therefore, we care about these new characters. Then, after the first book, you start to care about them in their own right. They become the protagonist and you stop searching for Bond so actively. I was trying to create a book where he is both present and absent.

The three new heroes are Sid Bashir, Johanna Harwood, and Joseph Dryden but let's talk about them in a moment. For people who haven't yet read your book, I would say to them that it's not accurate to say that Bond is missing from it. He is completely present throughout. You spend the whole book revealing Bond's character, his life, the training he provided to the new heroes, his relationships with the other Double-O agents, and so on. He even appears in flashback. Can you talk about the 'keeping Bond present' part of the book?

I took my cue from Fleming. I looked particularly at *From Russia with Love* and *The Spy Who Loved Me* [two books where Bond makes a late appearance]. I've always been interested in moments where Fleming shows us Bond through somebody else's eyes. When we're in Bond's mind, we have a sense of his inner life. We have a sense of somebody who struggles with the license to kill and the decisions that he has to make. Bond can be quite a melancholy, philosophical figure. When we see him from the outside, we see this taciturn, cruel, ironic mask that comes over him when he's sleeping. In *The Spy Who Loved Me*, when he knocks on the door, Vivienne Michel is worried that he's another gangster. She thinks, "I know it's another gangster because he looks like a villain."

I find it interesting that Fleming has created this hero who is both light and dark. At first glance, he could be the bad guy. He has to have that share of darkness to be a Double-O. That goes to the darkness of what Fleming created with this idea of a hero with a license to kill, which in many ways seems paradoxical. Usually, superheroes never kill. That's usually the line the hero will not cross. So I'm always interested when Fleming looks at Bond from the outside. Or when he looks at Bond from the villain's perspective.

In *From Russia with Love*, we have that fantastic passage where the Russians are plotting to demoralize Britain, which I co-opt for *Double Or Nothing*. They say that the strength of Britain lies in myth, the myth of Churchill, the myth of Scotland Yard, and the myth of Sherlock Holmes. "Have they no such man who represents the Secret Service and represents Britain?" Somebody replies, "There is a man called Bond." It's really interesting to me that in his fifth outing, Fleming says, I've created this myth of Britain. He's my consciously constructed myth, and I'm going to spend the whole novel seeing if I can deconstruct that myth or whether the myth can survive.

I looked at that. I thought I'd take my cue from that because Bond is about looking. That's particularly true in how it's been translated to cinema. We look at Bond. That's the activity. In *Double Or Nothing,* we have a look at Bond from Moneypenny's perspective as a long-term friend and his boss. From Harwood's perspective, as a lover. From Bashir's perspective, as his mentor. From Dryden's perspective, Bond is this gruff, possibly over-the-hill guy who's maybe a security risk. So you see him from all of these different perspectives and that allowed me to bring out something about his character, I hope. It's a character study of Bond, without Bond.

What do you think is revealed about Bond through those people?
What came to me was the multifaceted depth of Bond's character. I think there's this flattened idea of what Bond is from more casual Bond fans or those who know Bond more from a movie or haven't seen all the films and haven't read the books. Some posit that Bond can be boiled down to a series of gestures and icons—the gun, the martini shaker, the suits, and the cars. Those are certainly signals of Bond. What I found in looking at him from so many different angles and through so many different eyes is that we have this character that goes back to Fleming, who has a great deal of depth. He has a real vulnerability as a hero.

I thought a lot about how much he's lost—his parents, Vesper, and Tracy. Therefore, he has few meaningful relationships that he's prepared to engage in, and, to me, that goes back to the fact that he's guarding himself. When he does have meaningful relationships, like his friendship with Felix [Leiter], how tender those relationships are and what they mean to him. What defines Bond as a hero is the heart that never gives up. He never lets those close relationships down. That's why *Skyfall*, for example, hit so hard when M dies. It's the ultimate heartbreak. He's lost the parental figure again.

For me, he's this character who's vulnerable as well as indomitable. He has that humor, he's intelligent, he's curious, and he doesn't have many reasons to live beyond his duty. I hope that I was able to bring some of those facets out in the book.

What about the structure of the book?
I thought a lot about structures. I thought about how Fleming writes the same way as the classic quest structure where you have one man picking up the mission and going out. I thought it'd be interesting to use a different structure. Because I wrote an ensemble cast, I had a

cooperative structure rather than a singular structure. I thought, I have three and they'll be on different missions that overlap throughout the book.

Let's turn to your new Double-O agents. The premise hinges on introducing fresh characters, not pale imitations. They should be different; otherwise, what's the point? Can you talk about building your new Double-O agents?

I completely agree. The new agents can't be imitations of Bond because then they are watered-down versions and people will feel cheated. What's the point of that? I think all writing is political. Even if something isn't about politics, it's a political statement. Bond novels and movies are political. I want to keep Bond as Bond because I love that character. I feel like I have an opportunity to create these new characters that will widen the stage and invite more people to stand on it.

I thought a lot about the imaginary spy games I'd play when I was a kid. I'd spy on my neighbors, who, luckily, were tolerant people. I would turn their movements into mystery stories. For me, that fascination with spying and my love of writing grew together. In my imagination, I was Bond. I never played as a Bond Girl. That's no insult to Bond Girls. You have some amazing characters there but nobody aspires to be the supporting character. You want to be the main character of your own story. This seemed to me to be an opportunity to enable more people to see themselves as the main character.

Then that was emboldened by doing research into intelligence agencies, and seeing how diverse they are. It's one of the most diverse subsections [of intelligence work] because if all agents looked like James Bond, there'd be a real limit to the number of places that they could go undercover.

There's also this idea that I was intrigued by, that the CIA started to talk about, particularly after 9/11. It's this idea of "perspective blindness." If everybody in your organization comes from the same background, you'll all interpret the world in the same way. You will pick up the same clues, and you'll miss the same clues. You'll misinterpret information. It's a strategic asset to have people from all sorts of walks of life in your organization. That felt like real encouragement to open the door to a more inclusive world of James Bond. Then the next step was to come up with the characters. It was my choice to go with three main Double-Os for this story.

What about the characters themselves?

There were a few different triggers for the different characters. Starting with 004, Joseph Dryden, I read that a lot of Special Forces soldiers who were injured ended up becoming spies. They have such experience, and they go on multiple missions. A huge amount has been invested in them. They have all of the talents and all of the skills, but an injury keeps them from the front line. So they're often scooped up into intelligence services. I found that interesting.

They're warriors who rely on their bodies. But now, some injury has kept them from the front line. Then I thought, this is a way to bring Q branch in. What if somebody's body was augmented and changed? How would that change their relationship with their own body? What would that do to them psychologically? That felt like an interesting character crux. That was the beginning of Dryden.

Then I thought it would be nice to bring in Jamaica because, obviously, there's the Fleming connection, the Bond connection. I was also thinking that Fleming was writing post-World War II. Bond comes from the context of conflict and colonialism. I wondered, how do you position yourself in dialogue with that now? I want to both honor that connection with Jamaica and subvert how we see Jamaica and the novels in which Jamaica is this colonized space. Instead, celebrate the impact of the Windrush generation on Britain, and celebrate the contributions of immigrants to Britain. [The Windrush Generation refers to Caribbean immigrants who helped rebuild Britain after World War II.] I wanted to pick up the idea that we're here because you were there. I was writing this in the wake of the government here [in England] having this policy of creating a hostile environment for the descendants of the Windrush generation to try and encourage them to leave. I found that upsetting it doesn't represent what I want my Britain to be like. That was also on my mind. That was Dryden's heritage falling into place.

Then I thought it'd be really interesting…I've always loved that moment in *Tomorrow Never Dies* when Teri Hatcher turns up as Bond's ex-lover. I love the idea of the ex-lover reappearing. I thought it'd be really interesting if Dryden had a love interest in the army who comes back but is now working for the other side and is with the villain. I thought there was a radical potential to have the first gay Double-O and the first Black Double-O.

What about Sid Bashir?
Bashir's character came from thinking a lot about the idea of the mind of the Double-O.

If Bashir is the mind and Dryden is the body, then Harwood, who has had a relationship with Bashir and Bond, could be the heart. Body, mind, heart?
I did think of that, by the way, and having a five-man band. With Harwood, I was thinking about the idea of a license to kill. That sounds sexy on the surface, but when you think about it, they've been given enormous ethical responsibility. I wanted to dig into that. I thought that the opposite of a license to kill is the Hippocratic Oath, the doctor's oath to do no harm and heal anybody. Then I began to wonder, what would it take for somebody who'd taken the Hippocratic Oath—what would have to happen in your life and what person would you have to be—for you to flip on that and pick up the Double-O mantle and the license to kill?

    That took me into this space with Harwood where I thought her greatest asset is her adaptability in that she can be anything to anyone. She can be anything they need her to be in that moment. She's incredibly persuasive. She's incredibly flexible, resourceful, and changeable. But there's a danger in that as to your inner identity, knowing yourself and not believing other people's view of you but rather having an anchor. That's why Harwood is my favorite character to write. There are so many layers at work there. That was the impetus for her character.

Let's go back to Bashir for a moment.
For Bashir, it was this idea from the Koran that to save one soul is to save all of humanity. With Bond, we always want him to kill one person, usually one man, to save the world. So, it's always hinged on death. One death will save the world. I wanted to explore the opposite of that belief, which is that saving one person will save the world. Also, what would it be like if you grew up with that faith and you became a Double-O? Now, you would be given the power of death. How would you marry those two things together? That's Bashir's central arc throughout the book. It's the battle between strategy and philosophy for his heart and mind.

We start with three agents but end with two.
Yeah, we lost one at the end.

I assume it was always your plan to kill Bashir.
No, that came to me in the writing process, and it was totally unexpected. It shocked everyone. The editors were like, "What are you doing?" The original idea was that he would live and he would carry you [the reader] into the second book. Bashir is the character that you start the book with, and his death came about in two ways.

One of the reasons that they wanted to bring in these new Double-O agents was that they wanted a greater sense of jeopardy. We don't really believe that Bond can die. No matter what happens on the screen, we don't really believe it. Even when he does die in the cinema, the closing credits still come up as "James Bond Will Return." There is this sense of his character being immortal.

They said to me early on, "We'd like to increase the stakes." I got to the end, and I thought, "Well, that's the ultimate stake and the ultimate sacrifice. It also speaks to Bashir's arc; does he really believe that to save one life has to save all of humanity? Or does he believe that you have to take a life for the greater good? Does he think you have to do what's good for the most number of people? That's been his arc through the whole book.

As I got to the end, I thought the only answer, really, for this character is coming back to his faith and back to the faith of his mother, whom he lost as a child. In the end, he does believe that to save one life is to save all of humanity. But that comes at the cost of his own life. I felt so strange because I was in charge of it. I felt heartbroken as I wrote that scene. I also felt like the character was saying to me, this is the answer to my arc.

Bashir's death impacts not only the characters in *Double Or Nothing*, but it also impacts the direction of the second book, *A Spy Like Me*.

In *Double Or Nothing*, Harwood has made, in some ways, the greatest sacrifice in the book because her soul is on the line when she becomes a triple agent. When she becomes a triple, she has signed up for being mistrusted by the people she loves the most and whose love means the most to her in the world. She signed up for that to have a chance at getting Bond back. Of course, Bond was lost on the mission with Bashir.

We have this fraught love triangle going on. She loves both of them. She has to have Bashir believe that she's betrayed MI6 in order to embed herself with these terrorists and deliver the mole. She has all this on her shoulders as to whether or not MI6 can survive this treachery. The cost of that is that maybe Sid thinks that she's a traitor. For her, that's a huge sacrifice. There are moments in the book where she's curious and wonders, will I be able to make that sacrifice? Why did I agree to it?

For me, it goes back to her childhood when she learned that, in order to survive her father [and his mental illness], she had to learn to be incredibly adaptable. She learned to make identity malleable in the face of somebody else's delusions. It's a skill she can offer. It comes at this great cost, and people on the outside think that she's cold. That's why she's such an interesting character to write. There's so much internal conflict, which is expressed in her huge resolve. She's left in this incredibly painful position. Sid's was a painful scene to write. It was also one of my favorite scenes to write.

For *A Spy Like Me*, you had a couple of choices. Bring a new agent forward or spotlight Conrad Harthrop-Vane, 000, who has a relatively small role in book one.
We have new Double-Os in Book Two. Conrad comes more to the fore. I took his name from a list of Double-Os that Fleming gave in passing once. He's the son of somebody who had done some work in the past for the service. Writing his character has been really fun as a way to draw connections back to Fleming. It's a deep cut. Hopefully, it's a satisfying exploration in Book Two.

I consider him a shadow Bond. He's Bond if Bond wasn't charming. He's privately educated at a top university. He has all of the right skills, and he knows how to present himself exactly the right way. Bond is the star, and Harthrop-Vane is the man who wants to be the star. That's why he signed up to become a Double-O. It's because it suits his sense of himself. He's interesting to write because he's confronted with the limitations of himself. He comes from a background that is intertwined with espionage history here in the UK. It's the privately educated Oxbridge graduation [a combination of Oxford and Cambridge]. That was our spy history.

Then there's another character who is not a Double-O but is playing a Double-O-like role. Her name is Rachel Wolf and she's a professional thief employed by espionage services. She's been fun to write. She has a different sense of humor than the others. She brings a lot of joy to it. She's a Jewish character. Bashir was one way to explore faith and this is another way to explore a different faith but with some similar ideas.

A lot of my decisions come from a place of being irked by something. I haven't fact-checked this yet, but somebody who knows the espionage services told me that traditionally, Jewish people haven't been employed as spies in the British Secret Service because we're considered rootless wanderers. As someone from a Jewish family, I was irked by that and decided to correct matters.

As a nice Jewish boy, I'm glad that you are. In *The Moneypenny Diaries*, it's established that Moneypenny is half-Jewish. It's critical

to have positive representation in the media.
I think that representation is important. That was something I thought a lot about with Bashir's character and then again with Harwood, who is partly of Algerian descent. For me, growing up as not only a huge fan of Bond but of the action genre, the only instances of Muslim characters on screen since 9/11 in action stories are as villains. I wanted to challenge the stereotype and that narrowed view of culture. I think it does a lot of harm, and it's not reflective of contemporary intelligence services where this is a huge recruitment of people of Arabic descent. With Bashir's character, I wanted to say that there's a hero who doesn't look like James Bond. The idea of a hero is a broad one.

Where did the titles *Double Or Nothing* and *A Spy Like Me* come from?
From me. The title *Double Or Nothing* came early in the process; I wanted to somehow get "Double-O" in as a statement of intent and to say this is a little bit of a different book. Fleming is very good at drawing on idiomatic expressions for his titles. I thought "Double or Nothing" as a phase was similar to that. I also thought the idea of "Double or Nothing" sums up the ethos of a Double-O where they'll keep going and keep doubling down. Even when it's desperate, it's either that or nothing, and the world ends. That also established the stakes. As a way to bring in that idea, I decided to have this villain who's addicted to gambling.

    The title for *A Spy Like Me* came much later. I had *Double Or Nothing* before I even began writing the books. *A Spy Like Me* came up in a scene that takes place about halfway through the novel. It was one of those things where I wrote it and thought, "Oh, that'd be a good title." Then, I kept going. Then it took another year where we were all sitting around saying, "What about titles?" for me to say, "Well, there was this one ages ago that I thought would be a good title." Luckily, everyone liked it. We ended up using that. It speaks to the themes of the book. One of the main themes of the book is interrogating the identity of these different Double-Os. What drives them? What drives them to become Double-Os because Double-Os have this incredibly short life expectancy. What drives them to be committed to a life that might end at 45? It was playing around with those ideas.

You have a little fun with that critical piece of Bond lore. Fleming established that the mandatory retirement age is 45. You don't dispute that, but you say it's a euphemism because the Double-O agents will likely be dead by then. When you pitched Book One, did

you also pitch Books Two and Three, at least broadly?
Yes, yes. The idea from the beginning was that it would be a trilogy. Each novel is connected, but they can also stand as discrete entities. That was a real gift because I could think about these long-running character arcs. I didn't have to tie them up in one book.

I mapped it out pretty well. Although, it's changed organically in the writing. Book Three was much more open. The first thing I actually wrote was the last scene of Book Three. Although the plot was open, I knew where I was heading. I knew my ultimate destination. That destination remains the same even if how I get there changes a little bit as I go.

Do you save the manuscripts on your computer as Book One, Book Two, and Book Three?
Exactly, that's how they're saved. Because I'm a geek, they're saved under code words, so if anybody steals my laptop, they won't be interested in opening up the file. But it's the most boring code word that I could possibly imagine. Inside, it's Book One, Book Two, and Book Three.

Can you talk about the decision to name the character Johanna Harwood, a screenwriter of the first Bond movie. I imagine that you wanted to spotlight the real Harwood and draw attention to her contributions.
Exactly that. That was my hope from the beginning that I could name her Harwood. I didn't have a Plan B. I was grateful that she said yes. I sent her a letter saying, "I want to pay homage to you as the first woman to write Bond, the first Bond screenwriter, and the writer of my favorite Bond film, *From Russia with Love*. To thank you for what you did."

I feel like that generation of women faced so many obstacles in their way creatively and not creatively, within the creative field. If they hadn't fought for what they fought for, I wouldn't get to do what I do now. It was really important to me to shine the light backwards and to illuminate the real-life Johanna Harwood's role in Bond history.

It's been a role that hasn't really been duly celebrated or noted. Growing up and watching all of the DVD commentaries and all those other things, she wasn't mentioned. It was only coming to later research, as a Bond obsessive, that I realized what she did. I really wanted to honor her. I was grateful that she said yes. She sent me a letter after she read book one saying that she enjoyed it. It's the highest praise I could possibly receive.

After Bashir rescues Harwood from captivity, he brings her to a hotel room. If it were a movie, I would have expected a risqué line about how they were going to spend the next few hours, and then the screen would fade to black. That's not what happens in *Double or Nothing*. Instead, she wants food and room service. Then, Bashir washes her hair. It's a lovely moment that was nuanced and unexpected.

Thank you. I thought about that a lot. As you say, the narrative beat we expect next is that the sun rises over a bedroom where their clothes are scattered across the carpet. I thought this isn't that. A lot of times in this genre, female characters are restricted to being a prize. The man has gone through an ordeal, and there's a woman as a prize at the end of the ordeal. That goes back to chivalric literature.

I think that Fleming doesn't get enough credit for how much he invested in his female characters. He creates these brilliant characters with rich backstories, with inner lives, with agency, with motivations, with a lot of space on the page. I wanted to take that and to go further than that, and to have Harwood as a protagonist rather than a supporting character.

In that scene, I wanted there to be this tender moment of connection between the two. It needed to be in a way that felt realistic for both of them as protagonists, rather than one of them being an object to the other. She's been through this harrowing traumatic experience; her first instinct isn't going to be, let's hop into bed together. It's going to be medical. It's going to be psychological and emotional. Then through that, you have this moment of tenderness and intimacy between them. I hope it reads more compellingly because it feels real and not like a moment of the male gaze that has nothing to do with the narrative.

I love your dialogue which is whip smart. It crackles like the witty banter from a film noir movie. There's a moment where Harwood says that if she fails the loyalty test, Bashir will take the gun, put a bullet in her head and "save M the paperwork."

That's so nice to hear, particularly because I'm a massive fan of film noir. My love of dialogue comes from my love of those Humphrey Bogart-era films. There's a story about the Bogie and Bacall film *The Big Sleep*. After they first looked at the film, they decided it wasn't quite sexy enough. The response to that was to put in a scene of dialogue where they talk about horse racing. The whole exchange is a metaphor for sex. It's so telling that their response to "it's not sexy enough" was let's have them talk more.

I'm always drawn to Aaron Sorkin's dialogue that's working on multiple levels and that's always witty. There's also Georgette Heyer [the English novelist who wrote Regency Romances and detective stories]. From all these different genres, you have all this dialogue that is heightened with meaning and with sexual tension. I think that's what the best dialogue in Bond is. I wanted to bring that through,

Can you talk about how you handled Moneypenny, who is now in charge of the Double-O division?
We excerpted the first Moneypenny chapter before the book came out for *The Sunday Times,* and the headline was something like, "Moneypenny is now boss." ["Moneypenny Takes Charge in the New Bond Novel]. Moneypenny is the longest-serving female character in Bond when you put together the page and screen, and so she's the world's most overdue promotion. In that sense, I think we attach a lot of authority to her because she comes with all this experience. So she can play a much larger role than simply sitting behind the desk. I thought, Well, then let's put her in that position of power. Also Judi Dench has been so fantastic and influential in the films to me, it made sense.

I was pleased by it, but I didn't necessarily consider it a revolutionary statement. What's been so lovely is that it seems to feel that way that way for a lot of people. A lot of women in their 40s and 50s have said to me, "I was used to watching Bond with my brother. I'd always ask, 'Why couldn't Moneypenny have more of a role?' and he'd reply, 'Oh, she's only a secretary.' They're really happy to see her in this expanded role. I think Moneypenny is a real symbol for people and giving her that bigger role seems to have touched the cultural nerve in a good way.

Silly question. I've read the book multiple times, but I've also listened to the audiobook several times. When I hear Doctor Nowak's name, the first half of it also makes me think of the character named Doctor No. As in Doctor No-wak. Is that intentional?
That is entirely unconscious. You're the first person to point that out. I love that.

I have to ask you about Bill Tanner and the decision to make him a traitor.
That was an idea quite early on. I was thinking a lot about this idea of the old boy's network, which, in the history of espionage in Britain, has been its downfall. If you think about the Cambridge Five, the establishment has

trusted the establishment. [The Cambridge Five were a group of five British spies who passed information to the Soviet Union from the 1930s until at least the early 1950s.] If you went to the right school with the right people, you're considered okay. That's our weakness, from intelligence services to Prime Ministers. I wanted to explore that notion. Particularly because I'm writing in a different Britain than Fleming.

Fleming was from a class and a time when he could be confident about Britain. I wouldn't call him flag-waving by any means. He certainly is reflective about postwar society and where Britain might be going. In *You Only Live Twice*, for example, there's a lot of reflection on the modern Britain of his time. He was writing about a world that's come through World War II. Communism is looming, but there's still this confidence that he instills Bond with. Perhaps it's an imperial confidence. I think that was partly what made Bond so attractive to Britain. Britain had won the war but had been hobbled by it and was on rationing. Then here's this glamorous spy with this real sense of positivity and verve and glamour going on.

I'm also writing in a time of crisis, the climate crisis. I was writing after Brexit and during the pandemic. I feel like there isn't that same confidence that I can call on. I don't have the confidence of the white, straight, upper-class, privately educated male who's confident the world is made for them. I have not inherited that confidence. I don't feel that confidence when I see it in the world.

I don't know if I'm articulating this well because I never explained it before. But, in that way, I think I wanted to explore the idea of what it looks like if the core is rotten. And poor Tanner…that fell on his shoulders.

Were you nervous about the fan reaction?
It's funny because I was writing it in lockdown, and nobody knew what I was doing because it was still secret. I wasn't that nervous when I was writing it. It felt like this was right for the story. This is right for the characters. This is right for my intentions. It was only once the news became public that I began to get nervous about all of these things. It was daunting. It was hugely exciting and thrilling when the news was announced, but it was uncharted water for me. Anthony [Horowitz] and Charlie [Higson] are coming from positions where they are household names. They have that security in a way. Whereas for me, much earlier in my career, I'm a literary novelist.

When it was announced, I didn't know what to expect. I'd been told that it would be a big news story. You can understand something intellectually but not understand it emotionally. Part of me thought that maybe no one would even notice what I was doing. It was announced in *The Guardian*. I tweeted about it, and I went to make a cup of tea. When I came back to my computer, suddenly, there were thousands of notifications. That weekend, it was in the news all over the world in languages I couldn't identify. My face is really big in all the newspapers. That was otherworldly.

At first, it was positive. There was this real wave of positivity from the fans. Then it was picked up by certain elements of the media that attract more misogyny and trolls. I felt that wave. After about day two or three, I thought, "God, maybe I shouldn't even engage with online stuff. I shouldn't read the news. I should close myself off." Then I noticed through that noise that there was a lot of positivity from the actual Bond fans. I thought, hang on, in a way, it's like the playground. Just because there are bullies doesn't mean you shouldn't play with the cool kids who want to play. I won't give fuel to the bullies. Instead, I'll give fuel and, I hope, a platform to this incredible community. I think the Bond community is the most positive, creative, inclusive, supportive, and welcoming community there is. I've tried to magnify that and to engage as a fan with the community. I found that they've been welcoming to what I've been doing. So that's been a huge relief.

I'm sorry to hear that. However, I'm glad that you were able to also see and feel the support. As an outsider and someone who hasn't lived your experience, my impression is that more people are rooting for you than not.
Very much. It does feel like that. I take the responsibility seriously. As a lifelong fan of Bond, I've been given this opportunity to contribute to the canon. I want to represent Bond fans well. I've tried to engage with readers and say, 'I'm one of you,' rather than, 'I stand apart from you.' As a creator, I don't feel that way at all. I feel like we're one community.

It's such a joy to get to share this passion and connect with people from all over the world from different walks of life. [Sherwood has even attended a Bond fan's small virtual book club.] That's what's amazing about the Bond community. It only makes sense…for something to be this popular for so long, there have to be so many different angles to it. You see that in the fan community, everybody respects the different ways that people come to it and love it. I find that incredibly heartwarming.

After writing his first book, Anthony Horowitz told me that he wasn't sure that he wanted to write more because of the public scrutiny. Of

course, he came back and wrote two more. I mention this only to say that you're not alone.

Anthony has been so wonderful. I read all of his Alex Rider books when I was growing up. I hero-worship Anthony. I love Charlie's books. To get to meet them both was amazing. They've been so supportive. I've had long conversations with both of them about how to deal with some of the media side of it. They've been generous with their time and with their experiences. They have been incredibly encouraging. We've done a lot of events together now, which I love doing. I feel grateful to them.

Of course, you hope for the widest possible readership, but who are these continuation novels for?

Two answers. The first answer is me. They are the books that I wanted to read but didn't exist. Or, at least, I couldn't readily find them growing up. As somebody who loves fiction, loves the action genre and was looking for more female writers and more female heroes—in terms of being able to find them on bookshelves, being able to find them in university curricula—they weren't there. I've written an article, "Top 10 Female Spies in Fiction," which was fun to write. It's amazing how many of these brilliant female espionage writers we've had in the genre have been written out of the story. In many ways, it's the book I wish I'd had. It's my fantasy book; it's the book I always dreamt I could write.

Beyond that, I hope that it can satisfy Bond fans, people who have never read Bond before, and female thriller readers. That's not to say that I don't want male readers as well. I do. But look at the way the crime genre is segregated by gender. Even if you go to a bookshop and do a cursory look, you have psychological thrillers and what is sometimes called "domestic crime," written by women. Then you have action thrillers written by men. There's this real sense of "never the twain shall cross" and that the readers are kept quite separate. When you look at the crime genre overall, it's the queens of crime writing and women readers who drive the genre. I hope I can create a bit of cross-fertilization there and say that there's no reason for these things to be segregated. I hope the book satisfies deep Bond fans like me and like you, but that it also brings in new people. I've had a lot of people say to me, "This is the first Bond I've ever read." I feel honored to be a gateway to Bond for people.

Ian Fleming
Illustration by Pat Carbajal

APPENDIX

JAMES BOND WORKS BY AUTHOR

The publication dates provided are for the United Kingdom. Dates for the United States may vary. Short stories are indicated by quotation marks.

By Ian Fleming
Casino Royale (1953)
Live And Let Die (1954)
Moonraker (1955)
Diamonds Are Forever (1956)
From Russia, With Love (1957)
Dr. No (1958)
Goldfinger (1959)
For Your Eyes Only (1960)
(Collecting the short stories "From A View To A Kill," "For Your Eyes Only," "Risico," "Quantum Of Solace," and "The Hildebrand Rarity")
Thunderball (1961)
The Spy Who Loved Me (1962)
On Her Majesty's Secret Service (1963)
"007 in New York" (1963)
You Only Live Twice (1964)
The Man With The Golden Gun (1965)
Octopussy and The Living Daylights (1966)

By Arthur Calder-Marshall
The Adventures of James Bond Junior 003½ (1967)

By Kingsley Amis
Colonel Sun (1968)

By Geoffrey Jenkins
Per Fine Ounce (Circa 1968, unpublished)

By John Pearson
James Bond: The Authorized Biography Of 007 (1973)

By Christopher Wood
James Bond, The Spy Who Loved Me (1977)
James Bond and Moonraker (1979)

By John Gardner
Licence Renewed (1981)
For Special Services (1982)
Icebreaker (1983)
Role of Honour (1984)
Nobody Lives For Ever (1986)
No Deals, Mr. Bond (1987)

(John Gardner, cont'd.)
Scorpius (1988)
Licence To Kill (1989)
Win, Lose or Die (1989)
Brokenclaw (1990)
The Man From Barbarossa (1991)
Death Is Forever (1992)
Never Send Flowers (1993)
SeaFire (1994)
GoldenEye (1995)
COLD (UK), Cold Fall (US) (1996)

By Raymond Benson
"Blast From The Past" (1997)
Zero Minus Ten (1997)
Tomorrow Never Dies (1997)
The Facts of Death (1998)
High Time To Kill (1999)
"A Midsummer's Night's Doom" (1999)
"Live At Five" (1999)
The World Is Not Enough (1999)
DoubleShot (2000)
Never Dream of Dying (2001)
"The Heart of Erzulie" (2001, unpublished in its original form)
The Man with the Red Tattoo (2002)
Die Another Day (2002)

By Charlie Higson
SilverFin (2005)
Blood Fever (2006)
Double or Die (2007)
Hurricane Gold (2007)
By Royal Command (2008)
"A Hard Man To Kill" (2009)
On His Majesty's Secret Service (2023)

By Steve Cole
Shoot to Kill (2014)
Heads You Die (2016)
Strike Lightning (2016)
Red Nemesis (2017)

By Samantha Weinberg
Guardian Angel (2005)
Secret Servant (2006)
"Moneypenny's First Date with Bond" (2006)
"For Your Eyes Only" (2006)

(Samantha Weinberg, cont'd.)
Final Fling (2008)

By Sebastian Faulks
"Ian Fleming Thinks Even James Bond Goes Shopping" (2006, unofficial)
Devil May Care (2008)

By Jeffery Deaver
Carte Blanche (2011)

By William Boyd
Solo (2013)
"William Boyd Interviews James Bond" (2013)
"William Boyd Q&A with James Bond" (2013)

By Anthony Horowitz
Trigger Mortis (2015)
Forever and a Day (2018)
With a Mind to Kill (2022)

By Kim Sherwood
Double Or Nothing (2022)
A Spy Like Me (2024)

By Vaseem Khan
Quantum of Menace (2025)

Notes

[1] An earlier version of this introduction was published in *Fatherly*.

[2] Some Bond scholars would strongly contest the interpretation that *With a Mind to Kill* portrays Bond's final mission as a 00 agent

[3] "Bother" or "Oh, bother" is an expression that is used to express annoyance.

[4] For the full story behind the *Casino Royale*, see my book *The Lost Adventures of James Bond*.

[5] This is not the Steven Jay Rubin who wrote *The James Bond Films*.

[6] Fleming's "How to Write a Thriller" was published a few times in different forms, including in *Show* in August 1962. Source: Jon Gilbert, *Ian Fleming: The Bibliography,* p540, Queen Anne Press, 2012. The piece has also been published in *Talk of the Devil*, a collection of Fleming's writing, as "The Art, or Craft of Writing Thrillers" by Queen Anne Press in 2008. *Talk of the Devil* also contains two non-Bond short stories, "A Poor Man Escapes" and "The Shameful Dream."

[7] In *James Bond: The Authorized Biography of 007*, John Pearson indicates that Bond lives at 30 Wellington Square.

[8] Part one of the Anthony Horowitz interview originally appeared in my book, *The Many Lives of James Bond: How the Creators of 007 Have Decoded the Superspy*.

[9] "Raymond Benson Interview," May 11, 2004, MI6.com https://www.mi6-hq.com/sections/articles/interview_raymond_benson_before.php3 and Tom Sears and Chris Wright, "Raymond Benson Interview – Podcast #11," James Bond Radio, April 18, 2014

Afterword

by David Lowbridge-Ellis MBE

Unlike 007, I'm not a gambling man. But I'm willing to bet that most of you reading this have, at some point in your life, reckoned you could write a good Bond story.

I know I have.

It sounds so easy, doesn't it? All we need to do is follow the formula: a winning recipe, which has been followed, to a greater or lesser extent, for over fifty novels since the death of Fleming. All we need to do is adhere fairly closely to this basic recipe, choosing the right ingredients: a villain, a caper, a love interest, and some allies. And then the seasoning: the right locations, guns, cars, clothes, food, drinks.

Et voila!

Except, have we really thought this through?

Between the pages of the book you're holding, you find the people who have been entrusted with Fleming's legacy breezily reeling off what *they think* is the recipe (for instance, Jeffrey Deaver: "geopolitics, travel, a super bad guy, set pieces, and Bond's panache and smarts"). And while I noticed many similarities in what the various authors said, as I read more and more of Mark's brilliant interviews, I started to note more and more differences in how each author approached their time in Fleming's world. Things aren't as formulaic as they first appear...

One of the biggest points of contention was none other than James Bond himself. As the writers interviewed here observe, Bond is a character they did not create, so writing him comes saddled with a heck of a responsibility. This is not just a responsibility to the fanbase who have their own ideas about who James Bond is, but also a responsibility to themselves and how they see the character.

I often think of James Bond as a Rorschach Test; when people talk about James Bond, they reveal as much about themselves as they do about Fleming's character. Observe here, in this book, the authors who claim Bond is *not* someone prone to introspection, who find he's more enjoyable to read about when he's not wracked with self-doubt and dwelling on his failures. And then, contrast this with the authors who say the exact opposite: that Bond is most engaging when he's at his most vulnerable and how rewarding they find it to go inside his head.

So which one of these is the 'true' Bond? Perhaps checking The Fleming would help? Or maybe not...

Anyone holding an uncompromising reading of the character who feels the need to validate their viewpoint by citing Fleming had better brace themselves for someone to come back at them with evidence from the texts, which flips their reading on its head. Between the pages of Fleming's fourteen books, we find a Bond who is both a man of action AND a man of indecision; someone who is both violent AND caring; a sexist AND someone who respects women; both dark AND light; both traditional AND progressive.

A somewhat less psychological example of how hard to pin down he is: does James Bond wear anything in bed or sleep naked? Mark's revealing interview with Anthony Horowitz reveals that even this apparently trivial detail is up for debate, even with the highest of Fleming authorities.

There are some fans of Fleming who revere the Bond books as some kind of sacred texts. And while I count myself as someone who can readily quote those fourteen books chapter and verse, I will happily concede—like any true believer—that my own views are merely my own interpretations. We all take away from these books what we bring to them, and that includes the anointed few who have had the chance to write in Fleming's world. The best that any continuation author can do is hold true to their conception of the character, because no matter what choices they make, they can be sure that a Bond fan somewhere will disagree with them.

All of the authors interviewed in Mark's book felt the weight of expectation upon them, as a Bond Author. They were hyperconscious of the need to please as many people as possible, from the Fleming die hards to the people who have never read a Bond novel. Several of the authors concede they made certain choices to provoke—rather than placate—the audience. It's an impulse I cannot hold but applaud. Bond has to be refreshed to stay relevant, and I was fascinated to read about some of the tensions around this. John Gardner's persistent attempts to reflect the real-world AIDS epidemic were repeatedly shut down by the publisher. It's clear that Gardner felt a responsibility to his readership. But having Bond slip on a condom (even one with three gold bands to match his cigarettes!) appears to have been even more controversial than having him drive a Saab. Perhaps it was because it would have shattered the illusion that many sustain while reading a Bond novel of a world without real consequences.

Would Fleming have had Bond enjoying sex responsibly? It's a question we'll never know the answer to. But it's the sort of question a Bond continuation author has to wrestle with, especially if they're setting their novel in the present day. Bringing Bond up-to-date is a risky prospect, but setting him in the past or the time period we're familiar with from Fleming can be just as fraught with peril. The principal pitfall is the same: how to resist slipping into pastiche, particularly when Fleming's own style is so recognisable to us. As revealed in these interviews, some continuation authors made a close study of Fleming's imagery, his vocabulary, and his sentence constructions. Others tried not to think about it too much. And who can blame them!

Writing a Bond novel, then, is perhaps not the unmitigated joy it at first seems. And that's even before we approach the various other challenges, including—perhaps most intimidatingly of all—choosing a title!

Inevitably, we will enjoy some authors' take on Bond more than others. But I think we should consider ourselves fortunate that when each of these people were asked to have a go at writing Bond they all agreed to have a roll of the dice.

David Lowbridge-Ellis MBE is the award-winning creator of the acclaimed Licence to Queer. *A lifelong Bond fan and a teacher by vocation, in 2023, he was awarded MBE in King Charles's first Birthday Honours for his not-so-secret Services to Education. You can find him on Instagram, X, YouTube, Facebook, wherever you get podcasts, and at www.licencetoqueer.com.*

ACKNOWLEDGEMENTS

I should start by thanking the authors who generously agreed to speak to me for this volume. Those wonderful souls include Raymond Benson, Charlie Higson, Sebastian Faulks, Jeffery Deaver, William Boyd, Steve Cole, Anthony Horowitz, and Kim Sherwood. Thanks go to Simon Gardner for sharing his recollections about his father, John. From Ian Fleming Publications, I express my gratitude to the formidable Corinne Turner, who has played a critical role in overseeing numerous continuation novels of the modern era.

I would like to thank David Zaritsky of *The Bond Experience* who has generously hosted two online book launches and has supported my work in numerous ways; James Page of *MI6-HQ.com* who has continually spotlighted my books; Joseph Darlington of *Being Bond*; Anders Frejdh of *From Sweden with Love*; James Chapman of *Licensed to Thrill* and *Dr. No: The First James Bond Film;* Ajay Chowdhury of *Some Kind of Hero*; Brian McKaig of *The Bondologist Blog*; Gareth Owen of Bondstars; Alan J. Porter of *The James Bond Lexicon*; John Cox of The Book Bond; Lennart Guldbrandsson of Writing Bond; Tom Cull of Artistic Licence Renewed; Dr. Lisa Funnell of *For His Eyes Only: The Women of James Bond*; Shane Whaley of Spybrary; Matt Spaiser of Bond Suits; Remmert van Braam of the Bond Lifestyle; Steven Jay Rubin of *The James Bond Films*; Richard Schenkman of *Bondage*; Andy Lane and Paul Simpson of *The Bond Files*; Lee Pfeiffer of *The Incredible World of 007* and *Cinema Retro;* Tom Sears and Chris Wright at *James Bond Radio*; Bruce Scivally of *James Bond: The Legacy*; Benjamin Lind of *The Bond Bulletin*; Nicolas Suszczyk of *The Bond of the Millennium*; Victoria Hodges of The Bond Room Unlocked; Thomas Nixdorf of The Nixdorf Collection; Llewella Chapman of *Fashioning James Bond* and *From Russia With Love*; Phil Whitfield of *A Licence to Phil*; Tim George and Graeme Bibby of The James Bond Cocktail Hour; the gang at *Really, 007*; Phil Noble Jr., who named one of my books and who finds beauty in horror; *Archivo 007*; Greg Bechtlof of *MI6;* Bill Koenig of *The Spy Command*; Peter Lorenz of the *Illustrated 007*; Matt Sherman of Bond Fan Events; Spencer Draper of Damn Fool Idealistic Crusader; Scott Hettrick of Hollywood in High-Def; Clinton Rawls of *Comics Royale*; Roland Hume; and the inimitable Calvin Dyson.

I'm incredibly grateful to David Mamet and Don Winslow.

I want to thank the members of the group James Bond Collectable Books Worldwide and all its members including Matthew Bradford, Tony Jelly, Peter Crush, Jochem Gr, Ian Douglas, Martin Welles, John

Fairbrother, Gary Rosenfeld, David Lloyd, Ian Stubbs, Greg Williams, Tom Zielinski, Alan Tong, Ian Allison, Matthew Dewhurst-Grice, Jeff Gelb, Bazeer Flumore, Robin Harbour, Pete Beaumont, Michael Fenemore, Lance Salemo, Paul Shields, Matthew Wood, David Alexander, Rebecca Andrews, Craig Arthur, Thomas Eagle, Brendan Edwards, Tim Kitchen, Simon Read, Richard Skillman, Gary Webster, and the rest of the crew. Remembering Seán Ó Leannain and Wolfgang Johann Thürauf. Additional thanks to Dave Tulley, Paul Lally, Dave Tulley, Brian James Smith, and Anthony Lowbridge-Ellis,

My appreciation also goes to Gary J. Firuta, Jon Gilbert, Ryan Britt, Steve Clamp, Don Winslow, and Fergus Fleming.

I am in debt to Mark O'Connell of *Catching Bullets* for the use of his wonderful photos.

I'd also like to thank all the readers who expressed their enthusiasm for my previous works. Some of those wonderful people include Mark Ashby, Cal David, Glenn Hewett, Darren Noble, David Stephens, Brian Dobson, Oscar Rubio, Martin Hrdr, Michael Gallipo, David Stephens, Victor Tapia, Howard Pieratt, Steve Brock, Sean Hannam, Marc Hernandez, and Anagnostis Karras.

Thrilled to have Sean Longmore's stunning cover art grace this book. Pat Carbajal's phenomenal illustrations elevate it further—they're truly exceptional.

I'm thrilled to have Bruce Feirstein's witty foreword grace this book. His expertise and personal experience working in the "trenches" reflect his singular point of view.

Massive thanks to David Lowbridge-Ellis of *License to Queer* for his insightful afterword. Beyond his writing talent, David's kindness shines through.

I give huge thanks to my friends and Beta-readers Jack Lugo, William Kanas, Alan J. Porter, and Brad Frank for their advice, corrections, and overall input on the book.

Enormous thanks to Elizabeth Belasco, a meticulous, unstinting, and genial editor.

I also want to thank my family and friends for all of their support. For my mom, the honorable Sandra Edlitz, who always encouraged me to follow my dreams. I'd also like to thank my wonderful sister Tracy, who is also a great aunt. To my dear and beloved uncle Elliot Ravetz, who remains my biggest writing advocate. Additional love goes to Gail Ravetz, Mark Visceglia, Scott Edlitz, Katy Edlitz, George Berger, Dr. Joan Shapiro, and Dr. Irving Shapiro. I also want to remember my late father, Robert I. Edlitz.

Above all, I must thank Dr. Susan Shapiro, my impressive wife, and Ben and Doug, my two remarkable children. Watching your growth and evolution is the greatest privilege of my life.

NEWSLETTER

Dear Readers,

Want a sneak peek at my next book? Sign up for occasional updates and be the first to know when it arrives! Drop a line to WriteMarkEdlitz@gmail.com

I look forward to hearing from you.

Bonding along
Mark

ABOUT THE ILLUSTRATOR

Artist Pat Carbajal started as a political cartoonist at various national newspapers in Argentina. He then moved on to portrait art, illustrations, children's books, comic books, and storyboards for commercials.

Pat started producing art for the American market in 2007 when he illustrated covers for *Timeline of The Planet of the Apes* by Rich Handley for Hasslein Books. In 2009, he painted covers for the Bluewater Productions biography series, which were based on the lives of influential American women. Rock stars were the next subject for Pat. Bob Dylan, Jim Morrison, and Jimi Hendrix were the legends who were featured in *Rock and Roll Comics: The Sixties*, followed by Ozzy Osborne, AC/DC, and Guns N' Roses in *Rock and Roll Comics: Rock Heroes.*

The first graphic novel that Pat completely illustrated was *Allan Quartermain,* which was written by Clay and Susan Griffith and was published by Bluewater. Together with Clay and Susan Griffith, he created the character of The Raven for Bluewater's *Vincent Price Presents*, a classic horror comic book that starred Hollywood screen legend Vincent Price. Pat made his debut as a writer in the following issue of the comic.

He illustrated the cover and interior art for The James Bond Lexicon: The Unauthorized Guide to the World of 007 in Novels, Movies and Comics.

For Hasslein Books, Pat illustrated the covers and interior art for Lexicon of The Planet of the Apes and Back to the Future, as well as Total Immersion: The Comprehensive Unauthorized Red Dwarf Encyclopaedia.

This is Pat's fifth book with Mark Edlitz. Previously, he provided illustrations for The Many Lives of James Bond, The Lost Adventures of James Bond, James Bond After Fleming: The Continuation Novels, and Movies Go Fourth: 4th Films in Fantastic Franchises.

Pat creates exclusive designs for t-shirts with Rotten Cotton and produces comic book and cover artwork for Eibon Press and Vinegar Syndrome, with a series of horror graphic novels based on cult movies, including *Maniac, Lucio Fulci's Zombie,* and *The Beyond*, and a series of graphic novels based on the works of Joe R. Lansdale

Pat lives in Argentina.

ABOUT THE COVER DESIGNER

Sean Longmore is a freelance graphic designer from the UK. He currently works producing art for Blu-ray releases including Pierce Brosnan's *The Thomas Crown Affair*, Roger Moore's *Gold*, and various action films starring Michelle Yeoh, as well as producing Bond fan art when he finds time. He also works in the world of Doctor Who.

The first Bond film he saw in the cinema at age seven was *Die Another Day*. His late grandmother watched alongside with her fingers in her ears because it was too loud; he still adores it to this day and now watches every Bond film just a little bit too loud...

Sean can be found on Instagram at @seanlongmore.

ABOUT THE AUTHOR

Mark Edlitz has worked as a writer and producer for ABC News, NBC-Uni, CNBC, Discovery ID, and National Geographic Channel's *Brain Games*.

Edlitz's writings about pop culture have appeared in *The Huffington Post*, *Los Angeles Times Hero Complex*, *Moviefone*, and *Empire* magazine online.

He wrote and directed the award-winning independent film *The Eden Myth* and directed *Jedi Junkies*, a documentary about extreme Star Wars fans.

Edlitz's first book, *How to Be a Superhero* includes interviews with actors who have played superheroes over the past seven decades.

His second book, *The Many Lives of James Bond* consists of original interviews with artists who have created James Bond movies, novels, television, radio dramas, comic books, and video games. It also includes a large collection of interviews who have played 007 in different media.

His third book, *The Lost Adventures of James Bond* uncovers different scenarios for Timothy Dalton's abandoned third and fourth Bond movies, questions Toby Stephens about playing 007 on the radio, delves into the unproduced *Casino Royale* play, and exposes the secret history of *James Bond Jr*, the animated series about 007's nephew.

His fourth book, *Movies Go Fourth: 4th Films in Fantastic Franchises* is a celebration of the fourth movies in the most popular film franchises of all time. It offers behind-the-scenes stories of fourth films from such beloved series as *Star Wars*, *Star Trek*, and *James Bond.* It also explores infamous fourth films, including *Jaws: The Revenge*, *Superman IV: The Quest for Peace*, and *Batman & Robin*. This riveting book reveals the inside scoop on some of the biggest films in horror (*Halloween*, *Nightmare on Elm Street*), sci-fi (*Highlander*, *Terminator*, *Planet of the Apes*), action (*James Bond*, *Die Hard*, *Rambo*), and comedy (*Police Academy*, *Home Alone*). It also examines notable unmade fourth films, such as *Francis Ford Coppola's The Godfather: Part IV* and *Sam Raimi's Spider-Man 4.*

His fifth book, *James Bond After Fleming: The Continuation Novels* is a comprehensive guide and overview of all the post-Ian Fleming Bond novels.

Edlitz lives in New York with his wife and two children.

www.ingramcontent.com/pod-product-compliance
Lightning Source LLC
Chambersburg PA
CBHW082207070526
44585CB00020B/2320